THE

GREAT
BEAR
ALMANAC

THE
GREAT
BEAR
ALMANAC

GARY BROWN

LYONS & BURFORD, PUBLISHERS

Printed in the United States of America

Design by Howard P. Johnson

10 9 8 7 6 5 4 3 2 1

Library of Congress Cataloging–in–Publication Data

Brown, Gary.
     The great bear almanac / by Gary Brown.
       p. cm.
     Includes bibliographical references and index.
     ISBN 1–55821–210–8 (cloth); ISBN 1–55821–474–7 (paperback)
     1. Bears—Miscellanea. I. Title.
QL737.C27B765 1993
599.74'446—dc20   93–7686
                                                          CIP

To Pat

My friend and wife,
for the assistance and
many sacrifices.

Contents

Foreword

Bears engage our interest as do few other wild animals. They are as individual, entertaining, and almost as dangerous as people, and their attraction is only heightened by their relative scarcity. Most of us can't begin to recall all the deer we have seen, but we never forget a bear.

As THE GREAT BEAR ALMANAC suggests, it's been this way for a long time. The bear has attracted, amused, entertained, terrified, and inspired us for thousands of years, and its cultural significance and imagery grows more complex and rich with each passing century. I doubt that there is another wild mammal that appeals to so many aspects of the emotional spectrum—from humor to fear—or that has inspired such a wide variety of literature, symbolism, and lore.

Gary will tell you all about that, and much more. I will tell you a little bit about Gary himself. I've known him for maybe ten years, have worked closely with him on some of the most controversial conservation issues, and have come to admire him not only for his wisdom about bears, but for his good sense about almost everything else.

Not long ago, when Gary retired from the National Park Service, his coworkers threw a party for him. It was winter in Yellowstone but the chance to honor Gary drew a rare crowd of about two hundred people, some of whom made one hundred and eighty-mile round trips on snowmobiles in one night just to be there.

Gary is a popular man in the national parks for good reason. As much time as I'd spent with him, it wasn't until these people got together and started sharing Gary Brown stories—lasting until the various awards and citations were trotted out—that I realized just how much he had contributed to the national parks during his career, and just how important he had been in the world of bear management.

In addition to some authentic heroics in other aspects of his rangering career (his mountain-rescue record in the Sierras quickly approaches legend status), Gary has been one of the park service's leading champions of bears, one of the *real* experts. This hit me when one ranger, a very experienced bear handler, stood up at the party to tell how excited he had been when he first got the chance to work with Gary Brown. At Yosemite, in Alaska, in Yellowstone, and in countless management forums in between, Gary has been a driving force for bear conservation.

What came out of all that experience and commitment—at least as far as this book is concerned—is a person who not only knows a great deal about bears from firsthand experience, but also knows the resources through which to find the kind of information needed for an almanac of this breadth. I've done four bear books of my own, and so the literature of bears is something I fancy I know a lot about. But as I leafed through Gary's manuscript, I kept reading things that made me think, "I never heard of that! Where did he *get* that?"

There have been lots of bear books, but there has never been anything like this. I'm delighted, and now that it's done, I intend to pester Gary to write more about bears as soon as possible.

—Paul Schullery
Yellowstone
January 1993

Introduction

This is a family book for all ages, meant for the reader to digest alone or read to another person. Related on these pages are the observations, descriptions, anecdotes, research information, comparisons, and beliefs of many people about the bears of the world. The sources of the data and comments include scientists, bear authorities, naturalists, adventurers, explorers, and lay persons alike. The information is presented in a format whereby the reader need not be concerned with continuity—beginnings and endings—but where one may read a paragraph, table, half page, chapter or the entire almanac in a sitting, and enjoy the overall world of bears. The almanac is not a technical publication, though it may be utilized as a reference by "students" of all ages.

An "almanac" is a publication composed of lists, charts, and tables of useful information in many related and unrelated fields. This almanac is just that, except it has a single focus: bears. The many "fields" of bears are related and intertwined, not only within the world of the bears, but within the human world as well.

This book is organized into two segments, the first being a look at bears in their world—an examination of the natural history of a group of fascinating animals. The second segment discusses the influence bears have in the human world—in our lives. Obviously, there is considerable overlap and conflict between these two worlds. The human influence of anthropomorphic interpretation filters back into the bear's world, and I have often wondered in whose world we all truly live, the bear's or ours—or maybe both.

Bears are possibly the most dominant animals in our lives and have, through sharing the earth with humans, exerted distinct influences over our being. Mythical, exciting, revered, human-like, and dangerous, they have altered our behavior and actions. Statues, place names, common utensils, postage stamps, politics, toys, parks, entertainment, Teddy bears, sports, wilderness, and zoos are only a few everyday things that bring the bear to people.

Bears are described in a variety of ways, generally colored by our own perceptions. Bears' actions are often termed "unpredictable," which means we do not understand the purpose for their behavior and therefore judge it by our own. We anthropomorphize, assuming their behavioral motivations to be the same as ours, applying our values, images, and perceptions. For example, within the human vocabulary they are considered "gluttons" because they consume enormous amounts of foods in a short period. However, they must eat in this manner because of inefficient digestive systems, as well as their need to prepare to hibernate for up to six months without food. Thought to be "lazy" because they move slowly and sleep during the day, bears are actually being cautious, moving efficiently in search of food, and much of their activity occurs during the night, unobserved.

Bear descriptions and reports of their behavior are often conflicting, which is an indication of their unpredictability and varying nature. This creates confusion and uncertainty as to the "truth," but such variations may be in perfect keeping with each bear—an individual with its own personality, needs, traits, and character. (I would hate to attempt to characterize the human race with a single or even numerous words.) The only thing of certainty about the personality and actions of a bear is that it is unpredictable. Maybe this conflicting information is best described by Paul Schullery in the *Bears of Yellowstone*. "No two bears live exactly the same life. They are nearly as different in physical appearance and in personality as are people. In attempting to summarize their lives, it is easy to speak of norms, averages, and probabilities, but one of the marvels of an animal as complex as the bear is its endless capacity to surprise us."

The reader should keep in mind that behavioral descriptions in this book are *human* perceptions, and each description refers to most bear species. I list specific behavior only where it is common in the respective species.

The information available about some species of bears is extensive, collected and recorded by intensive research. However, there are unfortunate information gaps about specific species, populations, and countries. For example, there is minimal knowledge about the sun bears and spectacled bears, compared to that available about other species.

Information often varies or is conflicting within, and of course between, populations. I have provided averages and ranges, which I hope provide an impression, a perspective, and an understanding of the relationships within and between species.

Conflicting information is described by Ernest Thompson Seton in Adolph Murie's *A Naturalist In Alaska*. Seton, regarding the ferocity of the polar bear, notes that, "before me is a pile of data dealing with the moods and temper of the Bear. One portion proves that the creature is timid, flying always from man, shunning an encounter with him at any price. The other maintains that the White Bear fears nothing in the North, knowing that he is king; and is just as ready to enter a camp of Eskimo, or a ship of white men, as to attack a crippled Seal."

During my research for this almanac, the grizzly bear's dominance in the writings, technically and anecdotally, was quite evident. I had to guard against *Ursus arctos horribilis* completely overwhelming nearly every chapter. In 1904 William Hornaday, naturalist and author, spoke of the grizzly bear as one of the most celebrated species of bears in the world. At the time the species existed in great numbers, and was terrorizing the frontiersmen of our continent. Today, the grizzly bear continues to dramatically influence North America. Much of this almanac is devoted to the grizzly and its relatives of North America, but I found that other bears of the world have been celebrated in their own, though similar way, while at the same time inviting controversy, competing with humans for space and food. In many areas they are considered pests and are losing their individual battles, and possibly the war, with humans.

The term "grizzly bear" is synonymous with "brown bear," but is specifically used where necessary to emphasize the individual significance of *Ursus arctos horribilis*. And the Kodiak brown bear, *Ursus arctos middendorfi*, occasionally stands alone. Although the Eurasian brown bear populations in some countries are called grizzly bears, I maintain them in the brown bear category.

Bears are extremely popular in worldwide legend and story, perhaps only slightly overshadowed by African lions and the tigers of Asia. Hopefully, this almanac will peak your interest and encourage you to seek other informational sources about bears. But, most importantly, I hope these pages will cultivate an understanding and appreciation of all bears, and will ensure a respect for them—in their world *and* in ours.

When I began writing the almanac, the Soviet Union and

Yugoslavia existed and contained important bear populations. In order to simplify and provide continuity, and being uncertain of tomorrow's political upheavals, I refer to the Soviet Union as the "Commonwealth" and to Yugoslavia as the "Former Yugoslavia." Occasionally, in order to be more specific, I have split the continent of Eurasia and references are to Europe or Asia.

Many have been extremely supportive of me in this endeavor, researching and providing information, allowing me to present the bears in as complete a manner as the book will allow. Distinct appreciation is deserved by Bob Steele, III (Steele's Performing Bears); Kerry Gunther, supervisor of the bear management office in Yellowstone National Park; Dr. Charlie Robbins, Washington State University; Mary Olson of the Science Museum of Minnesota; Dr. Christopher Servheen, Grizzly Bear Recovery Coordinator, Missoula, Montana; Fred Dahlinger, Jr., Circus World Museum; Dick Knight and David Mattson of the Interagency Grizzly Bear Study Team, Bozeman, Montana; Harry Reynolds, III, Alaska Department of Fish and Game; and Barry Hughson of Canadian Parks Service, Ottawa, who was extremely helpful in providing information on Canadian bears.

And Paul Schullery, author and editor, for his knowledge, guidance, and friendship.

—Gary Brown
January 1993

Bears In Their World

"Always in season and accessible, ranged on the mountains like stores in a pantry. From one to another, from climate to climate, up and down he climbs, feasting on each in turn ... almost every thing is food except granite ... the sharp muzzle thrust inquiringly forward, the long shaggy hair on his broad chest, the stiff ears nearly buried in the hair, and the slow, heavy way in which he moved his head ... how heavy and broad-footed bears are, it is wonderful how little harm they do in the wilderness. Even in the well-watered gardens of the middle region, where the flowers grow tallest, and where during warm weather the bears wallow and roll, no evidence of destruction is visible."

JOHN MUIR, 1901
Our National Parks

1 The Beginning

Evolution

Bears have been evolving for about forty million years; today's bears descend from a family (Miacidae) of small tree-climbing carnivores. Fossils of the "Hemicyon," or half-dog, found in the rocks of the Miocene Epoch, display the physical characteristics of both bears and dogs, and indicate the related evolutionary descent of wolves, hyenas, weasels, other wild dogs, and bears.

Study of the evolution of any species is quite complex, as it requires reconstructing something that has long disappeared, with the evidence primarily in fossils and living relics. "Tracing the ancestry of the Polar bear requires an intimate knowledge of every aspect of its present life," writes Thomas Koch in *The Year Of The Polar Bear*, "and, possibly even more important, a wizard-like ability to guess the creature's past history." This is true of all bear species.

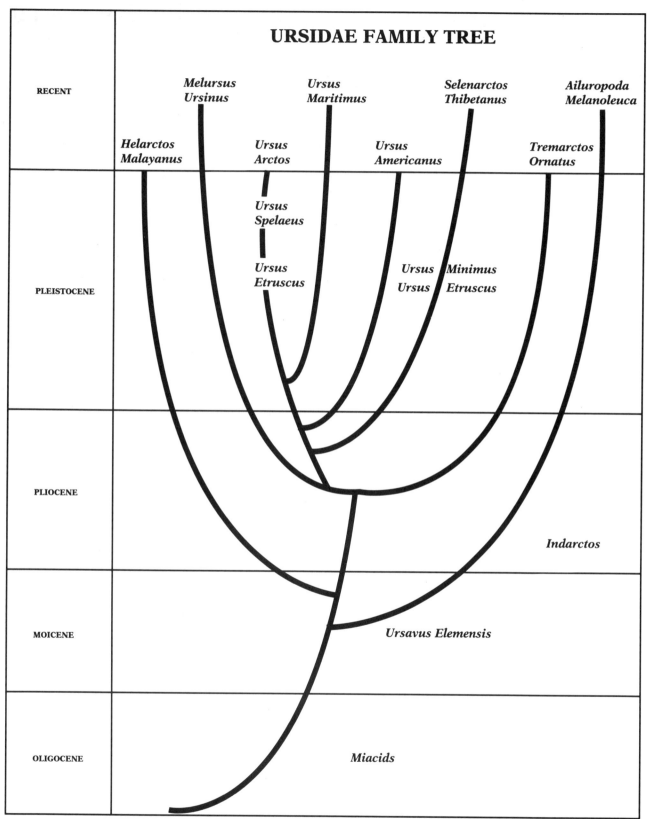

URSIDAE FAMILY TREE

RECENT				

Melursus Ursinus

Ursus Maritimus

Selenarctos Thibetanus

Ailuropoda Melanoleuca

Helarctos Malayanus

Ursus Arctos

Ursus Americanus

Tremarctos Ornatus

Ursus Spelaeus

PLEISTOCENE

Ursus Etruscus

Ursus Minimus
Ursus Etruscus

PLIOCENE

Indarctos

MOICENE

Ursavus Elemensis

OLIGOCENE

Miacids

Patricia Brown

ERA	PERIOD/EPOCH	DURATION	EVOLUTIONARY EVENT
MESOZOIC ERA 230,000,000 to 63,000,000	**Triassic Period**	230,000,000 to 180,000,000	*Members of the "dinosaur" family began appearing in mid-Triassic*
	Jurassic Period	180,000,000 to 130,000,000	*"Dinosaurs"*
	Cretaceous Period	130,000,000 to 63,000,000	*"Dinosaurs" had disappeared by mid-Cretaceous*
CENOZOIC ERA 63,000,000 to Present	**Tertiary Period**	63,000,000 to 2,000,000–500,000	
	—Early Oligocene Epoch	40,000,000–30,000,000	*Bears begin to evolve from small carnivorous mammals (Miacid)*
	—Late Oligocene Epoch	27,000,000	*First "true bears" evolving from bear-like dogs in North America*
	—Mid Miocene Epoch	20,000,000	*Ursavus elemensis, oldest true bear (fox terrier size) in sub-tropical Europe; modern bears are from Ursavus*
	—Pliocene Epoch		*Anancus arvernesis (early elephant);* Tapirus arvernesis *(early tapir);* Dicerorhinus megarhinus *(large, early rhinoceros)*
		12,000,000–3,000,000	*Giant panda appearing*
		10,000,000–5,000,000	Ursus *bears appearing*
		7,000,000	*Auvergne bear (*Ursus minimus*) appearing*
		6,000,000	*Very large predacious bears developing; evidence of* Protursus *(Spain)*
		2,500,000	Ursus etruscus, *modern bear, appearing*
			Ursus minimus
			Three lines of bears evolving in Europe: black, brown, and cave bears
			True bears come to North America with the black bears (subgenus Euarctos*) during the Pliocene*
	Quaternary Period*	2,000,000–500,000 to Present	
	—Early Pleistocene Epoch		*Giant panda-like bear appearing; black and brown bears widespread*
		2,000,000	Dicerorhinus etruscus *(rhinoceros)* *Predecessors of the modern bear are forest dwellers in Asia*
			Canis etruscus
			Ursus etruscus

*The beginning of the Quaternary Period is ill-defined, and ranges between 2,000,000 and 500,000 years ago.

Arctotherium, it was short-faced and had massive limbs. *Agriotherium* was extinct in most areas before the Pliocene Epoch.

PROTURSUS

A small bear of the Pliocene Epoch.

URSUS MINIMUS

The Auvergne bear, a primitive species that lived in Europe during the Quaternary Period. Small (100 pounds), approximately the same size as the present-day sun bear, *Ursus minimus* anatomically resembled the black bears. The Auvergne bear initiated the genus *Ursus* (eventually the American black, brown and polar bears), but was the immediate ancestor of the Etruscan bear.

URSUS ETRUSCUS

The Etruscan bear existed during the early Pleistocene Epoch. From European descendants, it populated much of Eurasia and North America, and is apparently the ecological successor of *Agriotherium*. Living and fossil evidence exists that polar, brown and black bears evolved from *etruscus*, when it separated into three distinct lines: the brown and black bears in Asia, and *Ursus speleaus*, the cave bear in Europe (thirty to forty thousand—possibly fifty thousand—years ago to ten thousand years ago).

URSUS SINO-MALAYANUS

Consisting of small and large forms, the early sun bear.

URSUS SAVINI

Savin's bear, a transitional stage between Etruscan bears and Deninger's bears. It was smaller, less heavily built and not as advanced as *Ursus deningeri*.

URSUS DENINGERI

Deninger's bear existed during the middle Pleistocene Epoch. It preceded, but was closely related to, *Ursus spelaeus* (cave bear). Though with the size and heaviness of the cave bear, it was more rangy and slight in build than the present grizzly and Kodiak bears.

ARCTOTHERIUM

The Hyena bear was probably a forest dweller. Short-faced, and with massive limbs, it was a large bear. The species *Arctotherium californicum* was larger than the present Alaskan brown bear.

URSUS (THALARCTOS) MARITIMUS TYRANNUS

The early polar bear. Very few fossil remains of polar bears have been found, but it is known that ancestors of the present-day polar bear moved into the arctic in the Pleistocene Epoch.

"... it is accepted that during the age of the glaciers, perhaps during the mid-Pleistocene, a sizable group of brown bears was isolated from the main population," explains Koch. "During this isolation, strong selection pressures forced them to change their style of life." *Tyrannus* was markedly larger and more *Arctos*-like than the present polar bear.

ARCTODUS PRISTINUS

The lesser short-faced bear was found in a few locations of eastern North America, mostly in

Florida. Its face was only slightly shortened, and the teeth were large and high-crowned, with very large canines. The lesser short-faced bear was smaller than *Arctodus simus*.

ARCTODUS SIMUS

The giant short-faced bear (bulldog bear) was not only the Mid-Pleistocene Epoch giant, but was the largest carnivorous land mammal ever. It occurred in North America, in the north central plains, Alaska, from Canada to central Mexico, and California to Virginia. The most common of early North American bears, the bulldog bear was quite common in California. It had a short, broad snout, and a low forehead with eyes set far forward. The body was short, with exceptionally long legs, the fore and hind feet turned forward, with all surfaces of the feet touching the ground. With powerful musculature, it was gigantic, measuring more than five feet at the shoulders, over eleven feet tall when standing, had a vertical reach of over fourteen feet (a basketball rim is ten feet high), and weighed one thousand five hundred to one thousand eight hundred pounds in the spring, more than a ton in the fall. Larger, but more rangy and slight in build, than the Kodiak brown bear, and "comparing canine teeth," according to one scientist, *Arctodus simus* would make a mature Alaskan brown bear look like a cub. Enormous specimens were found in Alaska and Yukon. Large and swift, the giant short-faced bear was the most powerful predator of its time. It kept black bears in trees and possibly humans off the North American continent. Possibly related to the lesser short-faced bear, it also appears related to the spectacled bear.

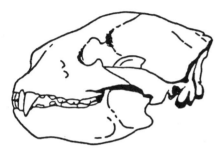

Skull of Giant Short-Faced Bear
(Arctodus simus)
Courtesy David Mattson, IGBST
(Interagency Grizzly Bear Study Team)
Bozeman, MT.

URSUS SPELAEUS

The European cave bear is one of the best-known Ice Age mammals. It inhabited mountainous and hill regions in the area of present-day Germany, France, and Russia, and lasted in Europe and Russia for two ice ages. Its head was very large, with a broad, domed skull and steep forehead, small eyes, upward-opening nostrils, and a grinding jaw. The body was stout, with long thighs, short and massive shins, large in-turning feet; the large bones are close in structure to those of the grizzly bear. Males weighed four hundred kilograms (880 pounds). The cave bear was a specialist, as it was a distinct herbivore, considerably more a browsing animal than predator. *Ursus spelaeus* was hunted and worshipped by Neanderthal man and has been found in burial positions.

TREMARCTOS FLORIDANUS

The Florida cave bear was widely distributed south of the continental ice sheet, along the Gulf Coast across Florida and north to Tennessee, with some evidence in California, Idaho, New Mexico, Texas, Kansas, Georgia, and Mexico. Its forehead was domed, teeth relatively small, neck elongated and body barrel-like. Limbs were heavy, the humerus and femur long, and the paws short. Large with a heavier build than short-faced bear, it was built more like the European cave bear, though not closely related to *Ursus spelaeus*. And, though larger and heavier, it is possibly related to the spectacled bear.

URSUS ABSTRUSUS The primitive black bear was small with a long, narrow skull, and was closely related to *Ursus minimus*, the ancestral black bear of the Old World.

URSUS AMERICANUS The American black bear was found over most of North America. Similar to the European cave bear and evolving from the same line, it probably descended from *Ursus abstrusus*, as did the Asiatic black bear, to which it is closely related. The black bears split from the brown bears in the late Tertiary Period. The black bears, subgenus *Euarctos*, came to North America during the Pliocene Epoch—before brown bears—and *Ursus americanus* and *Ursus thibetanus* have changed little since the early Quaternary Period. American black, Florida cave and short-faced bears were distributed south of the continental ice sheet.

URSUS ARCTOS The brown bear derived from *Etruscus*, and along the same line that produced cave bears. They evolved (recently) in the open spaces, lived mostly in non-forest or woodland areas and, not being a forest animal, had to stand and fight for their territory, food, and cubs. Spread widely across the Pleistocene landscape, with the earliest bears living in China, the brown bear succeeded *Arctodus simus* over much of its range.

URSUS MARITIMUS The polar bears are specialized descendants of the brown bear, and the youngest of the living species of bears. They possibly appeared 20,000 years ago, somewhere along the Siberian coast where the Asiatic brown bear population split.

Bears have evolved through an "orderly" development–variation and change generation after generation–adaptation, new characteristics–physical, behavioral. After forty million years, their evolution continues, as does ours.

Cave Bears

Cave bears (*Ursus spelaeus*) were an important evolutionary bear, and especially so beginning in the nineteenth century, when the study of their remains became more extensive. Becoming extinct as early as eleven thousand years ago, the cave bear had used predictable locations (caves) for shelter, hibernation, birthing, and safety. They appear to have lived and died in the caves. Some caves were utilized by bears and

Skull of Cave Bear (Ursus spelaeus)
Courtesy David Mattson, IGBST

humans (in the case of humans, as Paleolithic hunting stations) during different seasons and periods. These sites provided the hunters of the period opportunities to more easily locate and kill the bears in the caves and have access to the species for cultural and survival purposes. In recent times their remains have told a broad evolutionary story.

Early discoveries of bear skeletal material, found in the caves of central Europe, were thought to be from unicorns and dragons, as well as bears. Considered of medicinal value, the material was pulverized and utilized in medieval pharmacies, and numerous central European caves were "commercially" exploited. However, the material was being properly recognized by the mid-1600s, and because of the location of discoveries, the bear teeth and bones were considered to be of the "cave bear," but the exploitation of the caves continued. Phosphate fertilizer was produced from tons of cave bear skulls and bones taken from the d'Aubert Cave in the Pyrenees between 1890 and 1894.

Scientific exploration and study also began to occur, as caves provided excellent environments for fossilization and preservation of materials. Skulls, canine teeth, sometimes nearly complete skeletons, and other skeletal materials have been found not only in mountain caves, but in pits, tar pits, rifts, and in "open-air sites," such as river deposits and other sediments on valley floors.

Theories of the causes, or probable causes, of the extinction of the cave bears have been identified and thoroughly debated by numerous authorities.

▲ Changes in surroundings

▲ Changes in climate

▲ Changes in available foods

▲ Killings by the human populations

▲ Evolution into brown bears

▲ Lack of adaptation to the changing, cooling climate

▲ Degeneration (increasing dwarf forms; high percentage of pathological cases; increasing number of males and resultant imbalance of sex ratio)

▲ Diseases

▲ Discrepancy between body size and chewing/grinding surface of the teeth

▲ Smaller number of yearly births

Undoubtedly, there was a combination of causes, many of the above list being interrelated, with some quite insignificant in themselves or only of local importance. According to some authorities, a most probable explanation may be the degeneration theory (internal) or the body size/tooth surface discrepancy theory (internal), and climatic changes (external).

"The cave bear was occasionally hunted by man, but the great accumulation of bones in the caves represents animals that died in hibernation ...," explained Bjorn Kurten in *Pleistocene Mammals of Europe*. "Death in winter sleep was apparently the normal end for the cave bear and would mainly befall those individuals that had failed ecologically during the summer season—from inexperience, illness or old age. As a result the remains found are mostly of juvenile, old or diseased animals."

Extinction was gradual, over thousands of years, and is not significantly attributed to the Pleistocene *Homo sapiens* (humans). Fossil remains of cave bears have been dated from thirty thousand to forty thousand (possibly fifty thousand) years ago to approximately ten thousand years ago.

There are numerous cave bear grottos, caves, and "holes" considered significant and prominent in the modern-day discovery of the cave bear.

🐻 CAVE BEAR GROTTOS, CAVES, AND HOLES

Caves	Location/Comments	Caves	Location/Comments
Abri-Sous-Roche	Hungary, near Pilisszanto	*d'Aubert*	France, near St-Girons in the Pyrenees Mountains
Altenstein	Germany, between Liebenstein and Altenstein	*Drachenhohle*	Austria, near Mixnitz
Arma de Faje	Near summit of the Bricco di Peagna, near Calvisio, Finalese	*Drachenloch*	Switzerland, near Vattis, in the eastern Alps; Saint Gallen canton; contained rectangular stone tombs (stone chests) filled with bear skulls
Brillenhohle	Germany; bears used the cave seasonally and alternately with humans	*Dragons*	Austria; more than thirty thousand skeletons
Brixham	England, near Torquay	"*Erd*" *Cave*	Hungary, near Erd; contained bones of five hundred bears killed by Neanderthals forty-nine thousand years ago
Cave a Margot	France, on the Erve river near Saulges		
Cotencher	France, in the valley of the Areuse near Rochefort		
Cumberland	United States; Maryland	*Engihoul*	Belgium, near Liege, on the Meuse River

(continued)

Caves	Location/Comments	Caves	Location/Comments
Furgelfirst	Switzerland, between Santis and Kamor	*Rancholabrean*	United States; Florida; *Tremarctos floridanus*, Florida cave bear
Gaylenreuth	Germany; Muggendorf	*Regourdon*	France; arm bone of a bear found as an offering in a human grave
Grapevine	United States; West Virginia; lesser short-faced bear		
Grotte des Dentaux	Switzerland; Rochers de Naye; Vaud canton	*Salzofen*	Austria, in the Totes Gebirge
Hastiere	Belgium, near Hasitere-Lavaux	*San Josecito*	Mexico, state of Nuevo Leon; *Ursus americanus*, *Tremarctos floridanus*
Hellmichhohle	Germany; contained cave bear and brown bear bones	*Schnurenloch*	Switzerland; Simmental canton, Bern
Hohlenstein	Germany	*Schreiberwandhohle*	Austria; Dachstein
Igric	Hungary; Gyula in the Transylvania region	*Sibyllenhohle*	Germany; near the Castle of Teck, southeast of Stuttgart
Kents Cavern	England; Torquay	*St. Brais (Cave I)*	Switzerland; Bernese Jura; contains claw markings on cave walls
Labor-of-Love-Cave	United States; Nevada; *Arctodus simus*, *Ursus americanus* and *Ursus arctos*	*Steigelfadbalm*	Switzerland, near Vitznau, Luzern canton
Lachaize	France, on the Tardoire River	*Sundwig (Sundwich)*	Germany, near Iserlohn in Westphalia
Little Box Elder	United States; Wyoming, Converse County; *Ursus arctos* and *Arctodus simus*	*Tamar Hat*	Algeria
		Taza	Morocco
		Tischofer	Austria, near Kufstein close to Austro-Bavarian border
Montespan	France	*Tornewton*	England
Podkala	Italy; Podklanec, near Nabresina; near Triest	*Trou de Chaleux*	Belgium
		Tuc d'Audoubert	France, near St. Girons
Port Kennedy	United States; Pennsylvania; *Arctodus pristinus*	*Wildenmannistock*	Switzerland
		Wildkirchli	Switzerland; Appenzell canton; Santis Mountains
Potter Creek	United States; California; *Arctotherium simus*	*Wookey Hole*	England, south of Bristol

Classification of Bears

Bears are scientifically classified, like all animals and plants, in an orderly arrangement under a system of binomial nomenclature using the Greek or Latin languages of the early scholars. Carolus Linnaeus first classified *Ursus arctos*, the Old World brown bears, in 1758.

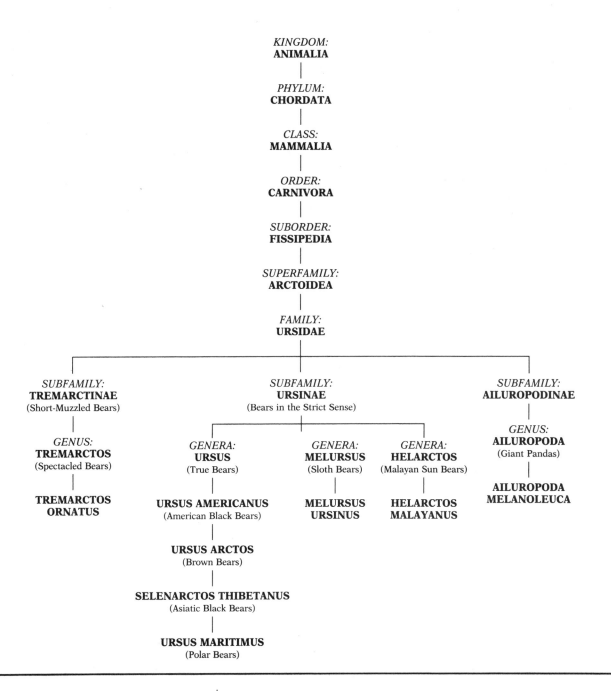

KINGDOM:
ANIMALIA

PHYLUM:
CHORDATA

CLASS:
MAMMALIA

ORDER:
CARNIVORA

SUBORDER:
FISSIPEDIA

SUPERFAMILY:
ARCTOIDEA

FAMILY:
URSIDAE

SUBFAMILY:
TREMARCTINAE
(Short-Muzzled Bears)

SUBFAMILY:
URSINAE
(Bears in the Strict Sense)

SUBFAMILY:
AILUROPODINAE

GENUS:
TREMARCTOS
(Spectacled Bears)

GENERA:
URSUS
(True Bears)

GENERA:
MELURSUS
(Sloth Bears)

GENERA:
HELARCTOS
(Malayan Sun Bears)

GENUS:
AILUROPODA
(Giant Pandas)

**TREMARCTOS
ORNATUS**

URSUS AMERICANUS
(American Black Bears)

**MELURSUS
URSINUS**

**HELARCTOS
MALAYANUS**

**AILUROPODA
MELANOLEUCA**

URSUS ARCTOS
(Brown Bears)

SELENARCTOS THIBETANUS
(Asiatic Black Bears)

URSUS MARITIMUS
(Polar Bears)

2 Bears of the World

Names and Taxonomy

Bears of the World
Original art by and courtesy of
Barbara P. Moore

Today's bears consist of eight species and numerous subspecies (the exact number of subspecies is debated) in approximately fifty countries on three continents. They are identified under an assortment of names: scientific, common, historical, contemporary, descriptive, literary, romantic, emotional, and popular. Some have had their scientific names changed. The sloth bear, originally considered a sloth ("bear sloth"), was in 1810 discovered to in fact be a bear, and, with a more drastic adjustment, the giant panda was a bear, then was not, and is once more.

AMERICAN BLACK BEAR

Scientific name and origin

- *Ursus americanus*
- *Ursus*: Latin word meaning "bear"
- *americanus*: the first Europeans on the east coast of North America found black-colored bears

Common names and origins

- black bear: black color
- cinnamon bear: cinnamon brown color
- glacier bear: bluish color, associated with glaciers
- Kermode bear: honors Francis Kermode for his scientific efforts with this subspecies

Continent

- North America

BROWN BEAR

Scientific name and origin

- *Ursus arctos*
- *Ursus*: Latin word meaning "bear"
- *arctos*: Greek word meaning "bear"

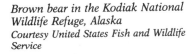
American black bear in Yellowstone National Park
Courtesy Yellowstone National Park

Common names and origins

- ❖ brown bear: brown color
- ❖ grizzly bear: grizzled color
- ❖ Kamchatkan bear: resides on Kamchatka Peninsula, Commonwealth
- ❖ Kodiak bear: resides on Kodiak Island, Alaska
- ❖ red bear: reddish brown color; resides in Himalayas
- ❖ silvertip: tips of hair silver color (grizzled)

Continent

- ❖ North America
- ❖ Eurasia

Brown bear in the Kodiak National Wildlife Refuge, Alaska
Courtesy United States Fish and Wildlife Service

The Polar bear: symbol of wandering freedom, in the Canadian Arctic
© Johnny Johnson

POLAR BEAR

Scientific name and origin

- *Ursus maritimus*
- *ursus*: Latin word meaning "bear"
- *maritimus*: located on or near the sea

Common names and origins

- *nanook*: Eskimo word for the polar bear or white bear
- polar bear: resides in polar regions
- sea bear: resides near the sea
- walking bear: travels great distances on the ice pack
- white bear: white color

Continent

- North America
- Eurasia
  (Arctic Ocean)

ASIATIC BLACK BEAR

Scientific name and origin

- *Selenarctos thibetanus*
- *Selene*: Greek word meaning "moon"
- *arctos*: Greek word meaning "bear"
- *thibetanus*: located in Tibet

Common names and origins

- Asian black bear: black color; resides in Asia
- Asiatic black bear: black color; resides in Asia
- *Bagindo nan tinggih*: he who sits high up in a tree (Malayan)
  collared bear: whitish collar; resides in Siberia/Manchuria
- Himalayan Bear: resides in the Himalayas
- moon bear: white crescent resembling moon on chest

Asiatic black bear in the Denver Zoo
© Gary Brown

- ❖ Russian black bear: black color; resides in Siberia/Manchuria
- ❖ Tibetan black bear: resides in Tibet

Continent

- ❖ Eurasia

GIANT PANDA

Scientific name and origin

- ❖ *Ailuropoda melanoleuca*
- ❖ *Ailuropoda*: black and white panda foot
- ❖ *melano*: black, darkness of hair
- ❖ *leuca*: white, colorless

Giant panda in its shrinking China habitat
© Terry Domico/Earth Images

Common names and origins

- giant panda: large (giant) bamboo-eater
- *huaxiong*: banded bear
- *maoxiong*: catlike bear
- *pae-shioung*: white bear
- panda: Himalayan word for "bamboo-eater"; originally associated with the "small" red, or lesser panda
- *xiongmao*: bear-like cat (great bear-cat)

Continent

- Eurasia

SLOTH BEAR

Scientific name and origin

- *Melursus ursinus*
- *Melursus*: dark (hair) honey bear
- *ursinus*: Latin; characteristic of a bear

Common names and origins

- *aswail (aswal)*: Ceylon and India names
- *bhalu*: India's favorite name
- Indian sloth bear: resides in India
- lip bear: extendible lips
- long-lipped bear: extends lips to suck up insects
- sloth bear: originally considered a sloth ("bear sloth"); sloth: Old
- English word for slow; sloths were slow and slept a great deal; names reversed upon realization it was a bear
- ursine sloth: bear sloth

Continent

- Eurasia

Sloth bear displaying its unkempt appearance
© *Mark Newman/Earth Images*

Sun bear in its Borneo habitat
© Terry Domico/Earth Images

SUN BEAR

Scientific name and origin

- *Helarctos malayanus*
- *Helarctos*: sun, bear
- *helical*: pertaining to the sun (chest marking)
- *malayanus*: located in Malaysia

Common names and origins

- *bruang (bruan)*: Sumatra name
- dog bear: has some resemblance to a dog
- honey bear: honey a major food
- Malayan bear: resides in Malaysia
- Malay bear: resides in Malaysia
- sun bear: yellow crescent (rising sun) on chest

Continent

- Eurasia

SPECTACLED BEAR

Scientific name and origin

- *Tremarctos ornatos*
- *Tremarctos*: tremendous bear
- *ornatus*: Ornate design on face/around eyes (spectacles)

Common names and origins

- *achupalla*: Andean word for "underbark eater"
- *ocunari*: Andean word for "cow-eating"
- *pucca mate*: Andean word for "red-fronted"
- spectacled bear: light-colored rings around eyes, like eyeglasses
- *ucumari*: Andean word for "bear with eye in hole"

Spectacled bear, an excellent tree climber in the Andes Mountains
© Mark Newman/Earth Images

❖ *yana puma*: Andean word for "black puma"
❖ *yura mateo*: Andean word for "white-fronted"

Continent

❖ South America

Subspecies

Several subspecies exist among the bears of the world. Distinctions have been made due to significant geographical, dietary, behavioral, and anatomical variations, as well as relatively isolated populations. These subspecies are recognized by many, though not all, bear authorities. Many other subspecies, addressed in the accompanying chart, are no longer recognized or are extinct.

Scientific Name	Common Name	Location
❖ **Ursus americanus**	American black bears	North America
❖ *americanus*	American black bear	North America
❖ *cinnamonum*	cinnamon bear	Northern Rocky Mountains
❖ *emmonsi*	silver black bear (glacier bear)	Northern British Columbia and Yukon; offshore islands
❖ *floridanus*	Florida black bear	Florida
❖ *hamiltoni*	Newfoundland black bear	Newfoundland
❖ *kermodei*	Kermode bear	Coastal British Columbia

Scientific Name	Common Name	Location
❖ *uteolus*	Louisiana black bear	Louisiana, Mississippi
❖ *machetes*	Mexican black bear	Chihuahua, Durango, Mexico
❖ **Ursus arctos**	Brown Bears	North America, Eurasia
❖ *arctos*	Brown bear	North America, Europe, Asia
❖ *beringianus*	Siberian brown bear	Commonwealth
❖ *gyas*	Peninsula brown bear	Alaska Peninsula
❖ *horribilis*	Grizzly bear	U.S., Canada
❖ *isabellinus*	Red bear	India, Himalayas
❖ *lasiotus*	Black grizzly	China, Mongolia
❖ *macfarlani*	MacFarlane grizzly	Northwest Territories
❖ *manchuricus*	Manchurian brown bear	Commonwealth
❖ *middendorffi*	Kodiak brown bear	Alaska (Kodiak, Afognak, Shuyak Islands
❖ *nelsoni*	Mexican grizzly bear	Mexico
❖ *pruinosus*	Horse bear	Tibet, China
❖ *syriacus*	Syrian brown bear	Caucus Mountains, Commonwealth
❖ *yesoensis*	Yezo brown bear	Hokkaido, Japan
❖ **Ursus maritimus**	Polar Bears	Arctic
❖ **Selenarctos thibetanus**	Asiatic black bear	Asia

(Also known as *Ursus thibetanus* and *Arctos thibetanus*)

Scientific Name	Common Name	Location
❖ *gedrosianus*		(Baluchistan region, Pakistan)
❖ *japonicus*	Japan black bear	three southern islands of Japan
❖ *thibetanus*	Asiatic black bear	Asia
❖ **Ailuropoda melanoleuca**	giant panda	China
❖ **Melursus ursinus**	sloth bear	Asia
❖ **Helarctos malayanus**	sun bear	Asia
❖ **Tremarctos ornatus**	spectacled bear	South America

Extinct Or No Longer Recognized Grizzly Bear Species of North America

Several legitimate species of grizzly bears have become extinct. However, considerable "splitting" occurred in the past, whereby species were divided based on infinitesimal differences in claw size, color, overall size, or features of the skull. Dr. C. Hart Merriam was the most notable splitter. He was an authority on bears, and along with many other biologists, believed that the variations he observed—primarily with skulls—regardless of magnitude warranted a separate species. Many of his separations were based simply on "individual" differences in the same group of bears. Merriam's subspecies enthusiasm was targeted at the grizzly bear above all other bears. From the early 1900s to 1918, Dr. Merriam split the grizzly bears into approximately eighty-six species, and a multitude of species existed for many years. In recent times the number of grizzly bear species has been reduced to a sensible and basic few. The list, excluding evolutionary species, identifies most of those that are no longer recognized or are extinct.

Common Name	Scientific Name	Location
❖ Absaroka grizzly	*Ursus absarokus*	Montana, South Dakota, Wyoming
❖ Admiralty Island grizzly	*kwakiutl neglectus*	Alaska
❖ Admiralty crested bear	*eulophus*	Alaska
❖ Alaska grizzly	*horribilis alascensis*	Alaska
❖ Alaska boundary grizzly	*internationalis*	Alaska, Yukon
❖ Alexander grizzly	*alexandrae*	Alaska
❖ Alsek grizzly	*orgiloides*	Alaska
❖ Anderson's bear	*andersoni*	Northwest Territories
❖ Apache grizzly	*apache*	Arizona
❖ Arizona grizzly	*arizonae*	Arizona
❖ Atnarko grizzly	*atnarko*	British Columbia
❖ Baird grizzly	*bairdi*	Colorado, Wyoming, Montana, British Columbia
❖ barren ground grizzly	*richardsoni*	Northwest Territories
❖ big-tooth grizzly	*crassodon*	British Columbia
❖ Black Hills grizzly	*rogersi isonphagus*	South Dakota
❖ broad-fronted grizzly	*phaeonyx latifrons*	Alberta, British Columbia
❖ California coast grizzly	*californicus*	California
❖ Canada grizzly	*shoshone canadensis*	British Columbia
❖ Chelan grizzly	*chelan*	British Columbia
❖ Chitna bear	*cressonus*	Alaska
❖ crested grizzly	*rungiusi sagittalis*	Yukon
❖ Dall brown	*dalli*	Alaska
❖ flat-headed grizzly	*planiceps*	Colorado
❖ forest grizzly	*selkirki*	Alberta, British Columbia

Common Name	Scientific Name	Location	Common Name	Scientific Name	Location
❖ Glacier Bay grizzly	*orgilos*	Alaska	❖ Pelly grizzly	*pellyensis*	Yukon
❖ great yellow bear	*inopinatus*	Northwest Territories	❖ Rindsfoos grizzly	*dusorgus*	Alberta
❖ Henshaw grizzly	*henshawi*	California	❖ Rogers grizzly	*rogersi rogersi*	Wyoming
❖ high-brown grizzly	*dusorgus*	British Columbia	❖ Rungius grizzly	*rungiusi rungiusi*	Alberta
❖ Idaho grizzly	*idahoensis*	Idaho			
❖ Innuit bear	*innuitus*	Alaska	❖ Sacramento Valley grizzly	*colusus*	California
❖ island grizzly	*insularis*	Alaska	❖ Shiras brown bear	*shirasi*	Alaska
❖ industrious grizzly	*kluane impiger*	British Columbia	❖ Shoshone grizzly	*shoshone*	Colorado, Wyoming
❖ Jervis Inlet grizzly	*chelidonias*	British Columbia	❖ Sitka brown	*sitkensis*	Alaska
❖ Kenai giant bear	*kenaiensis*	Alaska	❖ Sitka grizzly	*eltonclarki*	Alaska
❖ Kidder bear	*kidderi kidderi*	Alaska	❖ Sonora grizzly	*kennerlyi*	Mexico
❖ Klamath grizzly	*klamathensis*	California, Oregon	❖ Southern California grizzly	*magister*	California
❖ Kluane grizzly	*kluane*	Alaska, British Columbia, Yukon	❖ Stikine brown	*hoots*	British Columbia
❖ Knik bear	*eximius*	Alaska	❖ Stikine grizzly	*stikeenensis*	British Columbia, Yukon
❖ Kootenay grizzly	*pulchellus ereunetes*	British Columbia	❖ strange grizzly	*mirabilis*	Alaska
❖ Kwakiutl grizzly	*kwakiutl*	British Columbia	❖ Tahltan grizzly	*tahltanicus*	British Columbia
❖ Liard River grizzly	*oribasus*	Yukon	❖ Tanana grizzly	*phaeonyx*	Alaska
❖ Lillooet grizzly	*pervagor*	British Columbia	❖ Tejon grizzly	*tularensis*	California
❖ Lynn Canal grizzly	*caurinus*	Alaska	❖ Texas grizzly	*horriaeus texensis*	Colorado, Texas
❖ MacFarlane bear	*macfarlani*	Northwest Territories	❖ thickset grizzly	*crassus*	Yukon
❖ Mackenzie Delta grizzly	*russelli*	Northwest Territories	❖ Toklat grizzly	*toklat*	Alaska
❖ Mendocino grizzly	*mendocinensis*	California	❖ Townsend bear	*towndsendi*	Alaska
❖ Mexican grizzly (Nelson grizzly)	*nelsoni*	Mexico	❖ tundra bear	*kidderi tundrensis*	Alaska, Yukon
❖ Montague Island grizzly	*sheldoni*	Alaska	❖ Twin Lakes grizzly	*macrodon*	Colorado
			❖ Ungava grizzly	*unknown*	Unknown
❖ Mount Taylor grizzly	*perturbans*	New Mexico	❖ Upper Yukon grizzly	*pulchellus pulchellus*	Yukon
❖ Navaho grizzly	*navaho*	Arizona, New Mexico	❖ Utah grizzly	*utahensis*	Utah
❖ Nelson grizzly	*nelsoni*	Mexico	❖ Warburton Pike grizzly	*kwakiutl warburtoni*	Alaska, British Columbia
❖ New Mexico grizzly	*horrieaeus*	New Mexico, Mexico	❖ Washakie grizzly	*washake*	Wyoming
❖ Nuchek brown	*nuchek*	Alaska	❖ Yakutat grizzly	*nortoni*	Alaska
❖ Pallas grizzly	*pallasi*	Alaska, British Columbia, Yukon	❖ Yellowstone Park big grizzly	*imperator*	Wyoming
❖ patriarchal bear	*vetularctos inopinatus*	Northwest Territories	❖ Yellowstone Park grizzly	*mirus*	Wyoming

Other Bear Names

There are many historical and contemporary names ascribed to the different bear species. They include emotional and reactive impressions of those people whose lives have been touched or otherwise influenced by bears—people who have met, feared, worshipped, hated, killed, respected, and observed bear habits and characteristics. Many names are individual human perceptions and some simply geographical. They are often local, and many individual names become generic and are applied to other, if not all, bears. Individual bears were occasionally named because of their notoriety and many became legendary. The origins of many have been lost and forgotten with time.

The grizzly bear elicited more names than any other species of bears and possibly any other animal, including the descriptive "Old Ephraim," commonly used among early North American settlers of the 1800s and early 1900s. "The king of game beasts of temperate North America," wrote Theodore Roosevelt (Paul Schullery in *American Bears*), "because the most dangerous to the hunter is the grizzly bear; known to the few remaining old-time trappers of the Rockies and the Great Plains . . . as 'Old Ephraim'. . . ." The biblical character of Ephraim is the leader of a "warlike" tribe.

Old Ephraim, the grizzly bear, roamed most of the western North America.
© *Gary Brown*

Some historical and contemporary names ascribed to the
AMERICAN BLACK BEAR follow below.

- black bear
- black beast
- black food (Cree Indians)
- blue bear (glacier bear)
- brownie
- bruin
- camp robber of the wild
- cinnamon bear
- hairy beggar
- gap crosser (Appalachian Mountains)
- glacier bear
- happy hooligan
- island white bear (Kermode)
- Kermode bear
- king of American wilderness
- lava bear (central Oregon lava cones and flows)
- Mrs. Bear
- Mr. Bear
- outrageous nuisance
- phantom of the woods
- ridge runner (Appalachian Mountains)
- Smokey
- spirit of the forest
- Teddy
- the one going around in the woods
- variegated bear
- white bear (Kermode)
- yack-kay (Yankah)
- Yogi

The following names apply to the **BROWN BEARS**, including
the "grizzly bears" of Eurasia.

- Abruzzio brown bear (Italy)
- Alaskan brown bear
- Atlas Mountains bear
- bad man (Sherpas)
- bear cat
- black grizzly (China, Mongolia)
- big brown bear
- big hairy one
- blue tooth (Lapp)
- broadfoot
- brownie
- Caleb
- cousin (Asiatic Eskimo hunters)
- disgusting creature (Meto, Sherpas)
- dog of God (Lapp)
- dweller in the wilds (Ostyak)
- dweller in the woods (Ostyak)
- Eurasian brown bear
- fish-eating bear (Eurasian)
- four-legged human
- golden friend (Finn)
- Goliath
- grandfather of the hill (Ural Mountains)
- Grandmother
- great bear
- great food (Tungus)
- Great Grandfather
- Great Grandmother
- grizzly bear
- hairy-eared bear (Eurasian)
- himuga (Japan)
- holy animal (Lapp)
- honey paw (Tungus)
- horse bear
- illustrious pride (Finn)
- Kadiak bear (Kodiak)
- Kamchatkan brown bear
- Kashmir bear (Issabelline bear)
- king of beasts
- king of the woods (ancient Greeks)
- Kodiak bear
- Kodiak grizzlies
- light-foot (Finn)
- little mother of honey (Finn)
- lord of the mountains
- lord of the tiaga (Tungus)
- man bear (Tibetans)
- Manchurian bear
- Manchurian grizzly
- master of the forest (Lapp)
- Nomidaian bear
- old man of the mountains (Lapp)
- old man with the fur garment (Lapp)
- one who prowls at night
- owner of the earth
- red bear
- sacred man (Lapp)
- sacred virgin (Lapp)
- Siberian bear (Kamchatka)
- Sitka bear
- snow bear
- snow man (Kangme, Tibetans)
- step-widener (Lapp)
- Syrian bear
- takes large leftovers
- the one going around in the woods
- thick fur (Lapp)
- unaggressive giant
- wide-way (Lapp)
- winter-sleeper (Lapp)
- wise man (Lapp)
- woolly one (Lapp)
- worthy old man (Ural Mountains)

*(Specific to the **NORTH AMERICAN GRIZZLY BEAR**)*

- a mountain
- aklak (Eskimo)
- akshak (Eskimo)
- baldface
- bar (North American mountain men)
- barren ground grizzly
- bear cat (Alaska)
- beast
- beast that walks like man
- big feet
- big hairy one (Blackfoot Indians)
- big naked bear (Mohican Indians)
- bruin
- buffalo grizzly
- California grizzly
- chief's daughter
- chief's son (Cree Indians)

(Specific to the NORTH AMERICAN GRIZZLY BEAR)

- cinnamon bear
- colored bear (Iroquois Indians)
- cousin (Northeast Native Americans)
- dog bear
- dumb animal
- elder brother (many Native Americans)
- eldest brother (many Native Americans)
- enemy of man
- evil genius
- fine young chief (Navajo)
- food of the fire
- four-legged human (Cree Indians)
- fur bear
- fur father
- gentleman (Merriweather Lewis)
- glacier bear
- grand old gladiator
- grandfather (Northeast Native Americans)
- gray bear
- great bear
- Great Grandfather (Northeast Indians)
- grisly
- grizzle bear
- grouchy fellow
- hog back
- hohhost (Native Americans of northern Rocky Mountains)
- huge and ugly beast
- Kenai giant bear
- king of beasts
- king of brutes
- king of the plains
- lord of the woods
- Madame silvertip
- matohota (gray bear; Sioux Indians)
- Moccasin Joe (early frontiersmen; hind footprint)
- monarch of American beasts
- monarch of the country which he inhabits
- monarch of the mountains
- monarch of the plains
- monster (Lewis and Clark expedition)
- Old Caleb
- Old Eph
- Old Ephraim
- old man (Sauks Indians)
- old man in a furred cloak (Native Americans)
- old man of the mountains
- our greatest wild animal
- pig bear
- range bear
- real bear (Blackfeet Indians)
- red bear
- renegade
- roach bear (early frontiersmen; raised hackles)
- silver bear
- silvertip
- spitfire
- that hairy one (Blackfoot Indians)
- that which lives in the den
- that which went away (Koyokon)
- the monster
- the one of matchless might and unquestioned
- the thing
- Uncle
- unmentionable one (Blackfoot Indians)
- uzumate (Indians of Yosemite region)
- white bear (Lewis and Clark Expedition)
- yellow bear
- yackah (Native Americans, northern Rocky Mountains)
- Yakutat bear
- Yosemite (Miwok Indians)

There are fewer, but perhaps more exotic, names for the other six species of bears.

POLAR BEARS

- Arctic bear
- atertak (Eskimo; one who goes to sea)
- brownie (Scottish whalers)
- eternal vagabond (Eskimo)
- the farmer (nineteenth-century whalers; "Walked icy fields, his alone to tend")
- fierce fighter
- the great wanderer
- hairy foot
- he who is without a shadow
- ice bear
- king of the Arctic
- lord of the ice and snow
- maritime bear
- monarch of the north
- nanook (Eskimo; the ever-wandering one)
- nanvark (Eskimo; polar bear cub)
- nomad of the Arctic
- pigoqahiaq (Eskimo)
- sea bear (ancient Greeks)
- tiger of the north
- the traveler
- wahb'esco (Cree Indians of James Bay)
- walking bear
- water bear
- white bear
- white bruin
- white giant

ASIATIC BLACK BEARS

- basindo nan tenggil (he who like to sit high—day bedding)
- black bear
- black beast
- dog bear
- Formosa bear
- giant cat bear (Japan)
- Japan bear

- man bear
- medved (Russian; honey bear)
- Mongolian bear
- moon bear of Tibet
- pig bear

GIANT PANDA

- ailurus (early scientific; also common)
- bai bao (white leopard)
- bai hu (white bear or tiger)
- bamboo bear (German; bambushbar)
- black and white bear
- cat bear (hsiung-maou)
- chitwa (Himalayan; 1800s)
- clawed bear
- fiery fox (Himalayan; 1800s)
- fire-colored cat
- harlequin bear
- meng shi shou (Chinese; beast of prey)
- metal-eating bear
- mo (white leopard)
- monk among bears (hoshien)
- parti-colored bear
- pi (ancient name for panda; a white fox)
- pixiu (ancient name for panda)
- raccoon (Himalayan; 1800s)
- shi tie shou (iron-eating beast; entered villages and licked cooking pots)
- shining cat
- spectacled bear (hua-hsiung)
- white bear (bei-shung; pei-shiung)
- zhi yi (white bear or tiger)

SLOTH BEARS

- aswail
- baloo (wise old man; Rudyard Kipling)
- honey bear
- jungle joker
- lip bear

SUN BEARS

- ape man
- bruang
- dog bear (Thailand)
- honey bear
- Malay bear

SPECTACLED BEARS

- short-faced bear

Social Names of Bears

BOAR: adult male bear (from the Old English "bar" and West Germanic "bairoz"; wild pig, male pig)

CUB: young bear (novice or learner, the young of certain carnivorous animals; an inexperienced or ill-mannered youth)

DAM: female parent (normally used for a quadruped, common with dogs; rarely used to refer to a bear; possibly originated in California during the mid-1800s)

GROUP: a pack or sloth (sleuth) of bears

HE-BEAR: adult male bear

SHE-BEAR: adult female bear

SLEUTH: a grouping of bears

SLOTH: a grouping of bears

SOW: adult female bear (adult female hog, Old English "sugu")

Populations

The determination of bear populations is extremely difficult, with exact numbers impossible. Bears are not found in herds like deer, elk, or wildebeests, but are secretive, and normally solitary except for sows with cubs. They also are transient, frequently moving in search of food (and often for reasons unknown to humans), with some individuals altering state or country populations by moving across political boundaries. Polar bears, "the wanderers," are in a near-constant state of movement, frequently altering country and continental populations. Population information from many countries is often unavailable due to a lack of funding and research, political conflicts including war, lack of interest, and low priority on the list of pressing needs. For example, the sun bear population is listed as six hundred to one thousand bears; not a population count, it is at best a knowledgeable estimation.

Population Determination Methods

Numerous census methods exist, from roadside, boat, aircraft, and field sightings to incident trends (conflicts with humans), harvest reports, and trapping samples. However, all of these methods meet a single premise—the sample is representative of the population. The sample data, though

WORLDWIDE AND CONTINENTAL POPULATIONS

Worldwide Populations		Continent	Species	Population
• AMERICAN BLACK BEAR	630,000–725,000	• AFRICA	none	—
		• ANTARCTICA	none	—
• BROWN BEAR	206,500	• ASIA	Asiatic black bear	unknown
			brown bear	122,000
• POLAR BEAR	26,000		giant panda	700–1,000
			polar bear	4,500*
• ASIATIC BLACK BEAR	unknown		sloth bear	10,000
			sun bear	600–1,000
• GIANT PANDA	700–1,000	• AUSTRALIA	none	—
		• EUROPE	brown bear	18,000
• SLOTH BEAR	10,000		polar bear	4,500
		• NORTH AMERICA	American black bear	630,000–725,000
• SUN BEAR	600–1,000		brown bear	66,500
			polar bear	17,000
• SPECTACLED BEAR	2,000–3,500	• SOUTH AMERICA	spectacled bear	2,000–3,500

*Polar bear populations are nearly impossible to determine as many bears move from country to country during the course of a year.

not of the total population, is utilized (over time) to build a life table that depicts the sex and age structure (number of observed bears of a sex in a specific age group) of the population. Knowing the proportion of each age/sex segment allows the biologist in subsequent counts to sample one segment and determine by ratio an approximate total number for the population. As the count of a specific segment of a population improves, the total number (or high to low range) for the population becomes more reliable. Most importantly, the information identifies the trend of the population, indicating whether it is increasing, decreasing, or stable.

COUNTRY POPULATIONS

American Black Bears

• Canada	342,500–395,500	• United States	286,600–328,000
• Mexico	uncommon		

Brown Bears

• Albania	unknown	• Japan–Hokkaido	3,000
• Bulgaria	700–750	• Lebanon	extinct?
• Canada	22,500	• Mexico	extinct?
• China	unknown	• Mongolia	unknown
• Commonwealth	118,000	• Norway	160–230
• Czechoslovakia	700	• Pakistan	fewer than 200
• Democratic People's Republic of Korea	uncommon	• Poland	70–75
		• Romania	6,300
• Finland	450	• Spain	115
• France	20–30	• Sweden	500–700
• Greece	fewer than 100	• Syria	few
• India	rare	• Turkey	common
• Iran	few	• United States	44,000
• Iraq	few	• former Yugoslavia	1,600–2,000
• Italy	60–70		

Polar Bears

• Canada	15,000	• Commonwealth	3,000–5,400
• Greenland	common	• United States	1,800–2,000
• Norway	4,000–5,000		

Asiatic Black Bears

• Afghanistan	rare	• Japan–Shikoku	fewer than 100
• Bangladesh	very rare	• Laos	unknown
• Bhutan	unknown	• Nepal	unknown
• Burma (Myanmar)	unknown	• Pakistan	uncommon; small, isolated populations
• China	common		
• Commonwealth	common	• South Korea	fewer than 57
• Dem. P.R. of Korea	unknown	• Taiwan	uncommon; small, isolated populations
• India	low		
• Japan–Honshu	few; eastern population extinct	• Thailand	common
		• Vietnam	unknown

(continued)

Giant Pandas			
• China	700–1,000		

Sloth Bears			
• Bangladesh, Sri Lanka, southern India	7,600–8,400	• India	common
		• Nepal	common
• Bhutan	unknown		

Sun Bears			
• Bangladesh	very rare	• Kampuchea	unknown
• Borneo (Indonesia)	common	• Laos	common
• Burma (Myanmar)	common	• Malaysia	uncommon
• China	extinct?	• Sumatra (Indonesia)	unknown
• India	extinct? Possibly exists in sanctuaries	• Thailand	common
		• Vietnam	unknown

Spectacled Bears			
• Argentina	possibly a few	• Ecuador	information unavailable
• Bolivia	information unavailable	• Peru	800 to 2000
• Columbia	small, isolated populations	• Venezuela	1000

(total South American population: 2,000 to 3,500)

(Information sources: Christopher Servheen, *The Status and Conservation Of The Bears Of The World*; various state and provincial wildlife management departments.)

COMMON:	Considered common; population unknown	**RARE:**	Known to exist; rare observations
UNCOMMON:	Considered uncommon; population unknown	**EXTINCT?:**	Possibly extinct
LOW:	Exist in low numbers	**UNKNOWN:**	Known to exist; population unknown
FEW:	Exist in *very* low numbers		

North American Populations

Bears were more than simply common in North America as the early explorers and settlers approached, crossed and settled the continent. In September 1824, explorer and trapper James Ohio Pattie, while traveling in the eastern part of the present state of Colorado, encountered over 220 grizzly bears in a single day. Twenty men stood guard around the camp that night.

"In January, 1827," according to Tracy Storer and Lloyd Tevis in *California Grizzly*, "Duhaut-Cilly wrote that 'bears are very common in the environs; and without going farther that in five or six leagues from San Francisco, they are often seen in herds. . . .' "

Storer and Tevis also relate the comments of George Yount, an early American pioneer in California during 1831. Yount wrote that bears ". . . were everywhere—upon the plains, in the valleys, and on the mountains . . . it was not unusual to see fifty or sixty within the twenty-four hours. . . ."

Author Ernest Thompson Seton noted that the Black Hills region of South Dakota had grizzly bears "in bands like buffalo." One hundred thousand brown (grizzly) bears originally inhabited the present 48 contiguous states, however only 1,080 to 1,350 exist today.

American Black Bears Five hundred thousand American black bears roamed the North American continent when Europeans began to arrive.

BLACK BEAR POPULATIONS IN NORTH AMERICA

United States	Population	United States	Population
• Alabama	150	• Montana	14,000–29,000
• Alaska	100,000	• Nebraska	extinct
• Arizona	2,000–2,500	• Nevada	500
• Arkansas	2,300	• New Hampshire	3,000
• California	15,000–18,000	• New Jersey	250–300
• Colorado	7,000–15,000	• New Mexico	3,000
• Connecticut	fewer than 30	• New York	4,000–5,000
• Delaware	extinct	• North Carolina	3,500
• Florida	1,000–1,500	• North Dakota	few
• Georgia	1,700	• Ohio	extinct
• Hawaii	bears have never existed	• Oklahoma	100
• Idaho	20,000–25,000	• Oregon	25,000
• Illinois	extinct	• Pennsylvania	7,500
• Indiana	extinct	• Rhode Island	3–6
• Iowa	extinct	• South Carolina	90–100
• Kansas	extinct	• South Dakota	few
• Kentucky	450	• Tennessee	1,000
• Louisiana	300	• Texas	50
• Maine	20,000	• Utah	800–1,000
• Maryland	200	• Vermont	2,000
• Massachusetts	700–750	• Virginia	3,000
• Michigan	6,000–11,000	• Washington	27,000–30,000
• Minnesota	10,000	• West Virginia	3,000
• Mississippi	fewer than 25	• Wisconsin	6,000
• Missouri	50–300	• Wyoming	unknown

Canada	Population	Canada	Population
• Alberta	40,000	• Nova Scotia	2,500
• British Columbia	90,000–120,000	• Ontario	65,000–75,000
• Manitoba	25,000–30,000	• Prince Edward Island	extinct
• New Brunswick	15,000	• Quebec	60,000
• Newfoundland	6,000	• Saskatchewan	24,000–32,000
• Northwest Territories	5,000	• Yukon	10,000

Mexico	Population	Mexico	Population
• Chihuahua	unknown	• Sinaloa	unknown
• Coahuila	unknown	• Sonora	unknown
• Durango	unknown	• Tamaulipas	unknown
• Nuevo Leon	unknown	• Zacatecas	unknown
• San Luis Potosi	unknown		

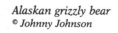
Alaskan grizzly bear
© Johnny Johnson

GRIZZLY BEARS IN NORTH AMERICA

United States	Population
ALASKA	32,000–43,000 (includes coastal and Kodiak brown bears)
IDAHO	20-30
MONTANA	800–1000
WASHINGTON	10-20
WYOMING	250–300
Canada	Population
ALBERTA	870
BRITISH COLUMBIA	10,000-13,000
NORTHWEST TERRITORIES	4,000–5,000
YUKON	6,000-7,000
Mexico	Population
CHIHUAHUA	extinct?

Brown/Grizzly Bears in Alaska The separation of brown bear and grizzly bear populations and distribution in Alaska is not perfectly definitive. The easiest system of division considers that the brown bears that inhabit the coastal areas, are larger than the inland grizzly bears, and have ready access to salmon, are Alaskan brown bears. The "inland" brown bears are grizzly bears; the brown bears (*Ursus arctos middendorffi*) isolated on the islands of Kodiak, Afognak, and Shuyak are the Kodiak brown bears. The highest densities, and largest populations, of brown bears in Alaska are coastal.* Brown bears of Canada and the contiguous 48 states are grizzly bears. (See Side Bar).

Polar Bears Polar bears are generally grouped in six closed populations: those of the Canadian archipelago; Greenland; northern Alaska; Siberia; Spitsbergen-Franz Josep Land; and Wrangel Island to western Alaska. The United States polar bear population is 2,000, located entirely in Alaska. In Canada, there are 1,200–1,600 polar bears in Manitoba, 200 in Newfoundland, and 12,000 in the Northwest Territories. The total Canadian population is difficult to estimate because the populations in Ontario, Quebec, and the Yukon provinces are unknown.

Distribution

T he family *Ursidae* and its members presently live on every continent except Africa, Australia, and Antarctica. There is no evidence of their previous existence in Australia and Antarctica. The present distribution of the world's bears is not only different from that during prehistoric periods, most species are today experiencing rapid and extreme distribution alterations as described in Chapter 9.

American black bears are the most common species of bears, distributed in forty-two of the forty-nine states (bears have never existed in Hawaii), and in eleven of the twelve Canadian provinces and territories in which they originally occurred. Previous distribution in Mexico is uncertain, but they presently occur in five and possibly four other states (previous distribution may have been in only those nine states). The species presently occurs more in the northern and western part of the North American continent, and its survival is considered assured.

*In total, there are 32,000–43,000 brown bears in Alaska, including grizzly bears. 2,700–3,000 are Kodiak brown bears found on the islands mentioned above.

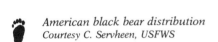
American black bear distribution
Courtesy C. Servheen, USFWS

Brown bears have the widest world distribution, and they too appear assured of survival, though the species has lost more than fifty percent of its range and population since the mid-1800s.

BEARS IN U.S. NATIONAL WILDLIFE REFUGES AND RANGES

National wildlife refuges and ranges are administered by the Department of the Interior.

They have been established to provide habitat and protection for a variety of wildlife, including bears.

American Black Bears

Agassiz, MN	McNary, WA	Tamarac, MN
Arctic, AK	Moosehorn, ME	White River, AR
Great Dismal Swamp, VA	Okefenokee, GA	Willapa, WA
Great Swamp, NJ	Ouray, UT	
Holla Bend, AR	Pungo, NC	
Kenai, AK	Red Rock Lakes, MT	
Kootenai, ID	Rice Lake, MN	
Lake Woodruff, FL	Seney, MI	
Loxahatchee, FL	Sherburne, MN	
Mattamuskeet, NC	St. Marks, FL	

Brown Bear

Aluetian Islands, AK
Izembek, AK
Kenai, AK
Unimak Island, AK

Grizzly Bear

Arctic, AK
Kootenai, ID

Kodiak Brown Bear

Kodiak, AK

Polar Bear

Arctic, AK

National Parks with Bears

United States	American Black	Grizzly	Polar
ALASKA			
Denali	X	X	
Gates of the Arctic	X	X	
Glacier Bay	X	X	
Katmai		X	
Kenai Fjords	X		
Kobuk Valley	X	X	
Lake Clark	X	X	
Wrangell-St. Elias	X	X	
ARIZONA			
Grand Canyon	X		
CALIFORNIA			
Lassen Volcanic	X		
Redwood	X		
Sequoia-Kings Canyon	X		
Yosemite	X		
COLORADO			
Mesa Verde	X		
Rocky Mountain	X		
FLORIDA			
Everglades	X		
MAINE			
Acadia	X		
MINNESOTA			
Voyageurs	X		
MONTANA			
Glacier	X	X	
OREGON			
Crater Lake	X		
TENNESSEE			
Great Smoky Mountains	X		
TEXAS			
Big Bend	X		
Guadalupe Mountains	X		
UTAH			
Bryce Canyon	X		
Canyonlands	X		
VIRGINIA			
Shenandoah	X		
WASHINGTON			
Mount Rainer	X		
North Cascades	X	X	
Olympic	X		
WYOMING			
Grand Teton	X	X	
Yellowstone	X	X	

Canada	American Black	Grizzly	Polar
ALBERTA			
Banff	X	X	
Elk Island	X		
Jasper	X	X	
Waterton Lakes	X	X	
Wood Buffalo	X		
(Alberta & Nwt)			
BRITISH COLUMBIA			
Glacier	X	X	
Kootenay	X	X	
Mount Revelstoke	X	X	
Pacific Rim	X		
South Moresby	X		
Yoho	X	X	
MANITOBA			
Riding Mountain	X		
NEW BRUNSWICK			
Fundy	X		
Kouchibouguac	X		
NEWFOUNDLAND			
Gros Morne	X		
Terra Nova	X		
NORTHWEST TERRITORIES			
Auyuittug			X
Ellesmere			X
Nahanni	X	X	
NOVA SCOTIA			
Cape Breton Highlands	X		
Kejimkujik	X		
ONTARIO			
Bruce Peninsula	X		
Georgian Bay Islands	X		
Pukaskwa	X		
St. Lawrence Islands	X		
QUEBEC			
Forillon	X		
La Maurice	X		
Mingan Archipelago	X		
SASKATCHEWAN			
Prince Albert	X		
YUKON TERRITORY			
Kluane	X	X	
Northern Yukon	X	X	X

Patricia Brown

Brown bear distribution, North America
Courtesy C. Servheen, USFWS

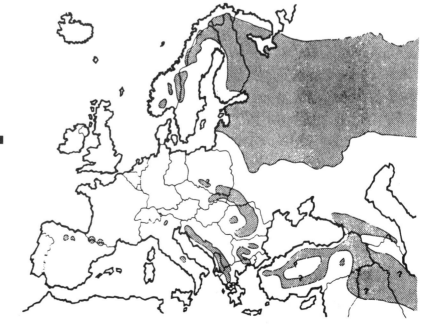

COUNTRIES WITH MOST SPECIES OF BEARS

India (4)   Asiatic black bear
brown bear
sloth bear
sun bear

China (4)   Asiatic black bear
brown bear
giant panda
sun bear

Canada (3)   American black bear
brown bear (including grizzly)
polar bear

United States (3)   American black bear
brown bear (including grizzly)
polar bear

Commonwealth of Independent States (3)   Asiatic black bear
brown bear
polar bear

Brown bear distribution—western Eurasia
Courtesy C. Servheen, USFWS

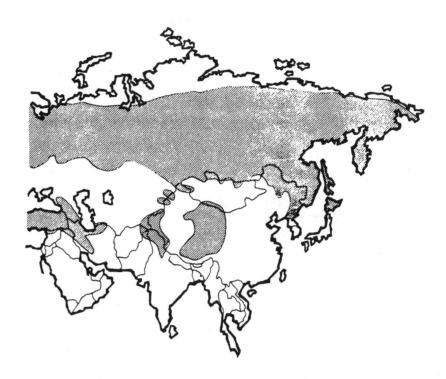

 Brown bear distribution—eastern Eurasia
Courtesy C. Servheen, USFWS

The polar bears' distribution is circumpolar, and is over most of its original habitat. Even though they are known for their enormous wanderings, they belong to the six specific population groups and remain in a specific geographical area during most of their lifetime.

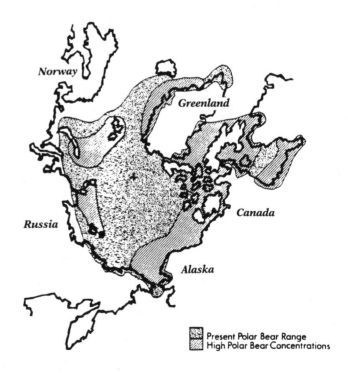

 Polar bear distribution
Courtesy C. Servheen, USFWS

Norway

Greenland

Russia

Canada

Alaska

▨ Present Polar Bear Range
▧ High Polar Bear Concentrations

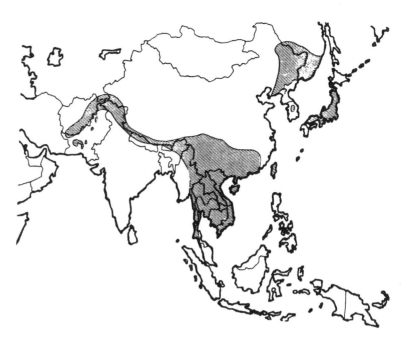

Asiatic black bear distribution
Courtesy C. Servheen, USFWS

Asiatic black bears are distributed throughout a large part of southern Asia, from Pakistan on the west through eastern Siberia into Korea and Japan.

Giant panda distribution—China
Renee Evanoff

Giant pandas are distributed in six small areas on the eastern rim of the Tibetan Plateau, most in a series of twelve Chinese reserves.

Sloth bear distribution
Courtesy C. Servheen, USFWS

The distribution of the sloth bears includes the forested areas of India, Sri Lanka, Bangladesh, Nepal, and Bhutan.

The sun and the spectacled bears might be considered true equatorial bears, as their distribution spans the equa-

Sun bear distribution
Courtesy C. Servheen, USFWS

Spectacled bear distribution
Courtesy C. Servheen, USFWS

tor. Small dispersed populations of spectacled bears occur throughout Ecuador, Venezuela, Columbia, Bolivia, and Peru. They may exist in Argentina.

Very little is known of the distribution of sun bears, except that it includes areas of Borneo, Burma, Java, Malaysia, Sumatra, and Thailand, and is drastically diminishing.

Early Discoveries of North American Bears

Early observations of bears were made by whalers, explorers, and scientists. Many were recorded, while others are assumed due to the early adventurers' activities in bear country. The first contacts with bears by these individuals and groups may have been not only observations, but actual encounters involving flight, injury, or death of bears and people.

The first non-Native Americans to observe a grizzly bear were most likely the Cabeza de Vaca party (de Vaca, Castillo Maldonado, Andreas Dorantes and Dorantes' slave Estevan) during their travels, from 1527 to 1536, through country that is now Texas and New Mexico. De Vaca's journal makes no mention of bears, but to have not encountered them would have been remarkable.

The first observations of American black bears by Europeans would have been the Norsemen during the tenth and eleventh centuries.

Observations

985	Bjarni Herjulfson sailed close along the coast of New England (American black bears).
1003	Leif Erickson located "Vinland" (American black bears).
1006–1007	Thorvald Erickson explored the northeast coast of North America. A few years later, Thorfinn Karlsefni resided for two winters in Erickson's Cape Cod camp. They both were in American black bear country.
1492	Christopher Columbus sailed to the North American coast (American black bears).
1524	Giovanni Verrazano sailed along the east coast of North America, later providing the first written description of area (American black bears).
1527 (November)– 1536 (July)	Cabeza de Vaca and three companions traveled extensively through grizzly bear country—what is now Texas and northern Mexico.
1540–1542	Francesco Vasquez de Coronado and his expedition traveled through American black and grizzly bear country, what is now Colorado, Kansas, Nebraska, and New Mexico. Pedro de Castaneda, a member of the expedition, wrote of "many bears."
1578	Hundreds of European vessels were fishing and whaling off of New Foundland.
1585	John Davis in Cumberland Sound, Baffin Island, observed polar bears. "In 1585 John Davis sailed into Cumberland Sound on the southeast coast of Baffin Island," notes Koch, "and observed 'So soone as we were come to an anker in Totnes Rode under mount Raleigh we espied four white beares at the foot of the mount. We, supposing them to bee goates or wolves, manned our boats, and went toward them: but when wee came neere the shore, wee found them to be white beares of a monstruous bignesse.' "
1602	Friar Antonio de la Ascension, with the Sebastian Vizcaino expedition to Monterey, California, recorded grizzly bears on the beaches.
1602	"The first published record of bears in Massachusetts...," according to James Cardoza in *The Black Bear of Massachusetts*, were by Gosnold during his expeditions to the Cape and islands in May and June (American black bears).

1666	Claude Jean Allouez observed grizzly bears in the Assiniboine River region of Manitoba, Canada.
1691 **(August 20)**	Henry Kelsey noted grizzly bears in Northwest Canada. Kelsey, employed by the Hudson Bay Company, is considered to have discovered the Canadian prairie. He provides the earliest known reference in the English language to a grizzly bear, according to Harold McCracken in *The Beast That Walks Like Man*.

Kelsey wrote, "To day we pitch to ye outermost Edge of ye woods this plain affords Nothing but short Round sticky grass & Buffillo & a great sort of Bear wch is Bigger than any white Bear & is Neither White nor Black But silver hair'd like our English Rabbit. . . ."

A later reference notes: "And then you have beast of severall kind
The one is a black Buffillo great
Another is an outgrown Bear wch. is good meat
His skin to gett I have used all ye ways I can
He is mans food & he makes food of man
His hide they would not me it preserve
But said it was god & they should Starve
This plain affords nothing by Beast & grass. . . ."

1804 **(April 29)**	The Lewis and Clark expedition encountered many grizzly bears as they crossed the continent. "The party made their night camp on April 28 twenty-four miles upstream from the junction of the Yellowstone and Missouri Rivers," explains Fred Gowans in *Mountain Man & Grizzly*. "At 8:00 A.M., shortly after breaking camp on April 29, Captain Lewis encountered his first grizzly."

Bear Anatomy and Physiology

The bears of today, having evolved from the same "source," show numerous similarities between species. Their evolutionary goal has been survival and Stephen Herrero, in *Bear Attacks*, notes that bears ". . . evolved from the way in which they adapted to and survived in their daily environment."

Descriptions

In 1607 bears were described by Edward Topsell, in *The History of Four-footed Beastes*, as "armed, filthy, deformed, cruel, dreadful, fierce, greedy . . . bloudy, heavy, night ranging . . . menacing . . . head-long, ravening, rigid and terrible. . . ." Today, a general description of the bears of the world includes:

▲ Found in eight species and numerous sub-species

▲ Live in temperate and tropical regions, having adapted to wide ranges of temperature and climate

▲ Six of the eight species live in forests

▲ Normally wide ranging

▲ The only large omnivore

▲ Generally have the same shape with variations in size and color

▲ Heavily constructed bodies

▲ Average weight at least ninety-nine pounds when full grown

▲ No obvious external differences in sexes

▲ Females of a species typically slightly smaller in weight

▲ Strong and durable

▲ Relatively short legs and necks

▲ Forelegs shorter than hindlegs

▲ Short tails

▲ Thick fur consists of short to long hair

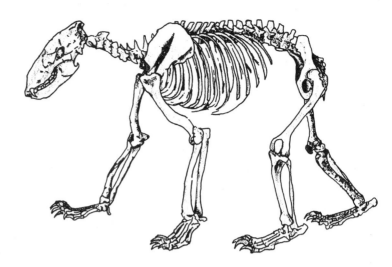

Skeletal bear
Renee Evanoff

- ▲ Large heads with rounded ears
- ▲ Unusually small eyes for their overall body size
- ▲ Lips that are free from the gums (mobile and protrusile)
- ▲ Forty-two teeth (sloth bear has forty)
- ▲ Enlarged molars
- ▲ Broad feet with five toes (giant panda has six)
- ▲ Strong, curved, non-retractable claws
- ▲ Forelimbs' bones separate, radius/ulna; human like
- ▲ Forelimbs move freely; capable of rotating forelimbs
- ▲ Strike, handle, and dig with the forefeet only
- ▲ Plantigrade when they walk, placing heel and foot down flat on the ground (flatfooted)
- ▲ Walk pigeon-toed (front feet turned inward)
- ▲ Shuffling gate when walking
- ▲ Provide an illusion of being slow and clumsy
- ▲ Illusion of clumsiness due to fat and fur
- ▲ Remarkably agile
- ▲ Fast runners
- ▲ Move with rhythm and precision
- ▲ Unable to jump upward from a standing start
- ▲ Sit on rump

- ▲ Susceptible to disease and pests common to humans
- ▲ Keen sense of smell
- ▲ Generally near sighted
- ▲ Snore
- ▲ Court with demonstrable affection
- ▲ Unusual reproduction (delayed implantation of the fertilized egg), sun bear excepted
- ▲ Low reproductive rates
- ▲ Spank their young
- ▲ Low natural mortality compared to other wildlife species
- ▲ Some species hibernate
- ▲ Generally omnivorous (polar bears somewhat an exception)
- ▲ No basic carnivorous technology
- ▲ Produce excrement similar to humans
- ▲ Highly evolved
- ▲ Intelligent
- ▲ Strongly curious
- ▲ Wily
- ▲ Generally solitary, except female with cubs
- ▲ Self-sufficient
- ▲ Independent
- ▲ Easygoing
- ▲ High degree of unpredictability
- ▲ Adaptable
- ▲ A symbol of wilderness!

"When a biologist once attempted to define the uniqueness of man as the only animal who could walk or run many miles, swim a river, and then climb a tree," wrote Paul Shepard and Barry Sanders in *The Sacred Paw*, "he overlooked the bears, who can do all of these faster and with more endurance than man, not to mention digging a fifteen-foot-deep hole or killing a horse with a blow of the forepaws."

American Black Bear (*Ursus americanus*)

The common North American bear we have come to love—the clown, the beggar, the bear of the national parks.

"To the early settlers who pioneered the eastern part of North America, the name 'black bear' was an obvious choice," relates Terry Domico in *Bears Of The World*. "Nearly all the bears in this region have black coats. . . . but as the white man pushed west, people began to encounter bears that resembled black bears in nearly every way except they had . . . brown fur." In western North America, more than half of the "black bears" are brown.

"Heavily hunted during the settlement of the eastern North America," Domico continues, "black bears were gunned down by the thousands for meat, fat, and fur. Huge expanses of forest habitat were cleared for farming. The bears became very scarce; what was left of the population withdrew, finding sanctuary in the few undeveloped places." However, appropriate bear management has paid dividends, as today the American black bear is the most numerous and widespread species of bear in North America.

"*. . . a beast taller than man and connected to the word freedom. . . .*"

DOUG CHADWICK, 1983

American black bear in Yellowstone National Park
Courtesy Yellowstone National Park

"By the time we reach grade school," writes George Laycock in *The Wild Bears*, "we already have a twisted idea of the character and behavior of the black bear. We are conditioned by children's books and television. Gentle Ben, Teddy Bears, Smokey Bear, we know and love them all and are sometimes shocked to learn that this roly-poly clown, or his mother, would do us bodily harm."

The American black bear is native only to North America. Living in a temperate climate, it is a forest animal, though its habitat is highly varied. It is also widely varied in coloration; the diversity among bears is greater in western North America than elsewhere. The color of an individual is relatively uniform, and a brown snout is the norm for all of this species. There is a blue-gray color phase (glacier bear) in Alaska and Yukon, and a white color phase (Kermode bear; "ghost bear") in British Columbia. The smallest bear of North America, the black has a straight, Roman nose, short hair, is lanky and has short, hooked claws. The American black bear hibernates, breeds at a young age and has a prolonged gestation period with delayed implantation. It dies relatively young. Adaptable, it accepts environmental changes well, being considered crafty and possessing considerable vitality. Known for its remarkable dexterity, this species is capable of opening screw-top jars and manipulating door latches.

Brown Bears *(Ursus arctos)*

The most widely known species of bear, primarily due to the notorious and controversial grizzly bear, the brown bear is, according to Clyde Ormand in the *Complete Book of Hunting*, ". . . ponderously large and possessed of unbelievable vitality." "Largest of the species," according to Laycock, "are those of the giant Alaska Kodiak, Peninsula [Alaska], and Kamchatka (USSR) brown bear subspecies." Possessing a dished-in face with a high brow, this shaggy bear with the distinctive hump between its shoulders is the most widely diverse species of bear in size and color.

The remarkable and distinguishing "hump" is actually a mass of muscle that, coupled with longs claws, provides the brown bear with great digging ability. Long guard hairs on the hump enhance this important feature of identification.

The brown bears include the grizzly bear of North America. It is native to the Old and New worlds and lives in a temperate climate. Its color is variable, though generally brown, and the color of individuals is relatively uniform. The most diverse bear in size and color, it is enormous in size. With its strong build, great strength, thick head, large hump of fat and muscle over the shoulder, it is the largest omnivore. It has a dished face (dished-in profile), short, round ears that are small compared to the skull, and long claws on the front paws. Its gestation period is prolonged and with delayed implantation, and it hibernates. Dignified, it is majestic and solitary.

". . . this species is so variable in size and coloration that it confused the late nineteenth-century naturalists who described them," explains Domico. "Many of these biologists thought each variation was a new species, and the resulting list of new bear 'species' became so lengthy that nearly every mountain range could claim to have its own species of brown bear."

Grizzly Bear *(Ursus arctos horribilis)*

North America's "unpredictable" bears, this subspecies has long been one of the most celebrated of all bears, having captured the attention and imagination of humans due to its size, temperament and conflicts with humans. A feared species, not only of much western legend, but of considerable fact.

"The story of the . . . grizzly bear," according to Harold McCracken in *The Beast That Walks Like Man*, "is an extraordinary heritage of legendary lore and historic melodrama, that goes back to the time when the saber-tooth tiger and the mastodon roamed where our farms and cities thrive today." As an example, Merriweather Lewis described the grizzly bear as a ". . . monster animal, and a most terrible enemy. Our man had shot him through the center of the lungs; yet he had pursued him furiously for half a mile, then returned more than twice that distance, and with his talons prepared himself a bed in the earth two feet deep and five feet long; he was perfectly alive when they found him; which was at least two hours after he had received the wound."

The grizzly bear is a North American subspecies of the brown bear (though a few populations of brown bears in Eurasia have at times been called "grizzlies"). It lives in a temperate climate and is the most open-country bear. Diverse in color, which is brownish (but varying from blond to black), it lacks a uniformity in color on the body and head; the fur there often gives a grizzled appearance. Large, though smaller than other brown bears, the grizzly is strongly built, with a large hump of fat and muscle over the shoulder, a thick head with a dished face and short, round ears, and long, obvious claws on front paws. They hibernate and have a prolonged gestation period with delayed implantation. Dignified, the grizzly bear triggers the emotions of humans.

"The term 'grizzly' is a colloquial name that refers to the animal's coloration," writes Domico. "It usually has a dark coat with shimmering silvery-tipped hairs that give it a 'grizzled' appearance. . . ."

The grizzly bear, according to McCracken, "is invulnerable to all of life's hazards, except the artificial weapons of man, but he has a cast-iron constitution. As a species [sub-species], they are just about nature's healthiest children. Susceptible to practically no physical disease or lesser ailments, they have the natural ability of thriving on a remarkably wide variety of diets. Although carnivorous by physical evolution, they are widely omnivorous in adaptability."

Polar Bear (Ursus maritimus)

The "wandering bear," of monstrous size, was called a polar bear (Nanook) long before the North Pole was discovered. Considered by many the most overall dangerous species of bear, and a formidable adversary, polar bears are one of North America's most magnificent animals. Arctic explorer Peter Freuchen said of the polar bears, "No more beautiful animal walks on four feet," relates Ben East in *Bears*. This traveling "sea bear," according to East, "is the great white or cream-colored survivalist of arctic snow and ice."

The polar bear ". . . is a noble-looking animal," describes John Muir in *The Cruise of The Corwin*, "and of enormous strength, living bravely and warm amid eternal ice. They certainly do not seem to have been fed upon lately to any marked extent, for we found them everywhere in abundance along the edge of the ice, and they appeared to be very fat and prosperous, and very much at home, as if the country had belonged to them always. They are the unrivaled master-existences of this icebound solitude. . . ."

Though grizzly bears are the most feared, polar bears are the most overall dangerous. Ian Sterling, a noted polar bear biologist, commented that "once polar bears reach maturity, they seem immortal."

The polar bear lives in an arctic (polar) climate, is the greatest wanderer of all bears, and is considered by many as the largest and most carnivorous of modern bears. Yellowish white in color, with a black nose, the polar bear's body is elongated with low, well-developed shoulders, a long, relatively thin, but well-developed neck, highly developed hind quarters and a small head. It has a straight profile, a Roman nose with a bulge at the bridge of the snout, large feet with membranes up to 1/2 the length of the toes and long and thick claws. Four inches of blubber cover the rump and legs (except inside the back legs). The polar bear does not hibernate (excepting pregnant sows), and it has a prolonged gestation period with delayed implantation. It considers anything that moves as food.

As autumn passes through the arctic, ". . . the sun has already disappeared below the horizon," writes Charles Feazel in *White Bear*. "Its cheering rays won't be seen again for more than a hundred days. The huge Newfoundland dog lies curled beneath the building that is wrapped in a deepening blanket of snow. . . ." "And in the gathering gloom, in the pack ice now frozen into solid sheets, there are bears. Hundreds of bears. Thousands of bears. Masters of darkness. White ghosts in the black night. No human, nothing in nature, challenges their supremacy: in the darkness of winter, the ice belongs to Nanook."

Asiatic Black Bear *(Selenarctos thibetanus)*

The moon bear of Tibet, the Himalayan black bear, and the Tibetan black bear are names provided this bear with the thick neck mane. A white crescent-shaped, medallion-like mark on its chest accounts for the name, moon bear.

Though often trained to perform in captivity, the Asiatic black bear has a nasty disposition. "Wherever they occur," relates Domico, "moon bears are constantly in trouble with humans. In addition to raids on domestic livestock and grain, there are numerous records of these bears mauling and killing people."

"It is a bear of eastern Asia," write Paul Shepard and Barry Sanders in *The Sacred Paw*, "filling in the habitat that lies between that of the brown bear to the north and the sloth bear and sun bear to the south." However, the Asiatic black bear is being seriously affected by humans marketing the bear and its parts, as well as by habitat loss.

The Asiatic black bear lives in a temperate climate. Coloration is black, often with a white throat, and there is a highly pronounced, long, manelike mantle of hair around the neck, throat, and shoulders. The fur is soft, and the ears are thickly haired and relatively large. The head appears round and the body is muscular and broad, with heavier front quarters and shorter legs than the American black and brown bears. Legs and hindfeet are slender, and the claws are short. The Asiatic black bear spends most of its day in trees, as protection from humans and other predators. It has a prolonged gestation period with delayed implantation and hibernates in northern regions of its range. Though shy and cautious, it is more aggressive than the brown bears of Eurasia.

The Asiatic black bears, with their strange appearance, many names, outstanding learning ability in captivity, and unpredictable temperament were described by Rudyard Kipling as "the most bizarre of the ursine species."

Giant Pandas *(Ailuropoda melanoleuca)*

A national treasure of China, the World Wildlife Fund's symbol of world conservation, and a mystery in the wild, these popular and appealing bears have long been the focus of a classification controversy. Though originally considered bears, their diet of bamboo, an uncertain ancestry, the inability to vocalize in the same manner as other bears, unbearlike foot pads, and remarkable eye patches all provided doubt as to whether they were true bears. Research—including genetic studies—however, indicates giant pandas are "specialized" bears. According to George Schaller *et al.*, in *The Giant Pandas of Wolong*, "... pandas are related both to bears and to raccoons but more closely to the former. ..."

"The color pattern of the panda's pelage (fur) is unique among mammals ...," writes Schaller *et al.* "The giant panda

---

 ### THE PANDA CONTROVERSY

Disagreement has long dominated discussions of whether giant pandas should be classified with bears or with the family that includes raccoons and lesser pandas. At present, they are placed in both, as well as in a distinct and separate family. They were originally called giant pandas because of their bone and teeth similarities with the smaller red panda. Confusion reigns.

Giant pandas have traits that are similar to raccoons and bears, but they have some unique characteristics of their own; several distinguishing characteristics include:

- Coloration: highly visible, distinct black and white markings
- Dentition: heavy jaws and large teeth with multiple crowns for grinding
- Vocalizations: they bleat, unlike the growl or roar of other bears
- Shape of male genitalia: penis is very small (rodlike) and S-shaped

- Forepaws have an opposable (sixth) digit that is an extension of a wrist bone
- Scent gland: located in the anal region and used for marking
- Small intestine: shorter and less complex than that of other bears
- No heel pad on hind foot; no human-like track

They resemble bears with their shape, reproductive behavior, including delayed implantation, their walk or gait, and their number of teeth.

During the early 1980s, serological studies were conducted in which the degree of rejection by various bears and the raccoon to molecules of protein of the same bear was measured. "When certain proteins (transferrins) from the black bear, *Ursus americanus*, are mixed with the blood of other animals, a measurable reaction occurs," relate Shepard and Sanders. "The degree of reactivity can be quantified and is interpreted as the degree of relatedness between animals descended from a common ancestor."

The degree of genetic difference—with higher numbers indicating greater difference—between the study animals was found to be:

- American black bears: 0 (own proteins)
- brown bears: 6
- sun bears: 8
- spectacled bears: 8
- **giant pandas: 18**
- red pandas: 52
- raccoons: 55

The study provided immunological evidence that giant pandas are more bear than raccoons and red (lesser) pandas, and they evolved from the bears, splitting off twenty million years ago. However, as with any controversy, questions, differing opinions, and disagreements continue.

---

requires no detailed description; its striking, black-and-white image is known throughout the world."

The giant panda, rare in the wild (and captivity), lives in a temperate climate. Its black and white hair gives it the most distinctive coloration pattern of all bears. It is stocky, with a relatively short body (squat and barrel-shaped), a broad, massive, and round head with a short muzzle. The legs are stout and powerful, relatively short, and it possesses a specialized head and paws to handle bamboo stems. The forepaws are flexible and there is a sixth toe that forms a kind of opposable thumb. Its dentition is typical of carnivores, as is the digestive tract, but digestion is poor due to a herbivore diet. The pupils of the eyes are vertical slits, as opposed to the horizontal orientation of other bears. Fur is coarse, extremely dense, and woolly, giving a cuddly appearance. A giant panda does not hibernate, but has a prolonged gestation with delayed implantation. Retiring and elusive, it is a solitary animal and a highly specialized and aberrant bear.

"No other animal has so entranced the public . . . ," relates Schaller, ". . . an almost mythical creature in which legend and reality merge."

Sloth Bear *(Melursus ursinus)*

These very active and elusive, long-lipped and poorly groomed bears are highly specialized to allow them to seek and feed on termites. An unusual face, minus two front teeth and with a long lower lip, provides sloth bears with tubular vacuuming systems for the suction of insects. Originally classified as a "bear" sloth due to its sickle-shaped claws and the habit of hanging from tree limbs, it was appropriately identified as a bear in the early 1800s.

The sloth bear lives in a subtropical (monsoon) climate. Its fur is black, with a whitish Y or V mark on the chest, and the coat is long, shaggy, and unkempt, with heavy fur on the back of the neck and between the shoulders forming a mane. The belly and underlegs are nearly bare. The blunt, hook-like claws are highly developed, and the pads of the toes are connected by a hairless web. The sloth bear has a specialized, bulbous snout, with wide nostrils, pronounced lips, and a lower lip that can be stretched over the outer edge of its nose. The tongue is long and flat, and the palate is bony and hollowed out. There are no upper incisor teeth, which enhances the tubular space used to suck termites. It is a rangy bear, long in appearance. The sloth bear does not hibernate, and there is prolonged gestation with delayed implantation.

Sloth bears' specialized termite hunting is described by Shepard and Sanders. "To get them the bear smashes a rotten log or tears open a termite mound with its long claws. At the same time it alternately blows away the dirt and wood chips and sucks up termites so noisily that it can be heard 100 meters away. It is called the 'lip bear' because its long lips form the end of a tube for this staccato in-huffing and out-puffing."

Sun Bear (*Helarctos malayanus*)

The world's smallest bears, the "Malay bears" live north and south of the equator. Considered "one of the most dangerous animals a human can encounter in the jungle," according to Domico.

Sun bear research has long been a low priority on the Malay Peninsula and in other areas where the bear occurs, so minimal information is available on this small, strange and fascinating animal that is also referred to as the "honey bear."

The sun bear occurs in a tropical climate; its population spans the equator. One of the rarest tropical forest animals, it is also the smallest and most lightly built bear (one hundred pounds is considered big). Black to dark brown in color, it has a whitish to pale orange/yellow horseshoe-shaped chest marking that is thought to resemble the sun; hence name. Its fur is short, the hair unusually thick for a tropical climate, and there is no hair on the soles of the paws. The head is short, wide and flat, with small, beady eyes, a highly flexible snout, and an extremely long, slender tongue. The muscular body has short, bowed legs (the front legs are quite powerful), large, inwardly set feet (making the bear bandy legged), and long and sickle-shaped claws. The sun bear does not hibernate and its gestation period is not prolonged, nor is there delayed implantation.

Spectacled Bear (*Tremarctos ornatus*)

The only South American species of bear, the spectacled bears are found in the Andes Mountains. Little is known about these rare bears, due to minimal investigation and the remoteness of the areas where they occur. Rings of gold color around the eyes are referred to as spectacles, thus the species' name.

The spectacled bear lives in a tropical climate, its habitat and range spanning the equator. The animal's color is black, or brown shaded with black, with yellowish white bands across the base of the nose and sometimes across the forehead, jaws, cheeks, throat, and chest. The highly visible markings are variable enough to be used to identify individuals. The fur is thick, with medium-length hair, and the head is large, with heavy jaw muscles and a short-faced profile. The spectacled bear has thirteen pairs of ribs (other species have fourteen pairs). It does not hibernate and the gestation period is prolonged, with delayed implantation. More vegetarian and tree dwelling than most species of bears, it is shy and cautious.

Size

The size of individual bears has long caused heated discussions and continual misjudgment. A bear's size is normally expressed in terms of weight, which is difficult to judge due to individual variations in height, thickness of fur, and physical stature, as well as the observer's proximity to the bear and particular level of stress. Under calm circumstances a bear's weight is often misjudged, but during a close encounter accurate weight determination is impossible by nearly all except possibly a seasoned field scientist. "The grizzly's reputation for ferociousness toward people," notes Terry Domico in *Bears Of The World*, "makes the animal seem much larger."

To the untrained eye, all bears are "big," as human perception of weight is most often much greater than an animal's true size. During a survey in Great Smoky Mountains National Park, responses to the weights of American black bears ranged from four hundred to four thousand pounds. The actual weights were ninety-five to one hundred fifteen pounds.

"The boar was small," according to Ben East in *Bears*, "hardly more than 150 pounds, but still big enough to be a formidable antagonist . . . the men guessed him at four hundred pounds."

In nearly all species of bears, the male is relatively larger than the female, though differences vary. For example, the difference between the sun bear females and males on Borneo is minimal, while on the Malaysian mainland the males may be more than one third larger.

Bear Weights: *Males vs Females*

AMERICAN BLACK BEARS	Males 33% larger
BROWN BEARS (Kodiak)	Males 40%–50% larger
GRIZZLY BEARS	Males 38% larger

POLAR BEARS	Males 25%–45% larger
ASIATIC BLACK BEARS	Males slightly larger
GIANT PANDAS	Males 10%–20% larger
SLOTH BEARS	Males slightly larger
SUN BEARS	Males 10%–45% larger
SPECTACLED BEARS	Males 33% larger

The Largest Bears

The brown bears and polar bears are without doubt the largest bears. However, there are conflicting and contradicting beliefs and statements concerning the largest individuals or species of these bears.

Brown Bears

"Of all the bears in the world, the Kodiak is the largest," according to Pat Cherr in The Bear. "He is the largest land-dwelling flesh-eater in the world."

"A full-grown Alaska brown bear is the most impressive wild animal on this continent," relates Clyde Ormand in Complete Book of Hunting. "The Alaska brown bear (Ursus) has for decades been considered North America's largest carnivore. . . ."

"There is little question," according to Ben East in Bears, "that on the average the brown bear is the biggest land carnivore left on earth."

"... the bear that most sportsmen call the Kodiak, the biggest bear on earth and also the biggest land carnivore . . ."

BEN EAST
The Ben East Hunting Book.

Adult male Kodiak brown bear in the Kodiak National Wildlife Refuge, Alaska
Courtesy Vic Barnes, U.S. Fish & Wildlife Service

"On Alaskan islands and in Siberia," write Paul Shepard and Barry Sanders in The Sacred Paw, "the brown bear vies with the polar as the largest predatory land mammal. . . ."

"The world's largest bears," notes Frederick Drimmer in The Animal Kingdom, "dwell along the narrow margin of the coastal land that stretches from Alaska to British Columbia and the neighboring islands. It is strange that these big brown bears, close kin to the grizzly, never wander inland very far. . . . The Kodiak Bear, Ursus middendorffi, is famous for its huge size."

"These mighty (brown) bears," wrote Roger Caras in North American Mammals, "are the largest meat-eating land animals left on the planet."

Polar Bears

"One of the most formidable of all carnivores," notes Cherr, "he [the polar bear] is tremendous in size."

"They [polar bears] grow to a very large size," writes Don Dehart in All About Bears, "with the large males, which are on a par with the Alaskan brown bear. . . ."

"Polar bears are the largest of the North American bears," according to Peter Clarkson and Linda Sutterlin in Bear Essentials.

"The white bear is a huge animal . . . ," note Shepard and Sanders.

"As to maximum body size probably the polar bear exceeds the coastal brownie," according to bear-hunting guide Duncan Gilchrist, in All About Bears. "A lifesize white bear may indeed be the world's most impressive mount."

"Polar bears," writes Domico, "are among the largest members of the bear family."

"Judged by skull size, the yardstick the Boone and Crockett Club uses in scoring trophy bears, the polar does not quite equal the brown, for the reason that his more slender head counts against him," notes East in Bears. "In weight he rivals the giant brown bear of Alaska. Perhaps the greatest difference between the sea bear and the land bears is in his [the polar bear's] looks."

"Only the Alaskan brown bear rivals it [the polar bear] in size," writes Erwin Bauer in Bears In Their World. "On average, Kodiak and polar bears are roughly the same size and are the largest carnivorous land mammals on earth."

"He [the polar bear] is the second largest meat-eating land animal in the world," according to Caras.

". . . the largest predators that stalk the earth," Feazel writes of the polar bears. "If he wished Nanook could slap a giraffe in the face."

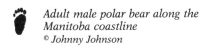

Adult male polar bear along the Manitoba coastline
© Johnny Johnson

LARGEST BOONE AND CROCKETT SKULLS

Longest skull	Inches
Polar bear	18 8/16
Alaskan brown bear	17 15/16
Grizzly bear	17 6/16
American black bear	14 12/16

Widest Skulls	Inches
Alaska brown bear	12 13/16
Polar bear	11 17/16
Grizzly bear	10 5/16
American black bear	8 14/16

Scoring and Ranking		Total Score
Alaska brown bear	1	30 12/16
Polar bear	1	29 15/16
Grizzly bear	1	27 2/16
American black bear	1	23 10/16

"The polar bear," writes Drimmer, *"is one of the largest carnivorous animals in the world, narrowly surpassed by the gigantic Alaskan brown bear. (In a sense it has a claim to the title of the largest carnivore, since the brown bear is carnivorous in theory and not in practice.)"*

"The polar bear," according to Koch in The Year of The Polar Bear," *has held the position as the largest terrestrial carnivore for thousands of years."*

The individuality of bears (thin, rangy, long-legged, thick skull, weight, height, posture, activity, and many other physical and behavioral features) provides enormous variation and considerable difficulty, if not near impossibility, in judging what species, or even in some instances what individual, is the largest. The ". . . brown bear is broad-shouldered and dish-faced, the polar bear is narrow-shouldered and Roman-nosed," notes Lopez in *Arctic Dreams*. "His [the polar bear's] neck is longer, his head smaller. He stands taller than the brown bear but is less robust in the chest and generally of lighter build."

Comparative Sizes of Skulls

The Boone and Crockett system described in Chapter 6 scores a skull by the total of the length and the width, and ranks the bears accordingly. This is a tangible means of size comparison, but not totally indicative of total size, as individual variations occur. For example, a large, heavy bear may have a small, short, or narrow skull, providing it with a total skull size unrepresentative of its overall body size.

Weight

Weights of bears vary between species, with polar bears and Alaskan brown bears more than ten times heavier than sun bears. Such differences between species, though due in part to genetics, are most often a result of variations in habitat, primarily diet. For example, the Alaskan brown bears of the coastal regions of North America, with a major source of fish and more lush vegetation, are nearly twice the weight of the inland brown bears (grizzly bears).

Causes of individual weight differences between bears of the same species, and sometimes the same habitat, may include individual health, age, the sex of the bear, individual ability to locate food or digest specific foods, and the level of ability to withstand human impacts on the habitat.

Seasonal fluctuations in weights of individual bears is common. Fall (pre-denning) weights are normally much greater than spring (emergence) weights. Weights are affected by seasonally available foods.

American black bears of eastern North America are consistently larger than those of the western states. (Weights are averages from a specific sampling.)

	Adult male	*Adult female*
❖ *New York*	*273 pounds*	*196 pounds*
❖ *California*	*216 pounds*	*127 pounds*

Wyoming/Montana grizzly bears are larger than those of the Yukon Territory. (Again, weights are averages from a specific sampling.)

	Adult male	*Adult female*
❖ *Wyoming*	*539 pounds*	*334 pounds*
❖ *Yukon Territory*	*315 pounds*	*209 pounds*

Bear weights are obtained when bears are harvested during a hunt, when illegally killed (poached), and when immobilized for management and research. The weights below from some states and provinces are "dressed" weights of bears harvested by hunters or taken during management actions.

Weights of Mature Males

	Average	*Range*	*Heaviest recorded*
❖ **American black bear**	*250*	*125–600*	*803*
❖ **Brown bear**	*725*	*500–900*	*2,500+*
❖ **Grizzly bear**	*490*	*350–700*	*1,496*

	Average	Range	Heaviest recorded
❖ **Polar bear**	1,150	900–1,500	2,210
❖ **Asiatic black bear**	250	200–255	440
❖ **Giant panda**	220	176–275	—
❖ **Sloth bear**	220	Up to 300	—
❖ **Sun bear**	100	60–110	143
❖ **Spectacled bear**	210	175–275	385

North American Bear Weights The weights listed below are provided by the wildlife management agencies of the respective states and provinces.

	American black bear	Grizzly bear	Polar bear
UNITED STATES			
❖ Alabama	426	—	—
❖ Alaska	440	850*	***
❖ Arkansas	570	—	—
❖ California	680	—	—
❖ Connecticut	200+	—	—
❖ Florida	624	—	—
❖ Georgia	520	—	—
❖ Idaho	***	550	—
❖ Maine	500+	—	—
❖ Maryland	385	—	—
❖ Massachusetts	467+	—	—
❖ Michigan	615+	—	—
❖ Mississippi	400	—	—
❖ Montana	***	790	—
❖ Nevada	435	—	—
❖ New Hampshire	468+	—	—
❖ New Jersey	582	—	—
❖ New York	750	—	—
❖ North Carolina	720	—	—

(continued)

	American black bear	Grizzly bear	Polar bear
❖ Oregon	456	—	—
❖ Pennsylvania	800+	—	—
❖ South Carolina	427	—	—
❖ Texas	570	—	—
❖ Vermont	514+	—	—
❖ Virginia	579	—	—
❖ Washington	***	Unknown	—
❖ West Virginia	485	—	—
❖ Wisconsin	700	—	—
❖ Wyoming	250	1,120**	—
CANADA			
❖ Alberta	600	***	—
❖ British Columbia	***	800+	—
❖ Manitoba	803	—	1,549
❖ New Brunswick	690	—	—
❖ Newfoundland	687	—	1,135
❖ Northwest Territories	***	528	1,780
❖ Nova Scotia	***	—	—
❖ Ontario	726	—	***
❖ Quebec	640	—	***
❖ Saskatchewan	500	—	—
❖ Yukon Territory	***	948	***
MEXICO			
❖ Chihuahua	110–330	—	—
❖ Coahuila	***	—	—
❖ Durango	***	—	—
❖ Nuevo Leon	***	—	—
❖ San Luis Potosi	***	—	—
❖ Sinaloa	***	—	—
❖ Sonora	***	—	—
❖ Tamaulipas	***	—	—
❖ Zacatecas	***	—	—

* Kodiak brown bears (males): 1,400–1,600 pounds
** Yellowstone National Park
*** Information unavailable

Bear Weights in Lore and Legend Lore and legend have provided some very impressive weights of bears:

Kamchatkan (Commonwealth) brown bear—2500 pounds

American black bear (during the 1800s)—1800 pounds

California grizzly bear (early 1900s)—2350 pounds

"Legendary" weights are not uncommon, even today. Ben East, in *Bears*, relates the comment of a zoo director about such weights, ". . . few grizzlies of record weight come from a part of the country where accurate scales are found." And Adolph Murie, in *A Naturalist In Alaska*, notes that "a bear a long distance from a scale always weighs most."

Height

The height of a bear is measured from the bottom of its paw flat on the ground to the highest point of the shoulder. What follows are the ranges or average heights for adult males.

▲ American black bear	2.5–3 ft.	▲ Giant panda	2.3–2.6 ft.
▲ Brown bear	3–5 ft.	▲ Sloth bear	2–3 ft.
▲ Polar bear	up to 5.3 ft.	▲ Sun bear	2.3 ft.
▲ Asiatic black bear	2.6–3.3 ft.	▲ Spectacled bear	2.3–3 ft.

In comparison, the height of an American bison is five feet; elephant eight feet; hippopotamus five feet; rhinoceros six feet; and a Siberian tiger three feet.

3½'

6'7"

Height/length measurements
Renee Evanoff

Length

The length of a bear is measured from the tip of the nose to the tip of the tail. Adult male average lengths (ranges) are listed below.

▲ American black bear   4–6 ft.   ▲ Giant panda   5–6 ft.

▲ Brown bear   7–10 ft.   ▲ Sloth bear   5–6 ft.

▲ Polar bear   8–8.4 ft.   ▲ Sun bear   3–4.5 ft.

▲ Asiatic black bear   5–7 ft.   ▲ Spectacled bear   4–7 ft.

In comparison, the length of an American bison is nine feet; elephant eleven feet; killer whale thirty feet; mountain lion eight feet; and a Siberian tiger thirteen feet.

Color

The coloration of bears is quite variable between species and within species. Color changes are not uncommon, due to maturation or seasonal fading and shedding in individual bears, or with the angle and intensity of the natural light of the moment. Variations may include totally different color or different shades of a color. (The underfur color normally remains the same, while the guard hairs change.)

American black bear cubs of the same litter may be different colors, and they may change as they mature from brown to black—or the opposite may occur. They may change before they reach one year old, or at two and three years.

A bear's underfur may be brown while the outer, guard hairs are tipped in black, and some bears are entirely of a single color. Several species of bears have yellowish or whitish chest markings on many individuals, while the chest mark, or medallion, is found on all members of the tropical bears—sloth, sun, and spectacled. The markings vary in shape and size.

Albinism Albinism, though extremely rare, occurs in all bear species. A "partial" albino American black bear, with a white breast and white front feet, was observed in Wyoming in 1948. There is record of a whitish American black bear with four cubs: one brown, two black, and one true albino. In Oregon, an American black bear had a light chocolate brown head and feet with the rest of the body a dirty white (not a true albino).

Ernest Thompson Seton makes reference to two albino American black bears in the eastern United States. An albino American black bear was killed near Kalispell, Montana in 1983.

Color Descriptions and Variations

AMERICAN BLACK BEARS
Black; brown; cinnamon; blond; white (Kermode bear); blue-gray (glacier bear); rich chocolate brown, light brown; silver; blond; yellow; sometimes white V-shaped throat or chest patch; face always brownish.

Color variations of American black bears are considerable, and are greater in the western part of the continent. Seventy percent of the American black bears are black in color, but only fifty percent of those in the Rocky Mountains are black. Black coats are found more often in moist areas such as New England, New York, Tennessee, Michigan and western Washington.

BROWN BEARS
Dark brown (almost black); rust; ash brown; cream; yellowish; frequently white-tipped hairs; less grizzled. More uniform than the grizzly bear in individual coloration.

EURASIAN BROWN BEAR
Wide variety of coloration: black; dark brown; reddish with a silver tip (red bear of India); bi-colored with yellow-brown or whitish cape across shoulders (horse bear of China).

GRIZZLY BEARS
Dark brown (almost black) to cream (almost white); yellowish brown; black hairs usually have white tips; intensity of color varies over body; pale-tipped guard hairs extend beyond the mat of fur and provide a "silvertip" or grizzled appearance; black grizzly bears are seldom grizzled; white collars on cubs not uncommon. The grizzly bear is named for color, not disposition.

American black bear sow and its cub. Note the color variation that occurs within this species
Courtesy Yellowstone National Park

The grizzly bear with its "grizzled" coloration
© Johnny Johnson

POLAR BEARS

White or cream; orange-yellow underhairs (hair is actually transparent, but appears white or cream); color varies with the seasons, often pure white following the molt; yellowish shade during the summer due to oxidation by the sun.

"The natural color of a fully grown polar bear is a creamy, yellowish white," writes Thomas Koch in *The Year Of The Polar Bear*. "Depending on his surroundings and the type of light, he may seem to be more one shade than the other. If it is a brilliant day, he will seem to be more white than yellow. If it is a dark, dreary day, he will appear more yellow than white.

In some zoo situations, polar bears have developed a green hue caused by a freshwater blue-green algae in the hollow hairs of their fur.

ASIATIC BLACK BEARS

Jet black; glossy; occasionally partly brown; muzzle brownish; white or orange-yellow crescent (horseshoe) on chest.

COLOR VARIATIONS IN THE U.S.

STATE	COLOR BREAKDOWN
Michigan	100% black
Minnesota	94% black; 6% brown
New England	100% black
New York	100% black
Tennessee	100% black
Washington (coastal)	99% black; 1% brown, blond
Washington (inland)	21% black; 79% brown, blond
Yosemite National Park	9% black; 91% brown, blond

Asiatic black bear of typical color—black with a white collar or crest
© *Gary Brown*

GIANT PANDAS	White, with black eye patches and ears; black forelegs with black extending in a narrowing band over the shoulder; black hindlegs; tip of white tail sometimes black; some brownish-black hair on the chest.
	The giant panda's coloration makes it highly conspicuous in the forest. "The color pattern of the panda's pelage," notes George Schaller *et al.* in *The Giant Pandas Of Wolong*, "is unique among mammals. . . ."
SLOTH BEAR	Dull black; sometimes rusty; white or cream V or Y on chest; gray/white snout.
SUN BEAR	Glossy, coal black; sometimes brownish; yellowish or whitish crescent mark on chest; crescent sometimes not present; muzzle and ear tips silver.
SPECTACLED BEAR	Jet black; yellowish line on face, which often forms rings around the eyes; white patch on chest. Markings are unique and allow identification of individual bears. The markings on the spectacled bear are much less conspicuous in Bolivia than over the remainder of its range.

The coloration of bears of the world is simply described as ranging from "black to white." Coloration as a means of identification of species, except the giant panda, is not as definitive as it may seem because of the enormous color variation within some of the species.

Fur

he bear's fur is among the most effective insulating coats worn by any wild animal," writes George Laycock in *The Wild Bears*. "The density of the coat keeps the animal [giant panda] warm, and the oiliness prevents water from penetrating," notes Schaller, ". . . an adaptation to a cool, moist climate."

The fur of bears, as that of most animals, provides many features for their survival:

▲ A factor in identification

▲ Protection from insects and other environmental threats

▲ Concealment from predators or enemies

▲ Indicates behavioral information (for instance, raised hackles)

▲ Protection from dirt and debris

▲ Insulation from cold and heat

The bears' fur consists of two hairs, the "guard hair" and the "underfur." Bear fur actually appears human when it is not coarse.

Bears shed (molt) their fur annually during the spring and summer, appearing quite shaggy as their old hair (guard hair and underfur) comes off and is replaced by new growth. The period of shedding varies with the climate, with an earlier shedding period occurring in warmer areas. Removal of the old hair is accomplished by rubbing against trees and rocks to facilitate the natural shedding and simultaneously serves the purpose of "marking." A bear's fur, as with other animals, appears its worst during shedding as it is uneven, with chunks hanging loosely from the body. A new coat is growing while the old is being shed and is normally in place by fall. "At this time of molt," describes Andy Russell in *Grizzly Country*, "grizzlies take on the look of mountain hoboes—ragged, unkempt, and tattered—until again transformed by new, much darker coats."

AMERICAN BLACK BEAR	Soft, dense underfur (insulation); long, coarse, thick (diameter) guard hair
BROWN BEAR	Long, thick fur; moderately long mane at back of head
POLAR BEAR	Most fur-clad species of bears, being completely covered except for nose and paw pads; fur is thick (650 hairs/.39 square inch) with tufted guard hairs; hollow, oily hair provides heat preservation while on land and buoyancy at sea; the hair has no insulating value when in the sea; the hair is two to six inches long; it collects heat: each hair is a hollow transparent tube that reflects and scatters the sun's rays to the black skin where the heat is absorbed; hairs change ninety-five percent of the sun's rays to heat
ASIATIC BLACK BEAR	Soft; shaggy; manelike mantle of hair around neck, shoulders and jowls; length varies with climate and habitat and is inversely proportional to fall fat accumulation
GIANT PANDA	Coarse; extremely dense and wooly; sparse on underside; feels slightly oily; resists compaction; fur is well suited for an animal that spends considerable time sitting on the ground in a cool, moist climate
SLOTH BEAR	Long; straight; unusually coarse and shaggy; mane (ruff) behind head, on neck and on shoulders; underlegs and belly almost bare; minimal hair on snout; fur often matted, unkempt
SUN BEAR	Very short; smooth; dense; dark skin evident; fur cowlicks, whorls on forehead and behind ears
SPECTACLED BEAR	Long (three to four inches); somewhat shaggy; thick; shiny

Skulls

Brown bear

Polar bear

Asiatic black bear

American black bear

Giant panda

Skulls
Courtesy David Mattson, IGBST

enerally, the skulls of bears are massive, typically long, wide across the forehead with prominent eyebrow ridges, a large jawbone hinge, and with heavy jaw muscles and broad nostrils. Combined with dentition, the structure of bears' skulls are very much carnivorous, though with omnivore modifications.

The skull may be the most important feature of an animal, housing the brain, providing a major protective and nutritional feature (mouth with teeth), and containing sensory/communication features. "Bear skulls undergo a series of changes from early life to old age, and in most species do not attain their mature form until seven or more years of age," observed C. H. Merriam in *North America Fauna, Biological Survey*, 1918.

Diet and other eating habits have influenced the individual development of the heads and skulls of each species. "Head shape and size . . . are influenced by dentition and jaw muscles," write Paul Shepard and Barry Sanders in *The Sacred Paw*. ". . . [skulls] are shaped to anchor the appropriate muscles. Because of the heavy jaw muscles it [spectacled bear] uses for crushing palm nuts, its skull shape is unusual, rather resembling that of the giant panda, which has massive molars for grinding bamboo shoots."

Brown bears normally do not bite to kill, but have grinding, crunching teeth with the massive muscles to accomplish the task. Polar bears are more carnivorous than other bears, and do bite to kill; their skulls are specifically shaped for the appropriate teeth and muscles to hold, chop, and slash their prey. Each of the eight bear species has its own distinctive skull shape and size.

AMERICAN BLACK BEAR	Broad, narrow muzzle; large jaw hinge; female head may be more slender and pointed
BROWN BEAR	Massive; heavily constructed; large in proportion to body; high forehead (steeply rising); concave (dished face); domed head; long muzzle; flat nose tip; ears barely observed as bumps; eyes tiny
POLAR BEAR	Large; small in proportion to body; long; snout long (warms air); Roman nose; large eyes
ASIATIC BLACK BEAR	Large; sloping forehead
GIANT PANDA	Massive; wide; zygomatic arches widely spread; constructed for attachment of powerful jaw muscles; short muzzle

SLOTH BEAR	Thick; long muzzle; small jaws; bulbous snout; wide nostrils
SUN BEAR	Wide and flat (unbearlike); short muzzle
SPECTACLED BEAR	Wide; short muzzle; lower jaw shorter than upper (overbite); unusual skull shape; resembles giant panda; young and female skulls narrow and long

Animal classification is primarily based on skulls (". . . details of skull and leg bones are the usual criteria for the biologists," note Shepard and Sanders) and in part led to the "splitting" of the bear species. Skull size is also the criteria for the "record size" bears of North America; the record lists are included in Chapter 6.

Teeth

A bear's teeth, combined with paws and claws, are its first-line tools for defense and obtaining food. The teeth are large, and though originally carnivorous, are adapted to an omnivorous diet of both meat and plant materials. The major difference between carnivore and omnivore dentition are the molars, which in bears are broad and flat. Dentition—the size, shape and use of the teeth—and jaw muscles influence the size and shape of a bear's head.

Bears have forty-two teeth, except the sloth bear which has only forty. Permanent teeth are normally in place by the time a bear is approximately two and a half years old. For each species the characteristics of the four kinds of teeth—incisors, canines, premolars, and molars—vary depending on diet and habitat.

	BEAR TEETH
Teeth	**Characteristic & Purpose**
Incisors:	*Pointed, not specialized. For cutting and biting.*
Canines:	*Pointed, long, sturdy. For grasping, ripping, and tearing (catching, holding, and killing other animals).*
Premolars:	*Not for shearing, as in carnivores; first three are unicuspids, with one root; last premolar has two roots—much larger; often missing in older bears. For holding and crushing.*
Molars:	*Heavy; "bunodont" crowns (flat, broad cusps). For crushing and grinding.*

AMERICAN BLACK BEAR	Premolars and molars for grinding
BROWN BEAR	Flat and broad crowns on molars; premolars and molars for grinding
POLAR BEAR	Canines larger and longer than for other bears; molars smaller than those of land bears; molars more for shearing; premolars more for biting than grinding
ASIATIC BLACK BEAR	Heavy molars (cause round-headed appearance)
GIANT PANDA	Massive (especially molars); highly modified for crushing and grinding (including posterior premolars, a condition not found in other bears)

SLOTH BEAR	Missing two upper incisors; forty teeth; cubs forty-two while nursing; two middle, upper incisors not replaced with permanent teeth; premolars and molars smaller than other bears (chew less vegetation); has poor teeth due to sucking and grinding dirt as they eat insects
SUN BEAR	Flatter teeth than other bears; canines long and protrude between lips
SPECTACLED BEAR	Large molars for crushing palm nuts; strong

Dental Formulae
(incisors—canines—premolars—molars)

bears	3-1-4-2 / 3-1-4-3	= 42
sloth bear	2-1-4-2 / 3-1-4-3	= 40
human	2-1-2-3 / 2-1-2-3	= 32

 The dental pattern of bears, as compared with human pattern. Most bears have 3 incisors, 1 canine, 4 premolars, and 2 molars in the top of the jaw, and nearly the same pattern in the lower jaw, except for three molars below instead of 2. With the exception of the sloth bear, bears have 42 teeth. Less-toothsome human beings have 32 teeth, including wisdom teeth.

Cavities and Abscessed and Worn-Out Teeth

Bears may have cavities, as they are one of the few wild animals susceptible to tooth decay, probably due in part to a sugary diet. Abscessed teeth are not uncommon and may contribute to the poor disposition of a bear. Any problem with a bear's teeth potentially affects its ability to eat, and in some situations has led to starvation.

Teeth "wear down" with age, and broken teeth are not uncommon. "One old male grizzly showed excessive tooth wear: four of the molariform teeth were worn in two, only two root stubs remaining in each, and one molar was missing," described Adolph Murie in *The Grizzlies Of Mount Mckinley*, "the upper and lower incisors were worn to the gums; the two upper canines were worn but still retained their shape, but the two lower canines were worn until only blunt stubs remained." This bear was shot breaking into a building.

Age Determination

A bear's age may be determined by the study of one of its teeth, in the same manner as growth rings are counted to age a tree.

A small vestigial tooth (premolar) is removed; softened with a nitric acid solution; sliced into thin sections that are then stained. The staining highlights the tiny rings, or "cement deposits" (cementum annuli) that are formed each year. The rings are counted under a microscope to determine the bear's age.

Ring width may provide a general indication of a bear's health—thin rings indicating poor development and health. Rings close together in a female bear's teeth may indicate lactation.

The cementum annuli are less well defined in polar bears, possible due to the lack of winter denning—growth is more continual.

Paws (Feet)

A bear's paws are important in locomotion (walking, running, climbing, swimming), killing, feeding, digging, lifting, raking, pulling, turning, sensing, and defense. Bears walk plantigrade like humans, paws with durable pads down flat on the ground, and pigeon-toed, forepaws turning inward. A bear's heat loss (thermoregulation) is primarily through its paws. "All the pads [paw soles] are surfaced with tough, cornified epidermis over a substantial mass of resistant connective tissue," describe Tracy Storer and Lloyd Tevis in *California Grizzly*. "This coverage of the foot is the sturdy, self-renewing 'shoe.'"

Bears have relatively flat feet (paws) with five toes, except the giant panda, which has six. Hind paws are larger than forepaws and resemble the feet of humans, except the "big toe" is located on the outside of the paw. Bears are renowned for their forepaw dexterity; they can pick pine nuts from cones, unscrew jar lids, and delicately manipulate other small objects. "The grizzly, though apparently awkward and lumbering, is really one of the most agile of beasts," noted Enos Mills in *The Spell of the Rockies*. "I constantly marveled at . . . [the] bear's lightness of touch, or the deftness of movement of his fore paws."

Claws are curved, longer on the hind paws than the forepaws, and unlike a cat's, non-retractable. (See more on claws later in this chapter.)

Specialized Paws

Giant pandas have a sixth digit, forming an opposable thumb (enlarged wrist bone with independent movement),

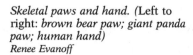
Skeletal paws and hand. (Left to right: brown bear paw; giant panda paw; human hand)
Renee Evanoff

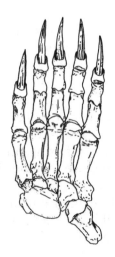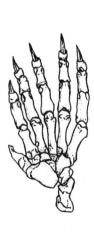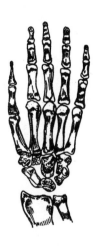

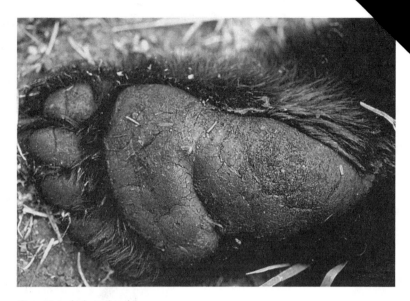

 Grizzly bear hindpaw
© Gary Brown

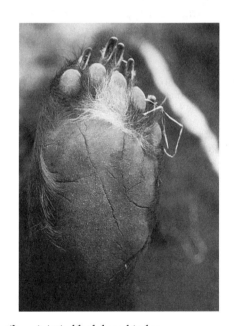

Asiatic black bear hindpaw
© Gary Brown

which allows them to handle bamboo stems and leaves with dexterity and precision. Polar bears have swimming membranes that join more than half the length of their toes, and the paw pads are non-skid on ice due to a tread of tiny nipples on the soles. Some bear species have paws with specializations geared toward their natural habitat.

AMERICAN BLACK BEAR	Sole black or brownish; naked, leathery and deeply wrinkled
BROWN BEAR	Sole black, brownish, sometimes whitish; wrinkled
POLAR BEAR	Sole black; paws broad, paddle-like; flatter than those of other bears; pads concealed by hair; paws heavily matted with short, stiff hairs on soles; hair between pads for protection from cold; paws unique for swimming, shoveling snow, and traveling on and through snow
ASIATIC BLACK BEAR	Forepaws not deeply divided (leaves more solid track); pads are bare; heel pads of forefeet larger than those of most other bears; hindpaw narrow and tapers toward rear
GIANT PANDA	No heel pad on hindpaws; forepaws adapted with a sixth toe (a thumb, one and a third inches long) for grasping bamboo stems; opposable thumb has independent movement; forepaws flexible
SLOTH BEAR	Huge paws compared to body; minimal hair on soles; hairless skin web between toes; paws extremely sensitive to touch; delicate finger (toe) control

SUN BEAR	Paws similar to those of Asiatic black bear; no hair on soles
SPECTACLED BEAR	No hair on soles, except band of hair between second and fourth toes

The tracks left behind by these paws that vary with the species and individuals are based on genetic characteristics. A bear may be identifiable by its paws.

Claws

Non-retractable claws, fixed in an outstretched position, are a bear's more specialized tools used for battle, digging (forepaws), climbing, and handling foods. Tiny objects are deftly manipulated with paws and claws, just as humans use their hands and fingers. "I have seen a big brown bear delicately turning a feather over and over in its paws," writes Terry Domico in *Bears of the World*. Claw lengths of species and individuals within the species will vary with the time of year, amount of digging, and type of terrain where the bear travels and digs. Foreclaws are normally longer than hindclaws.

Black Bear

Grizzly Bear

Grizzly and black bear claws
Renee Evanoff

AMERICAN BLACK BEAR	Color black, grayish brown; short and round; thick at base; tapered to sharp point; foreclaws and hind claws nearly same length; foreclaw sharply curved
BROWN BEAR	Color dark, almost black; large and slightly curved; longer and narrower than those of other bears; foreclaws four to five inches long; hindclaws shorter and more curved than foreclaws; claws more blunt than those of other bears; used for digging
GRIZZLY BEAR	Color quite variable (black, brown, grayish to white, sometimes ivory, especially in older bears; tan, amber, yellowish; may whiten with age; sometimes streaking with light and dark stripes)
POLAR BEAR	Color black; immense; thick; shorter than those of the brown bears; two to three inches; less worn than the brown bear (no digging, except in den preparation); used to climb ice and hunt
ASIATIC BLACK BEAR	Color whitish, sometime quite white; short; curved; strong; used for digging and climbing
GIANT PANDA	Color darkish to whitish; sharply curved; used for hooking stems, not digging
SLOTH BEAR	Color ivory or white; sickle-shaped (deeply curved); blunt; four inches long; use to dig

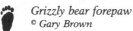
Grizzly bear forepaw
© *Gary Brown*

SUN BEAR	Color ivory; long; sickle-shaped; sharp; used for climbing; most curved and sharpest of all bears; up to four inches long
SPECTACLED BEAR	Light colored (whitish); huge; curved; strong and hard; used to scratch and dig in hard soil

"The claws of the grizzly/brown bear are one of its most distinguishing characteristics," explains Duncan Gilchrist in *All About Bears*. "Experts note that they are longer and straighter than those of the . . . [blacks]. They are never shorter than two and half inches. At the other extreme I have seen claws that reached six inches in length.

"A large grizzly/brown bear claw is an item of beauty," describes Gilchrist, "that is often used as the basis of a piece of jewelry."

Tracks

Tracks of any animal species are the exciting and intriguing sign left behind as they move through their habitat. A single bear track will increase the hunter's flow of adrenalin, peak the hiker's perception of wilderness, and heighten the alertness of both.

"I went up from the camp along a sandy stretch and was surprised to discover what I took to be the fresh print of the

Grizzly bear tracks in the sand along a lake beach in Yellowstone National Park
Courtesy Yellowstone National Park

bare foot of a man," wrote Frederick Dellenbaugh in *A Canyon Voyage*. "Mentioning this when I returned, my companions laughed and warned me to be cautious and give this strange man a wide berth unless I had my rifle and plenty of ammunition. It was the track of a grizzly bear." (Frederick Dellenbaugh was an artist and topographer for Major John Wesley Powell's second expedition on the Green and Colorado Rivers, in 1871 and 1872.)

Tracks are as individual as human fingerprints, and particular bears may be identified by this spore (width/length ratio, specific cracks in the sole, broken claws). Tracks within an individual species of bears will vary due to age, weight, sex, or the type of surface over which the bear is traveling. (Track measurements are of average adult males and do not include claw length.)

AMERICAN BLACK BEARS	Track distinct (less so when more hair on paws); toes loosely spaced from a curved arc; claw mark length not more than the toe pad length; claw marks normally not visible; claws appear like toe marks; intermediate pad is wedge shaped; single round heel pad often not visible; hindpaw track similar to human track; forepaw track 4½ inches long and 4 inches wide; hindpaw track 7 inches long and 4 inches wide
BROWN BEAR	Track often indistinct; toes close together and form a relatively straight line; toe pads joined; foreclaws twice as long as toe pads; claws occasionally not evident in track; single round heel pad sometimes not visible; forepaw track 6 to 8 inches long and 7–9 inches wide; hindpaw track 12–16 inches long and 8–10½ inches wide
GRIZZLY BEARS	Forepaw 5¼ inches long and 5½ inches wide; hindpaw ten inches long and six inches wide
POLAR BEARS	Tracks often indistinct due to hair and normally visible only in soft snow or mud; have fringed edges due to hair; toes form arc much like tracks of American black bear; claws commonly not visible in track; forepaw 5¾ inches long and 9 inches wide; hindpaw 13 inches long and 9 inches wide
SLOTH BEARS	Claws appear in forepaw tracks only; similar size to grizzly bears

Identification of Tracks

▲ Use a tracks field guide (see bibliography)

▲ Know what species of bears occur in the area

▲ Forepaw and hindpaw tracks are different

▲ Consider type of track surface (hard soil, snow, mud, etc.)

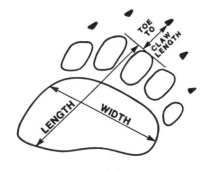
How to measure tracks
From *Bear Attacks*, by Stephen Herrero, New York: Lyons & Burford, 1985.

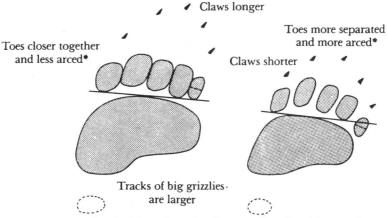

Claws longer

Toes closer together and less arced*

Toes more separated and more arced*

Claws shorter

Tracks of big grizzlies are larger

Heel pad of front foot often does not show for either species

GRIZZLY BEAR
Left front foot track

BLACK BEAR
Left front foot track

(Illustration from Bear Attacks *by Stephen Herrero)*

▲ Small toe may not always be evident

▲ Heel pad of forepaw often not evident

▲ Claws not always evident

▲ Consider relative size

▲ Track of a running bear will be different from that of a walking bear

▲ Hind paw track often slightly in front of forepaw print

Shoulder Hump (Brown Bear)

Brown bears have a hump between their shoulders that is covered with long hair and is normally a reliable means of species identification. The long hair often accentuates the hump when the "hackles" are raised. This distinguishing feature is a distinctive mass of muscle that provides the brown bears with their exceptional digging ability and the powerful striking force of the forepaws.

Tails

Bears' tails were originally large, but disappeared several million years ago as bears evolved from dog-like carnivores. Bears now have short, stubby tails, no more than "furry flaps of skin" hidden in the surrounding fur; they are the shortest relative to body size of all carnivorous animals.

The tails of polar bears are well insulated and have extra blood vessels to prevent them from freezing. A sloth bear tail is relatively longer than the tails of most other bears. Giant panda tails are one third to one fifth the length of their bodies at birth, but become smaller relative to body size as the bear grows.

Bears' tails generally function as protection for the anal region, though giant pandas also have a more specialized use for theirs; when marking (scenting) with its urine and anal glands' secretion, giant pandas utilize their tails like a brush to spread the scent.

Adolph Murie, in *The Grizzlies Of Mount McKinley*, relates a legend describing the grizzly bear's loss of its tail. "The loss of his tail made his temper uncertain and he became very temperamental and sometimes dangerous. When he was angry, he had not enough tail to take up the excess energy in slow writhing, as do cats and the energy then went into his legs and he charged toward whatever annoyed him. And he had not tail enough to put between his legs and run away, like a dog."

Tail Size (Inches)

▲ American black bear	4.8
▲ Brown bear	4–4.8
▲ Polar bear	2.8–4.8
▲ Asiatic black bear	4.4
▲ Giant panda	4–6
▲ Sloth bear	6–7
▲ Sun bear	1.2–2.8
▲ Spectacled bear	2.8

Baculum

The baculum is the penis bone, resembling an ivory hammer handle, found in several animal species (seals, walruses), including bears. "The genital of a Bear after his death waxeth as hard as horn . . ." wrote Edward Topsell in *The History Of Four-footed Beasts*. He obviously and erroneously believed the bone formed after death. Actually, a bear is born with a baculum that grows continually throughout its life; the size of the baculum can indicate the age of the bear. The baculum of a five-year-old American black bear is approximately 5½ to 6½ inches in length.

The baculum of the giant panda is very different from those of the other bear species, and other carnivores for that matter, being ". . . short and rodlike, with winglike expansions," according to Domico.

Believed to contain magical powers and provide strength and fertility, the baculum has long been sought by numerous cultures. The baculum of the polar bear is highly prized by the Eskimos, and the bacula of some older bears have been found broken, which stirs the question of how—ardor, or violence of battle? The broken baculum is the source of many native legends.

The damaged baculum is also evident in cave bears. "In several instances healed fractures of the penis bone have been observed," describes Bjorn Kurten in *Pleistocene Mammals of Europe*. "It has been suggested that they might be due to fighting between males in the breeding season."

Vision

The eyesight of bears has long been thought to be generally poor. However, more recent studies have shown it to be reasonably good, though there is still much to be learned of the visual capabilities of each species.

Generally, bears' eyes are various shades of brown, small (except those of polar bears), have round pupils (except giant pandas' which are vertical slits), and are widely spaced and face forward. They are important and useful feeding tools, and are reflective and mirror the faintest glow of the moon.

A general description of a bear's vision would include:

▲ Possibly equal to human vision

▲ Nearsighted due to feeding close to the ground (except polar bears)

▲ Exhibits color vision

▲ Good peripheral and night vision

▲ Good depth perception

▲ Binocular

▲ Eyes set relatively close together, facing forward

▲ Recognizes form, but not detail, at relatively long distances

▲ Observes moving objects better than stationary objects

Bears approach objects due to nearsightedness and stand upright to increase their sight distance.

Polar bears may have the most specialized eyes, providing very adaptable and excellent vision that exceeds that of other species of bears. They are large—almost as large as human eyes—and have an extra eyelid to filter snow glare. Depth perception is excellent and they are capable of good underwater vision due to nictitating membranes that protect the

An Alaskan grizzly bear stands for a better view in Katmai National Park
© Johnny Johnson

eyes and serve as lenses. Polar bears' eyes adapt to a wide range of light conditions, including darkness for hunting at night or during the dark winter. "The polar bear's visual world is marked by intense, glaring sunlight, contrasted by long, dark polar nights," relates Thomas Koch in *The Year Of The Polar Bear*. "Days are often punctuated with blizzards, sleet, and the constant, driving wind. With these factors present, the bear's vision is rarely given optimum conditions to view his surroundings. When traveling on the ice during good conditions, polar bears are able to identify immobile objects lying on the ice as far as one mile away."

However, a whaler's journal describing a blind polar bear demonstrates that good vision may not always be necessary. "From the appearance of the bear's eyes, the men surmised that the bear had been blind for a considerable period of time," relates Koch. "Even though the bear was blind, he was still fat, indicating that he hunted successfully, using only his hearing and smelling senses."

The ability to distinguish color, and activity at all levels of light (day and night) are excellent indicators of good vision. Some biologists believe the vision of bears is at least average, and at least two have expressed the thought that though bears act as if they have poor eyesight, it just may be they do not trust their eyes as well as their trustworthy noses. "Much of the anecdotal information on bear vision," according to Paul Shepard and Barry Sanders in *The Sacred Paw*, "assumes that the animal approaches strange objects because it does not see them well at a distance, but crows and coyotes do the same thing and nobody doubts their visual acuity."

Hearing

The ears of bears vary between species, both in size and in their location on the head. They range from large and floppy to small and hardly visible, and from those located well forward on the head to low and to the rear.

In general, a bear's hearing is fair to moderately good. "Hearing in bears is probably good," explains Stephen Herrero in *Bear Attacks*, "although most of the evidence is anecdotal." Bears, he also notes, ". . . probably hear in the ultrasonic range of 16–20 megahertz, perhaps higher." "The grizzly's sense of hearing is far more sensitive than man's," writes Thomas McNamee in *Grizzly Bear*, "and it is undoubtedly an important aid in the pursuit of such subterranean prey as pocket gophers, ground squirrels, mice, and voles, which grizzlies locate blindly and pounce on with noteworthy accuracy."

"At 300 meters [328 yards]," write Shepard and Sanders, "the bear can detect human conversation, and it responds to the click of a camera shutter or a gun being cocked at 50 meters [54.7 yards]."

Specific Descriptions of Ears and Hearing

AMERICAN BLACK BEAR	Ears are small, rounded, and set well back on the head; hearing is good
BROWN BEAR	Ears relatively small and located forward on head; hearing is good, though the grizzly bear's is considered, by some biologists, to be unsurpassed by other bears
POLAR BEAR	Ears small, located low on head (for low profile and protection), and furred inside for protection; hearing sensitive; ear canals close while underwater
ASIATIC BLACK BEAR	Ears bell shaped and longer (relative to body size) than those of large bears and stick out sideways from head; hearing good
GIANT PANDA	Ears large, fitting of the bulky body and set well back on head; hearing good
SLOTH BEAR	Ears very large, furry and floppy; hearing good
SUN BEAR	Ears small; hearing excellent
SPECTACLED BEAR	Ears small and far apart; hearing good

"The use of hearing by bears is not as obvious as that of sight and smell," notes Adolph Murie in *The Grizzlies Of Mount McKinley*. "Even though it may not play a prominent role in their activities, I believe grizzlies do have an acute sense of hearing."

Smell

Whether low to the ground or held high in the wind, the nose of a bear is its key to its surroundings. "Smell," writes Herrero, "is the fundamental and most important sense a bear has. A bear's nose is its window into the world just as our eyes are."

The keen sense of smell—the olfactory awareness—of bears is excellent. No animal has more acuteness of smell; it allows the location of mates, the avoidance of humans and other bears, the identification of cubs and the location of

 The polar bear with its nose into the wind determine the direction of a food source along the Manitoba Arctic
© Johnny Johnson

food sources. ". . . the nose provides the leading sense in the search for nourishment," notes Paul Schullery in *The Bears of Yellowstone*. The nose of the bear is somewhat "pig-like," with a pad extending a short distance in front of the snout.

A bear has been known to detect a human scent more than fourteen hours after the person passed along a trail. "The olfactory sense of the bears ranks among the keenest in the animal world," according to George Laycock in *The Wild Bears*. "A black bear in northern California was once seen to travel upwind three miles in a straight line to reach the carcass of a dead deer."

The sense of smell of polar bears may be the finest—able to detect a seal several miles away—and, as Domico relates, ". . . male polar bears march in a straight line, over the tops of pressure ridges of uplifted ice . . . up to 40 miles to reach a prey animal they had detected."

An old, and much related, Indian saying may best describe the olfactory awareness of bears. "A pine needle fell in the forest. The eagle saw it. The deer heard it. The bear smelled it."

Strength

Bears possess enormous strength, regardless of species or size. The strength of a bear is difficult to measure, but observations of bears moving rocks, carrying animal carcasses, removing large logs from the side of a cabin, and digging cavernous holes are all indicative of enormous power. No animal of equal size is as powerful. A bear may kill a moose, elk, or deer by a single blow to the neck with a powerful foreleg, then lift the carcass in its mouth and carry it for great distances.

"The strength . . . is in keeping with his size," describes Ben East in *Bears*. "He is a very powerfully built, a heavy skeleton overlaid with thick layers of muscle as strong as rawhide rope. He can hook his long, grizzly-like front claws under a slab of rock that three grown men could not lift, and flip it over almost effortlessly. . . ." ". . . a brown [bear] . . . took a thousand-pound steer a half mile up an almost vertical mountain, much of the way through alder tangles with trunks three or four inches thick."

Strength and power are not only the attributes of large bears but also of the young. The author observed a yearling American black bear, while searching for insects, turn over a flat-shaped rock (between 310 and 325 pounds) "backhanded" with a single foreleg. The bear was captured the following day in a management action and weighed 120 pounds.

Odor

Bears have a definite odor, as do other animals, including humans. However, the odor of a bear is quite pronounced, though not necessarily repugnant (depending on the individual nose), and is considered by many hunters as the easiest for a dog to track. The Eskimos often located polar bear dens by the scent emitting from the den vent hole.

The American black bear has a somewhat different odor from that of the grizzly bear which, according to one bear biologist, smells musky and musty. Scientists, naturalists, hunters, and others who have experienced the odor of a bear agree that for them it could never again go unrecognized.

Body Temperature

The normal body temperature of bears is approximately ninety-eight to ninety-nine degrees Fahrenheit. The temperatures vary, as do those of other mammals, based on individual differences and levels of activity. Temperatures are normally taken while the bears are immobilized (for obvious reasons) and under physical and psychological stress, resulting in elevated temperatures and the near impossibility of determining a "normal" temperature. However, two adult, male grizzly bears in a captive situation recently had their temperatures taken under "normal" circumstances. They each swallowed a tiny temperature-sensitive radio transmitter placed in their food. Their recorded body temperatures ranged between 98.5 and 99 degrees Fahrenheit, with a mean temperature of 98.9. Interestingly, while the transmitters were still in their stomachs (before being passed with other feces), they were fed frozen fish at which time the "stomach" temperatures dropped to the low eighties.

A bear's temperature may drop a few degrees when the animal is sleeping at night or resting on a snowbank or in a cool day bed. A hibernating bear's temperature drops in relationship with the outside and den temperatures, but appears to have a safety mechanism, as it does not drop below approximately eighty-nine degrees Fahrenheit.

Thermoregulation

Bears, like all mammals, must regulate their body heat. A bear's fur is an extremely effective insulation during the winter, maintaining body heat while absorbing heat from the sun. However, it does not allow adequate cooling during warm weather. As they don't have sweat glands, bears must cool themselves through several unique methods, shared by dogs.

▲ Balance energy expenditure and food intake

▲ Rest in shady day beds and cool summer dens

▲ Lie with bellies fully in touch with the cool ground

▲ Dissipate heat through slobbering tongues, panting like a dog; through their paws, which is the primary means of heat loss, as the pads are well supplied with blood vessels and are flat on the cool ground; and through areas with minimal hair such as the face, ears, nose, and the insides of hind legs

- ▲ Muscles behind shoulder contain a major supply of blood vessels and act as a radiator

- ▲ Shake off water as they emerge from a lake or stream

- ▲ Sprawl on snowfields or patches of snow

- ▲ Spread legs (thighs) wide

- ▲ Submerge in water

- ▲ Take mud and dust baths

Polar bears are faced with overheating like the other bears, but they also require additional heating during the subzero temperatures of the arctic winter. They have three to four inches of subcutaneous fat on their rumps and backs that provide additional insulation. However, they primarily bask in the sun and their outer fur functions as a unique system of heat transmission. Polar bear hairs, according to Charles Feazel in *White Bear*, have ". . . an empty core in the center of each strand. Each hair functions as a light trap, a conduit that takes the sun's rays . . . the last few inches to his dark skin. Polar bear skin is one of nature's most efficient UV [ultraviolet] absorbers. Ultraviolet light penetrates clouds, so Nanook's efficient solar collection system works even on overcast days." Also, a polar bear's long snout warms the cool arctic air as it inhales.

Giant pandas, according to George Schaller *et al.*, have a ". . . short, thick coat [that] provides excellent insulation; the animal readily sleeps on snow. The density and oily texture of the hairs probably prevent moisture from penetrating to the skin, an important adaptation in a damp, cool environment. And the hairs have a springy quality; they are resistant to compaction, which reduces heat loss when the panda lies on snow or cold ground."

A sloth bear, with its belly and underlegs nearly bare, is quite tolerant of heat.

Heart Rate

 normal heart rate for bears is ninety-eight beats per minute while awake and while walking, but it will increase with activity, as well as drop to forty to forty-five beats per minute during night sleep. The heart rates of some bears have slowed to eight to ten beats per minute when resting in a snow bank.

Respiration

The lungs of bears are relatively large and their breathing rate is six to ten breaths per minute while resting, forty to eighty when hot and panting, and sometimes over one hundred breaths per minute during extreme exertion. The oxygen intake (resting) is reduced by approximately one half during hibernation.

Pain

Bears have sensory end organs and experience pain stress from internal and external sources. Bear pain should not necessarily be compared with that of humans, which is possibly more complex. Generally, they do not appear to display obvious reactions, as humans do. Bears have numerous injuries due to the nature of their existence, and have been compared to professional football players who "live in a world of constant pain."

Persistent pain produces irritability and many "problem" bears, which display their discomfort by aggressive actions toward humans and other bears. They are found to have abscessed teeth or other wounds. Their wounds, or other problems, may be from natural or human sources:

▲ Abscessed teeth (appear to have more trouble with teeth than many other animals, probably due to sugary foods)

▲ External parasites (including bees that inflict obvious pain from stings as bears seek bee "hives")

▲ Fights with enemies or other bears

▲ Gunshot wounds

▲ Internal parasites (tapeworms cause considerable misery for bears)

▲ Loss of teeth in old age resulting in inability to eat

"Although the bears may cry in pain when stung by angry bees, they will persist until all the honeycomb has been eaten," describes Terry Domico in *Bears Of The World*.

Spring cub grizzly on the Alaskan tundra. Note the V-shaped collar of whitish fur, which sometimes occurs in grizzly cubs. A similar marking is permanent on the adult of the Asiatic black bear, shown at right.
© DANIEL J. COX

▶ An Alaskan grizzly bear
consuming salmon in the
Brooks River, Katmai National
Park, Alaska.
© JOHNNY JOHNSON

▼ Grizzly cubs swim toward their
mother, seeking a portion of her
salmon meal. Katmai National
Park, Alaska.
© JOHNNY JOHNSON

▲ An Alaskan grizzly searching for salmon in the Brooks River, Katmai National Park.
© JOHNNY JOHNSON

▲ A grizzly bear searches for salmon from a mid-stream perch.
© JOHNNY JOHNSON

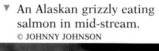

▼ An Alaskan grizzly eating salmon in mid-stream.
© JOHNNY JOHNSON

▲ A pair of grizzlies feeding on berries. Denali National Park, Alaska. © JOHNNY JOHNSON

▶ It is not uncommon for male bears from mid-life on to suffer scars like those evident on this Alaskan grizzly. Generally such injuries result from conflicts with other males during mating season. ALYCE PARSEGHIAN

▲ The relatively hairless face and
head of this grizzly is not
uncommon among juveniles up
to one year old.
© 1992 JOHN W. HERBST

► A grizzly bear silhouetted
against a Yellowstone sunset.
COURTESY YELLOWSTONE NATIONAL PARK

▶ Grizzly sow and cub, Katmai
National Park, Alaska.
© JOHNNY JOHNSON

▲ An ice-adorned grizzly in
Katmai National Park, Alaska.
© JOHNNY JOHNSON

▶ Grizzly bears play-fighting in
the water at the Calgary Zoo.
Note the massive claws, typical
for grizzlies.
GARY BROWN

▶ A grizzly bear plays
in early-season
snow. Katmai
National Park,
Alaska.
© JOHNNY JOHNSON

Digestive Tract

Bears have a simple intestinal tract, of which the colon is the primary site of fermentation. They have a long gut for digesting grass, but do not digest starches well. Their small intestine is longer than that of the true carnivores, and the digestive tract lacks the features of the true herbivores.

The barrel-shaped body of a bear is considered an indication of a long intestine. The brown bears' intestinal length (total and small) is greater than that of the American black bear's and giant panda's. Polar bears have the longest intestine.

The short intestine of giant pandas results in poor digestion efficiency. Only twenty to twenty-five percent of what they consume is digested; thus they must eat enormous amounts—twenty-two to forty pounds of leaves and stems daily—to gain minimal energy. They produce considerable feces, mostly undigested bamboo, passing it in only five to eight hours.

The alimentary system of a sun bear cub must, for the first several weeks following birth, be externally stimulated for the urination and defecation processes to take place. The sow licks the cubs to provide this simulation. The American black bear must also at times perform this function.

Scat (feces)

Scat, or feces, is the excrement of animals. Scatology is the scientific study of scat; scientists collect and thoroughly analyze bear feces to determine many things about bears, including what they have been eating, how much of each type of food, and during what season of the year they were eating the specific food. The information provides more knowledge about the bears' requirements and activities and assists in the appropriate management of their habitat.

Bear scat is also beneficial to the land. It scatters and fertilizes seeds of the plants the bear has consumed and provides humus that enriches the soil.

For the traveler in bear country, the observation of bear scat triggers excitement and anxiety: it is exciting to find an indication of a bear, but at the same time being unaware of its exact location provides anxious moments. However, bear scat may answer questions, too—how long has it been since the bear was here, how big is the bear and what has it been eating?

Typical grizzly bear scat
Courtesy Yellowstone National Park

Scat is a common sign of bear presence and activity. It may be distinguished by shape, size, and composition, though it is sometimes confused with horse and human excrement. "Bear scats are thick cords with blunt ends," describes James Halfpenny in *A Field Guide to Mammal Tracking in Western America*. "The quantity of scat is often great and you may see large piles. Bear scat often contains insects . . . plant remains are also common."

Diseases and Parasites

Bears are susceptible to a variety of bacterial and viral diseases and parasites, while being resistant to many others. Though these ailments may affect a bear's temperament, they are a minor factor in overall bear mortality.

Parasites

Bears are host to more than eighty types of known internal and external parasites, including more than fifty-five kinds of worms. Worms weaken a bear, which may lead to injury or death by other causes. External parasites are most common in the warmer climates, while quite scarce in the more northern areas of the world such as Alaska and Scandinavia.

Internal Parasites

- Ascaris schroederi (*intestinal worms*)
- *Cestodes (tapeworms)*
- Dirofilaria ursi (*blood parasite*)
- *Flukes (fluke fever)*
- *Hookworms*
- *Lungworm*
- *Nematodes (roundworms; very common)*
- *Protozoa*
- *Trematodes (intestinal and bile duct flukes)*
- *Trichinosis (trichinella worm)*

External Parasites

- *Black flies (pest to face and eyes)*
- *Fleas*
- *Lice*
- *Midges*
- *Mites (chiggers; mange)*
- *Mosquitoes (pest to face and eyes)*
- *Ticks*

DISEASE RESISTANCE

Bears are not susceptible to unique infectious diseases and appear resistant to viral diseases such as:

- Canine distemper
- Canine parvo
- Feline panleukopenia (distemper)
- Feline infectious peritonitis (inflammation of the membrane that lines the walls of the abdominal cavity and surrounds the viscera)

Bears are susceptible to:

- Anthrax
- Candidiasis (gastroenteric and encephalitic)
- Canine adenovirus type 1 (hepatitis; respiratory infection)
- Clostridium perfringens infection (gas gangrene)
- Enterotoxemia (diarrhea)
- Hepatic and bile-duct neoplasia (liver tumor)
- Liposarcoma tumors of the uterine horn
- Metabolic bone disease
- Ringworm
- Staphylococcal septicemia (blood poisoning)
- Tuberculosis (especially polar bears)
- Tumor on eyelids and scrotum

The trichinella worm is most prevalent in northern bears, and primarily the arctic, where nearly all polar bears and three of four brown bears have the parasite. Trichinosis may be fatal if the larvae in the blood stream lodge in the heart or brain. Humans can contract trichinosis by eating inadequately cooked bear meat.

Other Health Problems

- Actinomycosis (inflammation; tumors; "lumpy jaw")
- Arthritis
- Bites from other animals
- Broken teeth and lacerations while in research and management captivity
- Bronchopneumonia
- Cavities
- Flesh wounds from rocks or trees
- Fractures from falls
- Gunshot wounds
- Hemorrhoids
- Indigestion (especially giant pandas)
- Joint injuries
- Leptospirosis (bacterial infection involving the kidneys)
- Plague
- Pseudorabies (viral infection of the central nervous system)
- Q-fever (a tick-borne fever)
- Rabies
- Snowblindness
- Starvation (inadequate fat reserves before hibernation; inadequate diet due to poor teeth)
- Struck by vehicles
- Trauma
- Tuberculosis
- Worn, broken, or lost teeth

Ernest Thompson Seton wrote about an Alberta guide's observation of a grizzly and an American black bear "wandering aimlessly" with snowblindness.

Bear Health Care

Nature provides excellent health-care benefits:

- Fractures readily mend
- Natural resistances
- Animals survive amputations
- Animals withstand infection well

Bears contract tapeworms, especially bears that eat large amounts of fish, such as the Alaska and Kamchatka brown bears. Before hibernation, they instinctively seek and eat a blue clay, if available in their habitat, that rids them of these internal parasites. The American black bear does not appear to have this instinct.

Disease and Infirmities of the Cave Bears

Cave bears were also susceptible to various health problems. "When large predators are kept for many years in the confinement of cages, peculiar diseases of the spinal column develop," writes Terry Domico in *Bears Of The World*. "These

Bears in captivity and the wild have been known to become intoxicated by alcohol. Many stories of "drunk" bears, both fact and fiction, are related around the world.

There are documented accounts of Carpathian gypsies using liquor to control bears as they were being trained. The alcohol maintained the trainees in a docile condition.

A large bear, owned by a Spaniard in New Orleans who operated a "public house," was so conditioned to whisky and sugar that it would become troublesome unless it had its drink. When under the influence, according to the October 1855 *Harper's New Monthly Magazine*, the bear "rolled from side to side, whined like a child, leered ridiculously, and smiled foolishly, and was loving and savage by turns."

Two bears arrived in the small Massachusetts town of Florida in 1969, displaying an erratic, intoxicated behavior and a lack of fear. Speculation was that they were drunk from eating fermented apples.

The Burlington Northern Railroad experienced three derailments in Montana during the winter of 1988 and 1989, where a number of railcars of grain left the tracks. As the grain, described by an official as a "mountain of grain," began to rot (or ferment), numerous grizzly bears and a few black bears congregated to feed upon this aromatic and rich food source. The reports of drunk bears began to circulate and authorities agreed that the bears were displaying strange behavior. However, while most persons involved with the spills acknowledged that the bears' actions were unusual, they doubted the bears were intoxicated. They described the bears as "eating to exhaustion" where they would roll around on the ground, sleep, awake, and eat more. The bears had never had it so good.

include inflammations, fusing, and atrophy. An extraordinarily large number of cave bear remains are from diseased or physically degenerate bears." Cave bears' remains indicate they suffered with:

▲ Anchylosis of vertebrae (fusion of spine)

▲ Arthirical exostoses (bone tumors) of vertebrae

▲ Cavities

▲ Exostoses (tumors) of bones and mandibles

▲ Fractures of skull, humeri

▲ Hyperostosis of mandible (resorption of teeth)

▲ Necrosis in femur of young (tissue death)

▲ Nematodes (worms of the type found in recent mammal kidney problems)

▲ Osteomyelitis (inflammation of bone marrow, in young bears)

▲ Periostitis (inflammation of bone membrane)

▲ Rachitis (rickets; spinal disease; inflammation)

▲ Renal calculi (kidney stones)

Longevity

actors determining the lifespan of a bear vary between and within species. The "aging" of bears has not always been a common practice of states, provinces, and countries; therefore longevity records do not exist for some species of the world's bears and for other specific populations.

Principal Causes of Mortality
Interactions with humans

▲ Accidents
electrocution
struck by trains
struck by vehicle

▲ Habitat loss (indirect mortality)

▲ Hunting (including many chance encounters while hunting other game)

▲ Management/research
accidental
problem bear removed from population

▲ Poaching

▲ Self-defense

- ▲ Traps (some set for other animals)
- ▲ War
- ▲ Mines
- ▲ Shot

Natural Deaths

- ▲ Boulder rolling on bear
- ▲ Cubs crushed by sow
- ▲ Disease
- ▲ Enemies
- ▲ Old age
- ▲ Starvation due to loss of functional teeth*
- ▲ Parasites may weaken a bear; susceptible to other causes of mortality (see Diseases)

*When teeth become worn to a point of nonfunction, or are abscessed, bears are unable to chew the necessary foods; and adequate nutrition is no longer possible. They often can not emerge from their dens, having hibernated without an adequate storage of fat.

🐻 RECORD AGES (IN YEARS)

		WILD	CAPTIVITY
	Average	Oldest	Oldest
AMERICAN BLACK BEAR	18	31	44
BROWN BEAR	20	34	47
GRIZZLY BEAR	25	30	44
POLAR BEAR	25	34*	41
ASIATIC BLACK BEAR	25	—	33
GIANT PANDA	28	—	30
SLOTH BEAR	—	—	40
SUN BEAR	—	—	—
SPECTACLED BEAR	25	—	—

*34 years and 8 months

	AMERICAN BLACK BEAR	GRIZZLY BEAR	POLAR BEAR
UNITED STATES			
Alaska	25	35	*
Arizona	23	—	—
Arkansas	28	—	—
California	26	—	—
Florida	18	—	—
Georgia	17	—	—
Idaho	25	25	—
Maine	20	—	—
Maryland	11	—	—
Massachusetts	20.5	—	—
Michigan	31	—	—
Mississippi	7	—	—
Montana	30	34	—
Nevada	12	—	—
New Hampshire	39**	—	—
New Jersey	15	—	—
New Mexico	23	—	—
New York	42.75**	—	—
North Carolina	26.75	—	—
Oregon	30	—	—

Sources: Harvest or other state and provincial wildlife management records)

	AMERICAN BLACK BEAR	GRIZZLY BEAR	POLAR BEAR
Utah	16	—	—
Vermont	43.75	—	—
Virginia	20	—	—
Washington	28	—	—
West Virginia	27	—	—
Wisconsin	18.5	—	—
Wyoming	30	28	—
CANADA			
Alberta	27	29	—
British Columbia	*	34	—
Manitoba	28	—	30
New Brunswick	25.5	—	—
Newfoundland	22	—	30
Northwest Terr.	*	28	35
Ontario	25	—	*
Quebec	26	—	*
Saskatchewan	27	—	—
Yukon	27	33	*
MEXICO	*	—	—

*Information Unavailable
**Captive Bear

Bear Behavior and Activities

Disposition and Personality

Bears have a wide range of behavior, but generally are curious, suspicious, self-reliant, clever, cautious, independent and dangerous. The only certainty of a bear's behavior is unpredictability.

Behavior Characteristics

While there are behaviors common to most bears, there are more specific behaviors and characteristics documented within each species.

American Black Bear: Easily food conditioned; extremely clever; creature of habit; inquisitive; playful.

Brown Bear: Dignified; deliberate; fearless; bold; generally peaceful; solitary.

Grizzly Bear: Generally shy and peaceful; secretive; ferocious when provoked.

Polar Bear: Silent; cunning; casual demeanor; fierce fighter; untrustworthy in captivity.

Asiatic Black Bear: Easily annoyed; not necessarily fierce.

Giant Panda: Shy; restrained.

Sloth Bear: Bad temper; cranky; playful; aberrant; teases other animals.

"Bears are made of the same dust as we, breathe the same winds and drink of the same waters. . . ."

JOHN MUIR, 1871

Sun Bear: Good natured; older bears bad tempered.

Spectacled Bear: Timid.

Curiosity

 bear's curiosity may be attributed to many things, but most often a potential meal is the source. They will inspect odors, objects and sometimes noise to determine if the origin is edible or possibly a plaything. Actually, their intense curiosity should be considered investigation.

"It was not unusual to find the tracks of a bear leading straight up to one of the large [steam] vents, where evidently he had stopped to peer into the mysterious hot hole," Robert Griggs writes in *The Valley Of Ten Thousand Smokes*, following the 1912 eruption of Alaska's Mt. Katmai. "In one of the steaming areas Hagelbarger found a place where the hot ground had apparently excited the bear's curiosity, for he had dug into it until he started a small fumarole [vent with smoke and gases] of his own. The appearance of a cloud of steam under his claws as he broke into the hot crust must have given him a great surprise. It did not scare him away, however, for not satisfied with a single experiment, he tried again in several places, each time digging down till he started the steam before turning away."

Curiosity is often what brings a bear into the human world. "Young adult grizzly bears are particularly curious," according to Stephen Herrero in *Bear Attacks*, "and their curiosity is not yet tempered with a knowledge that humans can mean trouble."

> ### OLD BEARS
>
> "Old bears move slowly, their joints stiff with age. When angered, though, even the oldest whirls around with surprising fury, teeth and claws at the ready," describes Feazel. "The oldest, largest bears are often the worst tempered, having survived a thousand challenges by lesser bruins."

Intelligence

ear intelligence is difficult to assess, and should not be compared or measured in human terms. Bears are considered by scientists and naturalists to be highly intelligent animals, based on their ability to learn rapidly and to reason.

Curiosity, coupled with an excellent memory, may be the key to a bear's "intelligence." It leads to learning and knowledge, which is the basis of survival—adaptability to environmental changes and unusual circumstances. Bears learn and remember from a single experience—a food source, a threat, a trap, or a rifle shot.

"Bears are highly intelligent and individualistic," relates Terry Domico in *Bears Of The World*, "and are capable of nearly as many responses in a given circumstance as a human. Some biologists believe the highly adaptable brown bear is intelligent enough to be ranked with primates, like monkeys and baboons."

Bears display many "intelligent" actions that include:

▲ Hiding dark nose with a paw (polar bear)

▲ Hiding behind ice blocks (polar bear)

▲ Learning quickly in "training" situations

▲ The display of a cunning mind

▲ Sneaking

▲ Bluffing

▲ Concealing self in ambush; hiding from humans

▲ Beginning hibernation during heavy snowfall to conceal tracks to den

▲ Choosing alternatives

▲ Adapting to other influences (including human, if allowed)

▲ Baiting other animals (polar bear)

▲ Resourcefulness

▲ Capacity to reason

▲ Avoiding problems

▲ Outwitting humans

▲ Calculating

▲ Retreating in the face of great odds (human impacts)

▲ Hiding tracks (jump to side, step on own tracks, wade in stream)

▲ Using tools

▲ Backtracking

The bear "reached even deeper into his bag of tricks and came out with something new—backtracking," relates American black bear biologist Gary Alt, in Stephen Herrero's *Bear Attacks*, ". . . suddenly, his tracks simply vanished. There were no rocks, no water, nothing to conceal his tracks. I went back to the tracks. This time I noticed there were toe marks at both ends, even though there was no evidence . . . to indicate the bear had turned around. I followed them back about 50 yards and found where the bear had jumped off the main trail, walking away in a direction perpendicular to his old tracks."

Strong circumstantial evidence has existed for over two hundred years that polar bears use ice blocks or rocks to kill seals. Bear biologist C. Jonkel tells of polar bears using small rocks to spring traps.

Studies at the University of Tennessee psychology department indicate that American black bears are very intelligent, probably more so than many other mammals of the world. They open door latches and screw-top jars, recognize uniforms and vehicles. On one occasion, two five-year-old American black bears ran to a group of humans for security when a larger bear arrived. Enos Mills noted in *The Grizzly— Our Greatest Wild Animal*: "I would give the grizzly first place in the animal world for brainpower."

Associations Between Bears

With few species exceptions, adult bears are basically solitary. They are together during the courting/mating period, and as a family group of a sow and her offspring. Streams with spawning fish, dumps, and other major food sources may attract a concentration of bears resulting in a temporary proximity—a touchy truce.

"In a garbage dump in Yellowstone Park I have seen thirty grizzlies wallowing together with bodies practically touching," described Adolph Murie in *A Naturalist In Alaska*. "Here, apparently, wild natural habits are being lost, and the dump is making of our lone philosopher bears a bunch of gregarious characters. They perhaps are gregarious, however, only at the dump."

Males normally do not recognize their offspring and have no interest in them, unless as a food source, and sows with cubs usually do not associate with other family groups. Bears of different species do not associate, though a large bear may prey upon the young of another species.

Bears have minimal association with the species of other animal groups, unless of course there is a prey relationship. There are feeding associations that are quite beneficial for other animals. (See Interactions with Other Animals, later in this chapter.)

"Each unit, such as the lone bear, breeding pair, mother and cubs, sets of older cubs on their own, is independent and does not fraternize ordinarily with other units," explains Adolph Murie in *The Grizzlies of Mount McKinley*. "When bears do feed within two hundred to three hundred yards of each other, where they have been attracted by good rooting or grazing, a certain amount of uneasiness and watchfulness prevails, the degree of anxiety depending upon the types of bear units that are present and perhaps the extent of previous acquaintance."

Specific association behavior between bears of the same species includes:

American Black Bear: Suspicious of any intruder; non-gregarious; sow short tempered with mate following courting/

A teeth-bared association between Alaskan grizzly bears in Katmai National Park
© Johnny Johnson

mating; sow short tempered with cubs when she forces them out on their own; large males dangerous to smaller bears; brief congregations at food supplies; basically harmless in fight with same species.

Brown Bear: Adult males kill young bears and occasionally a sow; occasional congregations of sows with cubs; brief congregations at food supplies; have been known to fight to the death.

Polar Bear: Solitary; often tolerate close associations; occasionally play together; occasionally feed together on large food supply such as a whale carcass.

Asiatic Black Bear: Occasional family group, or pair of adults and two successive litters of young; walk in a procession of largest to smallest; basically harmless in conflict with same species.

Giant Panda: Closely share a small range; attempt to avoid each other; solitary and silent; rare face-to-face meetings.

Sloth Bear: Adult male occasionally with a family; occasionally travel in pairs; adult male gentle with cubs; mostly ignore each other; occasionally fight for food.

Sun Bear: Occasionally travel in pairs; pair of adults sometimes accompanied by infants.

Spectacled Bear: Adult male occasionally with family.

Hierarchy

Bears are generally shy and attempt to avoid trouble. They are socially hierarchic, with a definite determination of which bear is dominant and controls a situation such as feeding, breeding, or occupying a location. Hierarchy's *most important* function is to prevent these large and powerful animals from entering into seriously violent battles that would adversely affect the species. There may be threat displays with vocalization and body/facial language until dominance is established, or hierarchy may be subtly expressed and understood.

There is a linear dominance/avoidance system; the subordinate retreats, based on psychological factors, physical condition, including health, size, and age, knowledge from experience, and confidence. There is extreme sensitivity to the roar of large males, as indicated by the doubling of a subordinate's heart rate. Females with cubs may tolerate other females without cubs or their own independent young, but they are the most cautious of all bears.

Generally, size is power and young bears are subordinate. The dominance order is:

▲ Large, old males

▲ Females with new cubs (sometimes most dominant)

▲ Single subadult males

▲ Other adult males and females

▲ Other subadults

Unrestrained fighting may occur between males during mating season or between a sow protecting her young and another bear, but major confrontation is normally short and not fatal. Everything is based on the individuals. Their health varies, they grow older, larger, and more confident, and the hierarchical arrangement is constantly tested and occasionally readjusted.

Communication

Bears communicate their mood with expressive signals such as posturing, marking with odors and other sign, and vocalization. Their ability to communicate with facial expressions is poor, as they rarely display teeth or curl a lip like dogs, and their small ears, though possibly expressive, are positioned in most species as to be unnoticeable. But they strongly compensate with body language, attitude, and vocalization.

 *A yawning expression on a grizzly
bear in Wyoming*
Courtesy Yellowstone National Park

Vocalization

Bears are generally quite silent, but have a repertoire of vocalizations, each with a specific significance, for important intraspecies social situations and encounters with other species.

Some bear species, and individuals, are more communicative than others. Giant pandas vocalize infrequently, except when courting and in a few other social interactions. The sloth bear is especially noisy when mating, and the roar of the polar bear is described as the bellow of Chewbacca the Wookie in the movie *Star Wars*.

Vocalizations may be singular or multiple, and a particular sound may have more than a single meaning, depending on the situation. Various sounds may be expressed toward humans, bears, and other animals.

The cubs of most species vocalize in the same manner, whining, whimpering, and crying when upset, bawling, and crying when hurt, humming when content (nursing), and hissing when frightened.

Posturing

Posturing—the display of the body—may be a bear's most significant and productive act of communicating. When combined with vocalizations, posturing expresses attitude, dominance, subordination, and questions intent. It is an

BEAR VOCALIZATIONS

Species	Emotion	Emitted Sound
American black bear	• Annoyance:	chomp, cough, growl, huff, woof
	• Contentment: (eating)	mumble, pant, squeak
	• Disappointment:	howl, moan, sob, squall, wail
	• Fighting:	roar
	• Jealousy:	chomp, cough, growl, woof
	• Pain:	bawl
	• Resting:	yawn (loud)
	• Threat:	bellow, chomp, grunt, honk, huff, puff, snort
Brown bear	• Aggravation:	chomp, smack, woof
	• Anger:	growl
	• Anger: (extreme)	roar
	• Contentment (sow with cubs):	hum
	• Express transient feelings:	cough
	• Gastric problem:	belch
	• Nervous:	grunt, woof
	• Pain:	bawl
	• Summon young (sow):	bleat
Polar bear	• Agitated:	chuff
	• Anger:	hiss, rumbling growl
	• Aroused (highly):	roar
	• Contented:	purr
	• Display respect:	silent
	• Hurt:	bellow, roar, rumbling snarls
	• Uneasy:	hiss, rumbling growl
	• Upset (temper):	shriek, squall, whimper
Asiatic black bear	• Courting:	cluck
Giant panda	• Aggression:	growl, roar
	• Anxiety:	chomp, honk, grunt

(continued)

Species	Emotion	Emitted Sound
Giant panda *(continued)*	• Apprehension: (aggressive threat)	huff, snort
	• Apprehension: (defensive threat)	chomp
	• Birth (sow):	cry (loud)
	• Courting/mating:	bark, bleat, chirp, moan, roar, squeal
	• Distress:	grunt, honk, squeal
	• Friendly/social:	bleat
	• Meeting:	chirp, yip
	• Threat:	huff, snort
	• Warning:	bark, moan, yip
Sloth bear	• Anger (deep):	bark, scream, grunt-wickerings, snarl, yelp
	• Attack:	bark, grunt, roar
	• Danger:	snarl
	• Digging: (in company)	drone
	• Eating: (sucking)	huff, snuff (vacuum noise)
	• Fighting:	roar, snarl
	• Fright:	shriek
	• Hurt:	howl, squeal, whimper
	• Injured:	yowl, whimper
	• Mad (temper):	woof
	• Mating:	buzzing, melodious humming
	• Paw sucking:	babble, buzz, gurgle, hum
	• Play:	grumble
	• Resting:	buzz, hum
	• Sow with cubs:	croon
	• Teasing animals:	bellow
Sun bear	• Attack:	bark, grunt, roar
	• Paw sucking:	hum
Spectacled bears	• Alarm:	owl-like screech
	• Contentment:	soft purr

element of hierarchy. During posturing, a bear may display its size and stride, stand tall, specifically orient its body or head, and utilize any of many visual signals. It demonstrates its position and "bearing," while assessing the other bear. Posturing may include:

ORIENTATION (body)	Frontal (head high); side; sitting; lying down; body at higher elevation (standing tall); lying down and waiting; sitting down facing; standing bipedal (sniffing).
ORIENTATION (head)	Down; facing away; neck stretched; neck and head oblique; head dropped; staring; looking for clues; touching noses; bobbing head.
MOUTH	Shut; open; open with canines displayed; twisting muzzle; extending upper lip; moving jaw; clicking teeth; licking lips; snapping jaws loudly; yawning; spitting; panting; blowing wet bubbles; waving open mouth.
NOSE	Sniffing.
EARS	Back and up.
MOVEMENT	Approaching; retreating (walking, running); backing up; walking stiff-legged; charge; circle; moving downwind; strutting; paw gestures.

A stare or oblique neck is aggressive and a serious threat, while lowering of the head is submissive and a display of respect—a desire for peace. Extending the upper lip or blowing wet, smacking bubbles is definitely petulance. A bear may posture with humans much in the same manner as with other bears.

Marking (scenting)

Marking (signing, scenting) by bears is a highly ritualized, chemical and visual communication function performed by resident bears and transients. Marking is accomplished by several methods, including scratching, biting, rubbing, and scenting with urine or secretions from the anal gland.

Often marking appears to be just the act of a bear scratching its back against a tree or other object, but whether or not that is the intent, an odor, hair, or a rubbed area remains for the next bears to find. Tree marking appears to be the most common form of marking (or at least the most obvious to humans), and is most customary among males. Rubbing appears to be a separate marking "ritual" from biting or clawing an object.

A high frequency of marking occurs just prior to the breeding period and is also quite common during courting and mating.

The specific purpose of marking is not completely understood by naturalists and biologists, though there are numerous theories. ". . . it is clear to the human observer that few other animals in the Northern Hemisphere other than themselves could make so striking a five-fingered print," write Paul Shepard and Barry Sanders in *The Sacred Paw*. "Other than the bear, perhaps only the big cats give the impression of making a meaningful mark on a tree." The many theories include:

- *Male bears warning other male bears*

- *Signifying a dominance hierarchy between males*

- *Male bears indicating their dominance to avoid conflicts injurious to both bears*

- *Provides evidence for other bears to signal that it "was here"*

- *A sign of activity and presence*

- *A display of dominance (size)*

- *Marks a territory*

- *Marks a territory, though quite possibly does not necessarily mean "keep out," but "I am here, just be careful and do not crowd me"*

- *Males advising females (there may be an understanding that male markings allow a female to pass at any time)*

- *Females warning away other females (territorial mark)*

- *A means of identification*

- *A sign of belligerence*

- *An expression of well-being*

- *An expression of strength*

- *An expression of boredom*

- *An act of stretching*

- *An act of relaxing*

- *An act of manicuring (sharpening or blunting of claws)*

Theories for marking trees that are associated with breeding:

- *Announces presence in the area to a potential mate*

- *A means of promoting estrus in adult females of the area*

Announces that a potential mate is in the area

Serves as signal between males and females during breeding season

Black bear biologist Lynn Rogers has long studied bear behavior. He believes tree marking by an aggressive male bear indicates its dominance and is to avoid conflicts injurious to both bears.

Specific marking methods observed by scientists and other observers include:

American Black Bear: Tree rubbing with shoulder, neck, head, rump; tree biting; tree clawing; pushing tree over and rubbing on downed tree; rolling on ground at base of tree; leaving scat.

Brown Bear: Tree scratching; tree rubbing; may roll in urine before rubbing; tree biting; biting buildings, signs; rubbing on log in open area; pawing ground; leaving scat.

Giant Panda: Bark stripping; tree biting; tree clawing; ground pawing; rolling and rubbing on ground; tree scenting; spraying urine directly on trees.

Sloth Bear: Tree scraping with forepaws; tree rubbing with flanks; slashing tree with foreclaws.

Sun Bear: Tree scratching.

The giant panda has what appears to be the most involved method of marking. It has scent glands in the area of the anus that produce a secretion that smells acetic to humans. The tail acts as a brush to spread urine and the secretion at the scent areas, which are established along primary travel routes. The giant panda backs up to a surface, such as a tree, raises its tail and rubs. On rare occasions, the bear will continue to "back up" the surface, by walking with its hind legs until it is standing on its forepaws in a handstand, brushing with its tail, scenting as high as possible.

The marking of trees by rubbing or clawing is the most visible sign normally observed by humans. Marked trees are found along well-traveled trails and other travel routes. Some trees are used once, others year after year until the trail up to the tree may be as worn and rutted as a well-used bear travel trail. Tree marking may involve the bear stretching its body to scratch its back, leaving hair and odor; clawing and biting leaving scratches and tooth marks in the bark; worn areas at the tree base; and strips of bark on the ground. Limbs may be broken and chewed.

Marking by bears also occurred during prehistoric periods, as they appear to have "marked" the walls of caves. Extensive scratches found on cave walls and trees indicate seasonal occupancy by cave bears.

Bear Attacks

Bears attack other animals and humans for two basic purposes—for food and as a defensive reaction. Other than when preying on other wild animals, attacks are rare. A bear would rather bluff, chase, or scare away an intruder, or flee. However, if it attacks, the situation is serious.

Several reasons prompt a non-prey attack, and they are most often due to a short-distance contact with a person or other enemy:

▲ Defensive action

▲ Protection of cubs

▲ In confusion

▲ Travel route is blocked

▲ Protection of food source

▲ Their "space" is invaded

▲ During mating rivalry (males)

▲ Fear

In an attack, bears charge on all four legs, some in great, leaping bounds. They do not stand bipedal in an attack, unless in a final, close-quarters reaching action. They do not "bear hug," but strike, claw, and bite. The most effective method of attack is with a crushing blow of a forepaw; a single strike is so powerful that it can kill an adult elk, caribou, or moose.

Scientists, victims and other observers describe various actions of the species:

American Black Bear: Approaches low on four legs; swings powerful forelegs, with body strength behind them; bites and claws; hunts with ambush and surprise.

Brown Bear: Uses speed to run down prey; charges in great, leaping bounds (while uttering a deep roar); rears up in fight to grasp head or neck with teeth; swings powerful forelegs, with enormous body strength behind them.

Polar Bear: Uses stealth and sudden bursts of speed to approach prey; tucks forelegs under chest and pushes with hindlegs, or pulls self along on ice; stops when prey, such as

ATTACKS

"In an attack it [the bear] strikes around with its paws," according to Frederick Drimmer, in *The Animal Kingdom*. "The terrific strength of its weighty arms drives the claws deep into the body of its victims."

"When hunting large game, bears may stalk catlike, then run the prey down with a sudden spurt and kill it with blows of the forepaws and bites through the neck," describe Shepard and Sanders.

a seal, moves or looks; moves directly into wind; uses shadow or shields such as ice block and ridges; approaches within thirty feet; makes twelve- to fifteen-foot bounds; pounces with teeth and claws; uses its long neck to place its huge canines out in front of the body to grasp the seal on the ice or through its breathing hole in the ice; often synchronizes its feeding on seals with the seals' patterns of sleeping alongside their breathing holes; will occasionally enter the water to stalk seals on an ice floe, but mostly in vain; has been known to prepare a seal's hole so it is large enough for its paw, then waits in ambush for the seal; successful in less than one fourth of its attacks on seals.

Asiatic Black Bear: Sits or stands up and knocks prey over with blows of forepaws; claws and bites; bites limbs, shoulders and head if attacking a person; normally attacks only to protect food; climbing is principal means of defense.

Giant Panda: Pushes with body; swats with forepaws; lunges; grapples with tremendous shoulder strength, heavy forepaws and powerful jaws; bites neck.

Sloth Bear: Attacks savagely when surprised; spectacular charge and bipedal display; may attack unaware person at night; approaches low, head first and rears up to strike claws into head and upper body; bites and tears with teeth; stands and drives claws into humans' shoulders and temples; bites.

Sun Bear: Normally attacks only in defense; barks loudly when attacking.

Spectacled Bear: Timid; attacks only in defense; raises up and bites; strikes head and shoulders.

"In hunting seals on icefloes," write Shepard and Sanders, "polar bears slither on their stomachs, pause when the seal looks up and cover their black noses with their paws, then rush the seal from fifteen or twenty feet. When ringed seal pups are in chambers three feet down in ice, the bear digs and smashes his way to them. . . ."

". . . a large Grizzly Bear [apparently fleeing] . . . sprang upon the Canadian," wrote Osborne Russell in *Journal Of A Trapper*, ". . . and placing one forepaw upon his head and the other on his left shoulder pushed him [to] one side about 12 ft. with as little ceremony as if he had been a cat [while] still keeping a direct course as tho. nothing had happened."

Enemies

Bears' enemies are not necessarily other bears, animal species, or humans that precipitate direct mortality, but causes that result in indirect death, such as habitat degradation and food loss. Insecticides and other poisons are indirect threats.

"Although giant pandas have few natural enemies," notes Schaller *et al.*, "the periodic die-off of bamboo, their main food, threatens their survival."

Some "enemies," far inferior to the bear if they were in battle, only harass. Eagles will swoop down over bears, as do other birds such as ravens, magpies, and long-tailed jaegers. Ticks, fleas, mosquitos, flies, and other pests are also annoyances. Internal parasites weaken bears, and bears that kill porcupines may suffer serious infection and discomfort in their mouths and throats, be unable to eat, and possibly die of starvation.

Some enemies are a threat only to bear cubs, and there is an enemy common to all species—humans.

The Polar Bear Versus the Walrus

Muskox are a threat to polar bears only when they are circled as a group protecting cows and young. Wolves are a threat only to cubs, and polar bears simply avoid killer whales, but walruses are a different story.

Encounters between a walrus and polar bear are violent battles, and there are several recorded observations of a walrus killing a polar bear, though walruses are also killed. Polar bear authorities of the Canadian Wildlife Service, H.P.L. Kiliaan and Ian Stirling in *Observations On Overwintering Walruses*, describe ". . . a walrus that a polar bear killed with a blow in the head as it surfaced to breathe through a hole in the ice." They also noted another battle. "Tracks and blood in the snow around the walrus's breathing hole . . . indicated a fight had taken place very recently. The walrus was covered with blood and one tusk was broken. Despite a careful search, no bear tracks leading away from the site were found, suggesting that the bear may have been killed and sunk in the water."

"The polar bear and walrus, traditional rivals, occasionally come in contact while feeding on whale carcasses or while killing seals," wrote Thomas Koch in *The Year Of The Polar Bear*. "If a walrus is in the water, a polar bear will not enter. The walrus is the only polar animal that the bear really fears. If the two animals encounter each other on land, the

ENEMIES	AMERICAN BLACK	BROWN	POLAR	ASIATIC BLACK	GIANT PANDA	SLOTH	SUN	SPECTACLED
Alligator	X							
Bear (LARGER)		X	X	X				
Brown Bear				X	a			
Clouded Leopard							X	
Dog (DOMESTIC)	X		X	X		X		X
Dog (WILD)						X	X	
Eagle	X	a						
Human	X	X	X	X	X	X	X	X
Killer Whale			X					
Leopard						X	X	
Mountain Lion	X							
Muskox			X					
Porcupine	X b		b					
Snake (POISONOUS)	X							
Tiger				X		X	X	
Walrus (ADULT BULL)			X					
Wild Boar		X					X	
Wolf	X	a		a	a			

a–primarily a threat to bear cubs
b–quills in throat; starvation
Patricia Brown

polar bear will have an edge. When they meet each other in the water, the walrus has been known to grab the polar bear from below and, using his ivory tusks, which often grow more than thirty inches in length, to stab the bear in the back, driving the tusks to the hilt. The carcasses of polar bears and walruses have been found coupled in this manner."

Interactions with Other Animals

Bears consider any other animals as food, if they are capable of catching and killing the specific individual. There are many interesting interactions between bears and large and small prey. Sometimes the prey is too elusive, and the bear may in some situations become the prey. Feeding by bears often provides life for scavengers such as birds, martens, wolverines, coyotes, wolves, and foxes. Many interactions are not with what is typically considered prey or an enemy, but are opportunistic contacts, and historically some were staged by humans. Some are simply curiosity and "social" contacts.

African Lions

"When, a few years ago, a Los Angeles County grizzly was sent to Monterrey, Mexico, to be pitted against the man-killing African lion 'Parnell' the great Californian handled the African king as a cat would a rat. He killed him so quickly that the big audience hardly knew how it was done," described Horace Bell in *On the Old West Coast*, 1930 (as cited in Storer and Tevis, *California Grizzly*).

There is also a vague account of a circus (African) lion that jumped an American black bear during an act. The fight was fierce and both combatants were injured, but the lion's injuries where of the extent that it had to be destroyed.

 A confrontation between distant relatives in Churchill, Manitoba
© *Johnny Johnson*

Bison

The American buffalo (bison) shares much of its range with grizzly bears, but there is minimal conflict between them. A grizzly bear normally does not attack a bison, for it may be the loser. "The bear had two holes in it . . . all the bear's ribs on one side were broken," relates George Laycock in *The Wild Bears*, describing a dead grizzly bear, ". . . the buffalo came up winners."

"Upon examination it was found that both sides of the grizzly bear were badly battered and bruised to a bloody mass and the left side of the animal was punctured between the ribs by a hole 1½ inches in diameter," described Joe Way in Paul Schullery's *Yellowstone Bear Tales*. "The immediate area around the carcass was well torn up giving evidence of a severe struggle between the bear and some other beast. There were many large buffalo tracks which had cut up the ground in an arc around the carcass and there were several patches of buffalo hair."

"A veteran hunter in Dakota once watched a huge male grizzly attack a small herd of buffalo cows protected by five or six bulls," related Wayne Gard in *The Great Buffalo Hunt*. "As the bear approached, the bulls closed ranks and lowered their horns. When the bulls charged, the bear struck one of them so hard with his paws that he broke the back of the bull, killing him instantly. But the other bulls used their horns so effectively that soon the bear crawled off with mortal wounds."

Deer

Axis deer and sloth bears were observed feeding only thirteen feet apart and neither appeared disturbed by the other, according to Andrew Laurie and John Seidensticker in *Behavioural Ecology Of The Sloth Bear*.

Dog

A polar bear attempted to steal a dog's frozen fish and was bitten in the face.

Fox

Adolph Murie, in *The Grizzlies Of Mount McKinley*, observed an association between a bear and a fox. ". . . and he [the fox] may even play with a bear cub."

"Foxes [arctic fox] are found wherever polar bears wander," writes Feazel. "They wait impatiently for a chance to snatch scraps of seal meat after the bears eat the blubber. Bears usually tolerate the foxes' boldness but can grow impatient themselves, whirling to bellow a throaty warning or lashing out with massive paws. An arctic fox, however, depends for its winter survival on the white bear's leavings and won't be dissuaded."

Horse

Theodore Roosevelt told the story of a stallion that defended against a grizzly bear, breaking its jaw and chasing it away.

M.P. Skinner, in *Bears in the Yellowstone*, wrote of his horse that would attack bears "on sight." It killed two American black bears, "lashing out at them with . . . hind hoofs [lightning quick, crashing blows from the rear] and then quickly spring away before the return charge." He also relates that this horse had "driven several [grizzly bears] off, without ever having received a scratch. . . ."

Killer Whale

Though the polar bear swims six miles per hour, their major enemy, the killer whale, is capable of swimming thirty miles per hour.

A brown bear was observed resting on an estuary beach in British Columbia while several Orcas clearly observed it from the water.

Leopard

The sloth bear is known to drive away a leopard from its prey.

Moose

". . . if the mother [moose] catches the grizzly prowling about near her calf, she goes on the warpath and at least holds her ground," writes Adolph Murie who, as a marvelous observer, related other moose/bear interactions: ". . . watched a mother, followed by her very young calf, determinedly chasing a grizzly and doing her best to overtake it." ". . . a bull moose chasing a grizzly for some distance and striking at it."

An account is related of a Russian brown bear imitating the call of an elk (moose are called elk in Asia) during the rutting season, luring the unsuspecting moose to where it would be easier prey.

Mountain Goat

A goat was observed feeding near a grizzly, with neither indicating any aggression or fear.

Naturalist William Hornaday observed a goat use its horns to mortally wound a grizzly bear.

Grizzly bears and moose, in peaceful coexistence for this photograph, in Katmai National Park, Alaska.
© *Johnny Johnson.*

Mountain Lion

The Indians of California told stories of fights between grizzly bears and lions, with the lion normally the winner, and hunters and others relate stories of fierce conflicts with no clearcut winner, and most often two losers. They describe them as terribly noisy fights with the ground torn up where the skirmishes occurred. The bear would rise to meet the cat's thrusts and throw the cat to the ground. The cat would grasp the bear near the throat and use its hind feet to rake the bear's stomach and chest. The bear was stronger, but the clawing of the cat was highly effective, injuring the bear and causing it to release its holds. Normally they would part, both bloody and battered and neither the winner.

"The bear has been known to walk in on a feeding [mountain] lion, which reacted angrily, snarling and spitting," described Ben East, in *Bears*. "But in the end it fled without giving battle and the grizzly took over the kill."

Porcupine

". . . I have sat and watched a grizzly bear and a little porcupine feeding side by side on the grass near the snow banks," wrote William Wright in *The Grizzly Bear*, "neither one paying the slightest attention to the other."

"One day I watched an old bear, which was feeding in a swale, stop feeding and watch a porcupine that came waddling over a knoll only a few steps away," observed Adolph Murie. "This bear knew porcupines and permitted it detour to one side."

Bears are occasionally found with face and paws filled with porcupine quills, which may lead to infections and the inability to eat, with subsequent starvation. Ernest Thompson Seton described an emaciated dead bear with lips and mouth terribly swollen and "bristling with quills."

Pronghorn Antelope

Three pronghorns approached an American black bear sow with two cubs that were grazing on a hillside. Drawn by what appeared to be curiosity, the pronghorns moved to within fifty feet while the bears only occasionally glanced at them. Curiosity satisfied, they departed and the bears continued eating grass.

Rhinoceros

"Sloth bears avoid rhinos," according to Laurie and Seidensticker. However, "in one instance, a sloth bear roared when it encountered a rhino at close range, then ran away and was chased by the rhino 200 meters [656 feet] across an open river bed and into forest."

Seals

Polar bears are harassed by seals while swimming. "The seal, a proficient swimmer, is accustomed to remaining submerged for twenty minutes and is credited with swimming a hundred yards in ten seconds," writes Koch. "Seals can quite literally swim circles around a swimming polar bear."

Skunk

A grizzly bear was observed moving aside to avoid a skunk.

A family of skunks and an American black bear encountered each other at less than twenty feet. The bear stopped, but the mother skunk did not hesitate, and with a raised tail moved toward the bear, who retreated.

Tiger

A Manchurian tiger has been described luring an Asiatic black bear by imitating the bear's courting sounds.

Tigers will avoid sun bears; they must ambush or sneak up on a sloth bear.

James Corbett, famed Asian big-game hunter, witnessed a "very large" Asiatic black bear displacing a tiger from its kill.

Wolverine

"A mountaineer friend of Seton's [Ernest Thompson] told of two wolverines driving a black bear from the remains of an elk," noted Adolph Murie.

Murie observed a wolverine chase a grizzly bear off a carcass and, according to another reliable account, a Russian brown bear was driven away from a carcass by a wolverine.

Frank Dufresne relates the story of a thirty-pound wolverine accosting a grizzly bear on a narrow trail. The bear was ten times the size of the wolverine, but when the wolverine screeched, the young bear departed.

Wolf

A wolf and grizzly bear have fed side by side on a caribou carcass, while at other times a grizzly has fought off a pack of wolves to defend its food.

"As a rule, grizzlies and wolves occupy the same range without taking much notice of each other, but not infrequently the grizzlies discover wolf kills and unhesitatingly dispossess the wolf and assume ownership," writes Adolph

 An Alaskan grizzly bear in Katmai National Park confronts a wolf that it perceives as a threat to its food source
© *Johnny Johnson*

Murie in *A Naturalist In Alaska*. "In the relationship existing between the two species, the wolves are the losers and the meat-hungry bears are the gainers."

"When bears take possession of a kill in the presence of wolves," Murie explained, "they are much harassed, but they are so powerful that the wolves must be careful to avoid their strong arms. The wolves must confine their attack to quick nips from the rear. But the bears are alert, and usually the wolves must jump away before they come near enough for even a nip." Wolves are known to reverse the situation and chase a grizzly bear away from a carcass.

"The wolf, formerly abundant in New England," according to James Cardoza in *The Black Bear in Massachusetts*, "was apparently capable of successfully attacking bears." Cardoza relates the opinion of an individual in 1634 that believed there would be more bears ". . . if it were not for the woolves, which devour them; a kennell of those ravening runnagadoes, setting on a poor single Beare, will teare him as a Dogge will teare a Kid."

"One night we watched in awe as a young grizzly bear tried repeatedly to force its way past a yearling wolf standing guard alone before a den of young pups," described Barry Lopez in *Arctic Dreams*. "The bear eventually gave up and went on its way."

Bear Travel

Moving from one location to another is the most common activity of bears. It is closely associated with seeking food and resting. Bears, as David Brown notes in *The Grizzly in the Southwest*, "make well-defined pathways to and from characteristic bedding sites in heavy cover where they avoid the midday heat. These bedding sites are interconnected to favorite foraging areas and escape retreats by a system of well-worn paths that facilitate rapid movement with a minimum of noise."

Walk, run, wander, meander, climb, swim, and slide are all modes of travel that have a specific purpose for bears. East notes in *Bears* that "if scent or an unnatural noise alerts him [the bear] at close range, he is likely to . . . go crashing off through the brush like a runaway truck. But if he picks up danger signals at a distance, he will probably melt away with hardly more commotion than a shadow. For an animal of his size, he can move through thick cover with astonishingly little noise. . . ."

PURPOSES OF TRAVEL

- ▲ Avoid people
- ▲ Escape
- ▲ Move to and from daybed
- ▲ Move to and from den
- ▲ Play
- ▲ Return to previous habitat following translocation
- ▲ Seek a mate
- ▲ Seek food
- ▲ Purposes not understood by humans

Travel Routes

The routes traveled by bears are varied in topography and purpose. Some serve a specific purpose, leading to a known destination, while others are the result of exploration. Most commonly bears travel the routes of least resistance, while avoiding open areas. However, as George Laycock explains in *The Wild Bears*, "the grizzly can barrel, tanklike, through thick brush that would bring a man to a complete halt. . . ."

Cover and safety are important criteria in bears' travels, therefore ninety-five percent of their travel is away from roads and other developments. They are capable of negotiating most any terrain, including the densest vegetation or extremely steep ridges and cliffs. "The more rugged and inaccessible the general character of the topography of any particular region, there surely will the trails of white men, Indians, bears, wild sheep, etc., be found converging into the best passes," says John Muir in *The Mountains of California*.

Common Travel Routes

- Base of cliffs
- Bear trails
- Forest edges
- Game trails
- Glaciers
- Hillsides (rock ledges to walk on)
- Human-constructed trails
- Ice floes
- Open forests
- Open ridges
- Open seas
- Ridges
- Roads
- Shorelines (streams, ponds, lakes)
- Small passes between hills
- Snowfields
- Stream bottoms

Trails

Bears have routes with specific purposes and, as creatures of habit, repeated use transforms a route into a well-defined trail. Many years of use by generations of bears result in a trail of deep indentations in the ground, in a zig-zag pattern, due to the hindpaw stepping into the same location as the forepaw. Two well-defined ruts are formed with time. Where such a trail climbs over an embankment or up a steep ridge, the trail may become a stairway.

"We . . . came into the deepest bear trail I had ever seen," writes Harold McCracken in *The Beast That Walks Like Man*. "It was cut to an average of at least six inches into the solid ground . . . we marveled at how many thousands of footsteps by the padded feet of bears, through the untold expanse of years, it had taken to cut that primeval trail."

Travel Gaits

The common gait of all species of bears is the walk. They amble, or pace, with both legs on one side moving together—alternate paws on alternate sides—the paws striking the ground in the sequence of:

1
(right forepaw)

2
(left hindpaw)

3
(left forepaw)

4
(right hindpaw)

1
(right forepaw)

2
(left hindpaw)

3
(left forepaw)

4
(right hindpaw)

Bears do not always start walking with their right forepaw, of course, but they *always* follow the above sequence.

There general gait and appearance is:

▲ A shuffling, lumbering walk

▲ Plantigrade (feet flat on ground)

▲ Feet turned in (pigeon-toed)

▲ At normal walking pace, the hindfoot is often placed slightly forward of the forefoot track

▲ At a faster walking pace, the hindfoot is often placed well in front of the forefoot track

▲ A slow pace is a walk

▲ A hurried pace is a trot

▲ A frightened or angry pace is a gallop.

▬ WALKING

American Black Bear: Graceful; rhythmic; surefooted.

Brown Bear: Dignified; ponderous; travels a straight line if possible; head low, scenting; "swims" breaststroke through deep snow.

Grizzly Bear: Slow-motion shuffle appearance; fast moving; seeming slow, but truly rapid; somewhat graceful; silent; indication of power.

Polar Bear: Dignified; nimble; easy motion; fast moving; swift; weighty shuffle; front paws move in rhythm like paddles; requires twice the energy to walk as other mammals of equal size; energy-conserving pace; slides downhill on rump/forepaws.

Asiatic Black Bear: Dignified; deliberate motion.

Giant Panda: Moves with ease and silence; rolling gait; extremely long stride; body somewhat diagonal; head low; clumsy appearance; wiggling pigeon-toed (all paws); trots when startled; not built for traveling great distances.

Sloth Bear: Slow; shambling; feet set down in flapping motion; noisy; crashes through vegetation.

Sun Bear: Extremely pigeon-toed; front paws often cross.

Spectacled Bear: Wobbly.

The walk of the giant panda is different enough from other bears to be noteworthy. "Once seen, the giant panda's wiggling, pigeon-toed walk is never forgotten," write Desmond Morris and Ramona Morris in *Men and Pandas*. "Dwight Davis describes it, 'The head is carried well below the shoulder line, and the tail is closely appressed against the body. The stride is considerably longer . . . and as a result the gait is more rolling, with much more lateral rotation of the shoulders and hips than in *Ursus*. This gives a pronounced waddling character to the locomotion. The heavy head is swayed from side to side.'"

Bipedal Standing and Walking

Bears are plantigrade and capable of standing upright on their hind legs. They stand unaided to observe or increase sight distance, to fight, and to reach to feed, prey, or mark.

Some species of bears are capable of walking bipedally, though this is not a normal means of locomotion. They do not attack in this position, though they may raise their upper body to better reach and grasp their prey or enemy.

The American black, brown, grizzly, polar, sloth, and sun bears walk bipedally, but only a few steps. The giant panda and the spectacled bears do not walk bipedally. The Asiatic black bear walks bipedally extremely well. "Asian [Asiatic] black bears are very bipedal," according to Terry Domico in *Bears Of The World*, "and have been known to walk upright for over a quarter of a mile . . . on their hind legs."

Circus, menagerie, and other performing bears walk bipedally, being trained to perform stunts and walk distances in this manner.

Running

Bears, with the exception of the giant panda, run quite well. They are fast and agile, though their speed is maintained only for short distances. Many run with power, and are fifty percent faster than humans. "The grizzly can barrel, tank-like, through thick brush that would bring a man to a complete halt," relates Laycock. The stride of one galloping bear was recorded at seventeen feet between tracks.

Bears run to catch prey, inspect an unknown situation or movement, escape from a threat, to play, and for no apparent purpose.

An Alaskan grizzly bear in Katmai National Park stands to walk bipedally, though for only a few steps
© Johnny Johnson

SWIFTNESS OF THE SPECIES	
Species	MPH
American black bear	*25–30 MPH*
Brown bear	*35-40 MPH*
Grizzly bear	*35–40 MPH. Outruns a human by 30 yards in 100 yards; flees danger at a waddling gate.*
Polar bear	*25 MPH; 35 MPH short distance; easily overheat when running*
Asiatic black bear	*Quick, fast.*
Giant panda	*Quite slow; clumsy trot; does not gallop; seldom moves faster than a walk.*
Sloth bear	*Gallops faster than a running human; gallops with leaps; gallops when frightened.*
Sun bear	*Fast*
Spectacled bear	*Fast, agile*

 An Alaskan grizzly bear sow and its cub rapidly approach the photographer in Denali National Park
© Johnny Johnson

They run uphill and downhill with speed and agility. "The rumor [bears cannot run downhill without stumbling] is untrue," relates Stephen Herrero in *Bear Attacks*. "I have watched grizzly bears chase one another, and . . . elk and bighorn sheep—downhill, uphill, sidehill—wherever the pursuit leads. I have never seen a . . . bear stumble. . . ."

"He was going so fast," relates W.P. Hubbard, describing an American black bear in *Notorious Grizzly Bears*, "his hind feet were up by his ears when his front feet were under and behind him. He was all action, a big black bottom, with four stems churning for all they were worth."

Bears' endurance is exceptional. They have been known to run without a break for ten miles. A sow with two cubs is reported to have traveled more than twenty miles through mountainous terrain in one hour.

 A display of endurance as an Alaskan grizzly bear easily runs through deep snow in Katmai National Park
© Johnny Johnson

Navigation

B ears appear to have no difficulty navigating throughout their range. Obviously the size of the range might be significant, as one would not expect a giant panda to experience much difficulty when its home area is approximately one to three square miles. However, the ranges of other species of bears are hundreds of square miles (and those of polar bears are thousands of square miles), and the ability to navigate is remarkable. Bears also are unbelievably capable of finding their way home following a translocation to a totally new and unfamiliar area. Homing appears more developed in adults, and grizzly bears are more proficient than black bears in returning to their home range.

"Their [bears'] sense of topographical orientation transcends simple familiarity with specific features," writes Paul Schullery in *The Bears of Yellowstone*. "They can find their way home from country they have never before visited."

There has been very little scientific research of how bears nagivate. Some biologists believe bears may possess a level of sensory contact with their goal, and most believe that a familiarity with the area of release is not a factor.

Bear biologist Lynn Rogers, in *Translocation of Wild Animals* (Leon Neilsen and Robert Brown), describes the levels of the navigation ability of bears as:

- **American black bear** Excellent, strong swimmer; swims for pleasure and to feed.

- **Brown bear** Strong and skillful swimmer; swims to feed (fishing, frogging) and for pleasure.

- **Polar bear** "The swimmer." Exceptional and powerful swimmer for travel, feeding, and pleasure; excellent buoyancy due to thick, oily fur and blubber; normally swims (paddles) only with front legs/paws, with hind legs/paws used as rudders to steer (used otherwise as paddles); swims 6 miles per hour; male swims 100 yards in 30–33 seconds, female—100 yards in 40 seconds; can swim 60 miles without rest, leaving a wake as it moves through the water; its muzzle is submerged in rough water but is regularly raised to breath.

- **Asiatic black bear** Good swimmer.

- **Giant panda** Skeptical of water; will cross streams, but does not appear to voluntarily swim; swims to escape an enemy.

- **Sloth bear** Good swimmer; primarily plays in water; sits and splashes on self.

- **Sun bear** Good swimmer.

- **Spectacled bear** Good swimmer.

❖ Orientation to familiar landmarks (visual or otherwise)

❖ Movement in a particular compass direction without reference to landmarks

❖ Ability of an animal in an unfamiliar area to orient toward home or some other goal beyond the range of sensory contact

One American black bear was relocated 156 miles by air to an unfamiliar location. The bear quickly returned to its location of capture. Several Alaskan brown bears were moved more than 195 miles to unfamiliar territory. They all returned home.

A six-month-old grizzly bear cub became separated from its mother, following their translocation by air to a totally unfamiliar area. The cub traveled over thirty miles through rugged terrain to the location where it had been captured with its mother.

A brown bear in Alaska was translocated, according to Domico, ". . . by boat to Montague Island in Prince William Sound, a direct distance of nearly 58 miles. Twenty-eight days later the same bear was killed within 109 yards of its capture site. The return route must have required swimming some 7 miles . . . , then .5-mile . . . and 1.75-miles . . . to the mainland. All . . . accomplished at right angles to strong tides and in the frigid waters. . . ."

Polar bears may be the most amazing of bear navigators. Scientists are baffled by the white bear's ability to travel in straight routes across an ever-changing, ever-moving and drifting icepack, or how they remain in the same location when the ice beneath them is moving with the circumpolar drift.

Swimming

All bears seem to enjoy water, whether wading, floating, sitting or actually swimming. In general, they utilize bodies of water, streams, lakes, ponds, and the seas for pleasure and purpose. Water provides bears a means to escape from insects, cool off, feed (fish, frogs, bugs), relieve itching, travel, hide their tracks, play; it undoubtedly serves other purposes. They swim (sometimes long distances), wade, sit and splash, lie, soak, float, and scratch. Their buoyancy is excellent, especially that of polar bears. Bears swim "dog paddle" fashion and shake water off like dogs. They may go to water when wounded, possibly for healing or to die.

Bears not only enjoy wallowing in natural pools, but have on occasion bathed in developed pools. Tracy Storer and Lloyd Tevis, in *California Grizzly*, relate an account of a bear visiting Paso Robles Hot Springs in California. "A huge grizzly was in the habit of making nocturnal visits to the spring, plunge into the pool, and, with his forepaws grasping the limb [of a cottonwood that once extended low over the water], swing himself up and down in the water, evidently enjoying his bath. . . ."

Male American black bears swim between the mainland and offshore islands of the Pacific Northwest, seeking females during the mating season.

The author observed a large grizzly bear in the Savonoski River of Katmai National Park, Alaska swim from a gravel bar directly across a thirty-foot channel to the riverbank. Upon reaching the six-foot-high vertical riverbank, the bear turned upstream and swam sixty feet against a swift current (seven miles per hour), in what appeared to be an effortless manner, until it reached a more easily ascended embankment.

The polar bears are without question the "swimmers" of all bears. Their shape allows them to move through the water with relative ease, propelled with strong, powerful strokes. Swimming approximately three hundred miles between ice floes, they display enormous endurance in the water. They ". . . can swim tirelessly all day at a steady pace of six miles an hour," describes Charles Feazel in *White Bear*.

 An Alaskan grizzly bear swimming in a display of a bear's enjoyment of water
© *Johnny Johnson*

"Polar bears have been spotted swimming several hundred miles from the nearest land or ice floe. They can apparently swim for days without hauling out to rest. The bear shape cuts through the sea like the bow of a ship. Compared with other bears, polar bears are elongate, with stocky bodies behind their long necks and no humps at the shoulders. They have long, bowed forelegs that join with no chest between them . . . a bear's profile is a wedge, tapered toward the head . . . this shape is highly efficient in the water."

Polar bears are capable of leaping out of the water seven to eight feet in the air from a swimming start. They close their ears and nostrils when diving, and may remain under water up to two minutes, cruising ten to fifteen feet deep. Thomas Koch notes "this bear's peculiar habit of diving every few minutes or so while swimming, as if the diving were part of its escape mechanism," in *The Year Of The Polar Bear*.

Climbing

Bears climb trees to feed, rest, hibernate, play, or for safety. Young brown bears, American black bears, and Asiatic black bears climb naturally (they do not need to learn), which allows the mother to defend only the base of the tree. When threatened while aloft, cubs climb out on thin branches and sit where a larger and heavier enemy is unable to reach.

All species of bears, except the polar bear, are capable of climbing trees, though the adults of the larger species lose their climbing ability as they become heavier.

"Young grizzlies are good climbers: They can go up a tree like a black bear," describes Frederick Drimmer in *The Animal Kingdom*. "However, they lose this ability as they get older, and most full-grown grizzlies are too big and heavy to climb. Large grizzlies have been seen in trees, but they are exceptions. This is one of the major differences between the black bear and the grizzly."

The best climbers are those whose paws have naked soles that provide rough skin, short and sharply hooked claws, and a more-pronounced inward turn of the paws. The brown bears are poor climbers due to fixed wrist joints, poor claw structure—they're long and straight—and their weight.

The most common method of ascent among bears is by using the front legs to grasp the tree trunk and pull while pushing with the hind legs. The motion appears somewhat like an inchworm. Claws are hooked into available cracks for a better hold. A bear may on occasion grasp, pull and push, moving its legs in a sequence, as if it were walking.

Bears may also "ladder" up trees by using the tree branches as rungs. This method allows the larger bears, such as grizzly bears, to sometimes climb trees. If a tree is bent over or leaning, a bear may walk up the sloping surface in a normal manner.

The descent is made in reverse fashion, head up, walking down backward, though it may be sometimes accomplished by sliding down, or jumping down from low limbs.

🐻 CLIMBING ABILITIES

American Black Bear: Outstanding climber. Climbs regularly and easily to feed, escape enemies, or to hibernate in some areas. Climbing ability declines with age, with large adults climbing infrequently for food. Climbing is also the principal means of defense.

Brown Bear: Poor climber due to claw structure and body weight. Climbs to feed (pursue prey, seek human foods) and travel, even steep rock ridges; capable of laddering up only trees with low branches. Cubs climb trees.

Polar Bear: Does not climb trees; agile climber of ice ridges; climbs to travel and pursue prey. Can jump/scale over six-foot-high ice barriers; can jump down ten feet; can scale a thirty-five foot ice wall.

Asiatic Black Bear: Good climber. Climbs to feed, rest, sun, escape from enemies, and hibernate. Excellent climber in rocks and cliffs; frequently climbs trees. Climbing important in feeding habits; some older bears become too heavy to climb.

Giant Panda: Poor climber. Climbing is uncommon and less efficient than that of other bears; climbs slowly and clumsily, appearing inept; embraces tree, ascending with caterpillar movements. Climbs for defense—to escape dogs, humans, and other giant pandas—and to rest and sun. Females climb to escape courting males.

Sloth Bear: Excellent climber despite appearing slow and clumsy. Climbs to feed, rest; does not climb to escape enemies—runs or fights probably because its major predator is the leopard, an excellent climber. Can jump down ten feet, climb a smooth-bole tree or pole, and hangs upside down like a "sloth."

Sun Bear: Expert climber, nimble, skillful. Climbs to feed, rest. Cubs climb better than they run. Can nearly hang upside down with claws.

Spectacled Bear: Excellent climber. Climbs quite high. Climbs to feed, rest, sleep, escape; able to climb vines and small trees (less than four inches in diameter); spends more time in trees than other bears.

Playing

Humans appear to be most attracted to bears by their play, especially the humorous activities of cubs. A cub's active and amusing playfulness with its siblings and mother is not only sport, recreation, or idle activity as we would interpret, but a natural necessity for survival.

Play is actually "play fighting," and is extremely important to cubs as part of their education. The large variety of play fighting of the cubs, which they may engage in until five years of age, contributes to their preparation for survival in the "real" world. It may occur anytime and wherever they may be—in the den, in trees or on the ground, in water or on ice and snow. This playful education helps develop social attitudes and physical coordination.

"One of the most humorous play sessions I've observed," relates Herrero, "occurred . . . when two black bear cubs of the year came upon a young sapling pine tree. One bear climbed to near the top. Then the other bear followed, and their combined weight bent the tree to near the ground where one cub hopped off and the other was catapulted up as the tree straightened. Soon both cubs were up the tree again to repeat the sequence."

Adults also play very much like cubs, but it is a solitary activity except for females with their cubs. ". . . A big bear sat down like a dog at the top of the slide [long snowdrift]," relates Andy Russell in *Grizzly Country*, "a huge hind foot was elevated to scratch the back of an ear . . . with the paw still held up to its head, the grizzly took off in a plummet down to the bottom."

The play activities of some species in the wild are poorly documented, but there is evidence that the cave bears, like today's bears, enjoyed play. D.P. Erdbrink, in *A Review Of Fossil and Recent Bears of the Old World*, relates an explorer's description of a play area, the "toboggan of the bears." He noted the explorers found that, "a gentle slope, covered with

Alaskan grizzly bears in a play-fight
in Katmai National Park
© Johnny Johnson

cave loam, ending in a shallow subterranean pond, has been
the playground of local Cave bears, as indicated by numerous prints and even by imprints of separate hairs. . . ."

Play Activities

The activity list primarily pertains to recorded observations
of the play fighting of cubs. However, any activity in which a
cub may engage is probably enjoyed by an adult, and a few
adult activities are included.

- Bite and wrestle with sow
- Tag
- Push sibling under water
- Hide
- Roll on ground (tumble holding paws)
- High dive
- Paw

- Slide down snow banks
- Stand
- Mouth each other
- Nip
- Lie on back and grasp paws
- Box
- Climb on sibling
- Slap

- Climb on mother
- Shove
- Slide off mother
- Stomp
- Toss stick, catch in mouth
- Somersault
- Slide down icefields
- Bristle
- Roll on back

- Roll logs
- Climb (rocks, trees, stumps, ice floes)
- Romp
- Charge
- Run up and down trees
- Tumble
- Crawl through hollow logs
- Flip fish
- Swim through hollow logs
- Frolic
- Flip stick or driftwood
- Jump
- Slide down riverbanks
- Wrestle
- Poke
- Toss rocks or other loose items
- Stand on head
- Duck head
- Slide off sow
- Leap
- Crowd against sow
- Shadow box
- Knock each other off rocks
- Chase own tail
- Shove between sow's legs
- Play hide and seek
- Shuffling dance
- Roll down hill
- Hang upside down
- Slap paws together
- Swing on vines
- Sit and watch other animals
- Swim
- Jump up and flip
- Acrobatic leaps
- High-stepping run
- Tug of war
- Chase and tease monkeys
- Chase
- Lie on back in mud and kick
- Embrace
- Slide down snowfield on chest
- Nibble
- Lie on back and wave legs
- Roll in snow
- Slide down ice into water
- Growl
- Rock ice floes back and forth
- Splash water
- Lie on back and play with object
- Pounce
- Roll in water
- Grab hind paws and roll in water like a barrel
- Bite
- Waggle head
- Cock head and listen
- Slide down mud
- Jump out of hiding
- Run
- Run up and down tree
- Make and play with snowballs

"Next to the apes and monkeys, I regard bears as the most demonstrative of all wild animals."

WILLIAM HORNADAY,
Naturalist

"I was rewarded by seeing a small light-colored grizzly," describes noted explorer Charles Sheldon, in *The Wilderness of Denali*. "It was indulging in the most grotesque play imaginable, while not a hundred yards above it were more than thirty [Dall sheep] ewes quietly feeding, all completely indifferent to its near presence. The bear was repeatedly turning somersaults, rolling a few feet down the slope, and running short distances upward. Often it would lie on its back, throw up all four feet and attempt to strike them together. These antics continued for ten minutes or more, while only one of the sheep—a yearling lamb—looked directly at it. The others maintained their usual watch, apparently taking no interest in the bear."

"Suddenly, it jumped off [an ice wall] onto the almost perpendicular slope and came zooming out on the slick, wet ice of the glacier at a dizzy rate of speed," described Frank Dufresne in *No Room For Bears*. "Then, to my amazement, it came sailing over the lip of the glacier to plunge fifty feet into a lake." The bear then started climbing back up the slope to possibly try again.

Grooming

Bears are generally quite well groomed, utilizing a variety of methods to clean, smooth and otherwise maintain their fur and skin. Their grooming activities include:

- Bathing
- Combing fur with claws
- Licking fur dry
- Licking to remove dirt
- Nibble off dirt with teeth
- Rubbing against brush
- Rubbing against rocks
- Rubbing against trees
- Rubbing in grass

- Rubbing in gravel
- Scratching with fore- or hindpaw
- Scrubbing on grass
- Shaking off water like dogs
- Stretching in a catlike manner
- Swimming
- Wallowing in mud (removes insects and other debris, but is followed with other grooming measures)

The natural activities (walking through brush and high grass) of bears and their lack of pores also lend to cleanliness. The sloth bear is the major exception and is poorly groomed, while the polar bear licks and washes fastidiously after eating, even using snow if water is unavailable. "Like a cat, the bear washes his face with his newly cleaned paws," notes Charles Feazel in *White Bear*.

Scratching, this Alaskan grizzly bear displays one of many grooming habits
© *Johnny Johnson*

Paw Sucking

Paw sucking occurs with all ages of bears in most species, and captive bears appear to suck their paws more frequently than those in the wild. Though its purpose remains something of a mystery, research and speculation attribute this activity to various reasons that include:

▲ Obtaining footpad secretions

▲ Obtaining remnant food particles

▲ Paw cleaning

▲ An indication of contentment

▲ Psychological reasons

▲ Softening calluses

▲ Removing calluses

▲ Enhancing footpad sensitivity

▲ A means of displacement

▲ A pastime

▲ Boredom

An ancient theory, over ten thousand years old, speculates that paw sucking provides bears subsistence during hibernation, but this has been proven untrue. However, hibernating bears often sleep with their paws located directly against their face, and to add an element of confusion, recent studies have shown that American black bears shed their paw pads during hibernation and sometimes consume them upon awakening.

(Little is understood about paw sloughing. "In the den the skin of its paws is slowly sloughed off and replaced by new skin," according to Shepard and Sanders. "The factors that cause shedding of old pads are unknown at present," relates Lynn Rogers in "Shedding of Foot Pads by Black Bears During Denning.")

Sloth and sun bears suck their paws more than other bear species, babbling and gurgling as they carry out this activity for fifteen to twenty minutes each time. Asiatic black bears lie on their backs, placing their front paws together, and alternately suck each paw. Sun bears also lie on their backs, humming as they alternately suck their hind paws.

Reproduction

Reproduction is similar among bear species, though some variations exist in the timing of reproductive and denning activities, reproductive rates and litter size. (Reproductive rates of bears are highest in areas of abundant food—they must be healthy to reproduce.) Generally, the species of larger bears have less reproductive potential; however, the North American brown bears appear to have some decreasing potential with decreasing body size (due to declining habitat quality). The number of litters a sow produces during her lifetime depends on her longevity, age of first litter, survival of litters (how soon she is able to again breed), and her individual health.

"The grizzly has one of the lowest reproductive rates of the terrestrial mammals," notes David Brown, in *The Grizzly in the Southwest*. Giant panda reproductive potential is lower than American and Asiatic black bears of the same size.

Males become sexually active earlier than their boldness allows them to compete and participate. The polar bear is sexually mature at five to six years, though some authorities believe they are not bold enough until eight to ten years of age.

Bears have a mechanism, termed "delayed implantation," whereby the development of the embryo is temporarily suspended (see Gestation Period).

Courtship/Mating Period

"The ultimate social interaction is finding a mate. Mating itself is a brief act," notes Feazel in *White Bear*.

Courtship and mating periods vary between and within each species, depending on habitat and climate. The giant pandas and polar bears appear to have the earliest spring estrus periods, and the sloth and sun bears may breed nearly anytime of year.

In captivity, bears may mate at any time, possibly due to boredom and good health, but the sow usually does not conceive except during the normal breeding season. Cubs are removed from the sow earlier than in the wild, so litters may be at a two-year interval.

Courtship/Mating Activities

The male "comes to pay court with the delicate finesse of an animated locomotive running on a one-way track," notes Andy Russell in *Grizzly Country*, describing the arrival of the male when the female has come into estrus.

AGE OF SOW AT FIRST LITTER	
American black bear	• *Three to five years* • *Some seven years*
Brown bear	• *Five years*
Giant panda	• *Five–seven years*
Polar bear	• *Four–seven years*
Asiatic black bear	• *Three years*
Sloth bear	• *Undetermined*
Sun bear	• *Three years*
Spectacled bear	• *Four years*

American black bear	• June, July • As late as August in the north • Two- to three-week period	**Giant panda**	• March, April, May • Occasional fall estrus • Two- to seven-day period
Brown bear	• May, June	**Sloth bear**	• April, May, June (India) • Most of year (Ceylon) • All year (Sri Lanka)
Grizzly bear	• May, June, July		
Polar bear	• April, May • Three-week period	**Sun bear**	• All year • Two- to seven-day period
Asiatic black bear	• Late May • As early as March; as late as December • One- to two-day period	**Spectacled bear**	• April, May, June • One- to five-day period

"He kept herding her from below, as though his objective was to keep her up the slope," Adolph Murie describes in *A Naturalist in Alaska*. "When she traveled, he traveled on a contour below her. Once, when a sharp ridge hid her from him, he galloped forward and upward to intercept her . . . when he saw her again she was two or three hundred yards away. He galloped after her, his hoarse panting plainly audible half a mile away. But she made no real effort to escape, and he was soon herding her from below again. The chase continued all day."

The courting and mating activities of the bear species are quite noisy and diverse. Sloth bears may be the most vociferous while mating. They are very boisterous and emit a long, melodious call. Bears are polygamous and a single male may mate with several females, with copulation occurring "dog fashion"; however, a female giant panda crouches while the male squats.

Courting and mating actions among the different species include:

• Barking	• Chirping	• Kissing	• Roaring
• Biting	• Clucking	• Male holding female's neck	• Rubbing
• Bleating	• Head bobbing	• Moaning	• Squatting
• Caressing	• Hugging	• Mock fighting	• Squealing
			• Wrestling

"The male [grizzly bear] covered her for about an hour," relates Adolph Murie in *A Naturalist in Alaska*. "Much of the time the female wriggled about, apparently trying to escape while he held her with his paws in front of her hips and his head lying along her neck."

Gestation Period

Embryonic growth in all bears takes approximately two months, but due to embryonic delay (delayed implantation), the overall gestation period is considerably longer. Mating generally occurs during the summer, but implantation of the blastocyst (the fertilized ovum) is delayed until a more appropriate time for the female. When the ovum implants, the true gestation period begins.

The overall gestation period of bears varies considerably, and is probably due to delayed implantation. Bears are able to breed and give birth only when in their best condition. Therefore, if for some reason—such as inadequate food sources—the female is in poor condition, without the weight

GESTATION, BIRTH PERIOD, LOCATION

Species	Gestation Period (days)	Birth Period	Location
American black bear	• 235	• Late January/February	• Dens
Brown bear	• 180–210	• January/February	• Dens
Grizzly bear	• 235	• January/February	
Polar bear	• 240–270	• Late November/early January	• Dens
Asiatic black bear	• 200–240	• Winter/early Spring	• Caves • Hollows trees
Giant panda	• 97–163	• Late August/September	• Nests on the ground • Nests in caves or rock clefts • Nests in hollow trees or stumps
Sloth bear	• 210	• December/early January • All year in some locations	• Caves • Shelters under boulders
Sun bear	• 97	• All year	• On ground (in vegetation) • Hollow logs
Spectacled bear	• 240–255	• November through February (January most common)	• Nests on the ground • Nests under large rocks or tree roots

of fat reserves that is the "food" for her and her cubs during the winter, she aborts, and the blastocyst is absorbed by her body. Bear biologist Lynn Rogers has determined a correlation between an American black bear sow's body weight and implantation, and is able to predict the "likelihood of her giving birth." All species of bears, except the sun bear, have this wonderful physiological mechanism.

Birth Location

The locations of births among the different species of bears is influenced by habitat and topography, and whether the bears hibernate. The hibernating species most often have a true den.

Litter Size

Species	Average	Range	Years Between Litters
American black bear	2	• 1–5 • 3 not uncommon • 4 rare • 5 exceptional • First litter usually 1 • 6 once recorded	2
Brown bear	2	• 1–5 • Seldom 4 or 5	3
Grizzly bear	1.7–2.5	• 1–4	3
Polar bear	1.6–1.9	• 1–3 • 10% of litters 3	3–4
Asiatic black bear	2	• 1–4	2–3
Giant panda	1.7	• 1–3 • 3 exceptional • 3 in captivity in 1973	2
Sloth bear	1.72	• 1–3 • Seldom 3	2–3
Sun bear	2	• 1–3	3
Spectacled bear	1 to 2	• 1–3	Information not available

Giant pandas normally have two cubs, but only occasionally in the wild does the mother care for both; normally she abandons one of the two and it dies. (Only one survives in captivity.) "To hold, suckle, and carry two helpless young for four or five months until they are mobile is probably too difficult," notes George Schaller *et al.*, in *The Giant Pandas Of Wolong*. He also explains that the second cub is insurance, in case the other cub is not viable.

Don DeHart, a hunting guide, observed a brown bear on the Alaska Peninsula with six cubs, two of which were runts.

Interval of Litters

The interval (years between litters) may vary if the sow, following the period when she and her cubs separate, is unable to rebuild her weight and condition. Variations in food sources and forage seasons may determine the sow's preparedness, and density of bears, amount of human disturbance, and the sow's health and age are also factors. These elements also affect litter size.

Interbreeding

Interbreeding occurs in captivity. "One of the most revealing facets of the relation between the brown bear and the polar bear has occurred in some of the zoos around the world," explained Koch. "When given the opportunity to mate, these two different bears will produce fertile hybrids. This conclusively proves their close relationship in the not-too-far-distant past."

When polar bears breed with other *Ursus* bears, the "hybrid cubs show many characteristics of their polar bear parent, including body and head shape, a white coat at birth, and good swimming abilities," describes Charles Feazel in *White Bear*. "Some hybrids' coats darken as they mature."

"Successful breeding between polar bears and Alaska browns is not uncommon in captivity, and the polar bear has also been successfully crossed with the brown bear of northern Europe," explains Ben East in *Bears*. "In both cases the hybrid offspring are capable of producing young, too." The color of the offspring might be what you would expect. "Some are pure white, some silver-blue, some roan, and others grizzly brown," described Frank Dufresne in *No Room For Bears*. "Some have the big head and hump of the grizzly [brown]; others the snake-like neck and narrower head of the polar bear."

Interbreeding in captivity has included American black bear/grizzly bear; polar bear/brown bear; brown bear/Asiatic black bear; and brown bear/grizzly (same species, different subspecies). A female hybrid (polar) can be crossbred back to a polar bear. Captive interbreeding between bear species other than polar and brown bears is quite uncommon and occurs primarily in Eurasian facilities.

Bear Cubs

The human interest and fondness for bears is often centered around the cubs of the species. Cuddly in appearance and playful and amusing when most people first observe them, these youngsters are quite unattractive when they arrive in the bear world. They are born:

- ▲ With mother "half asleep"
- ▲ Almost helpless
- ▲ Blind
- ▲ Nearly naked (fine hair)
- ▲ Poorly insulated
- ▲ Toothless
- ▲ Unable to hear
- ▲ Unable to smell
- ▲ Weak
- ▲ Uncoordinated
- ▲ Noisy
- ▲ Demanding
- ▲ Able to detect temperature changes
- ▲ Able to move to warm objects
- ▲ Able to find sow's nipples

Grizzly bear cub, Katmai National Park, Alaska.
© Johnny Johnson.

CONDITION OF CUBS AT BIRTH

	Weight (ounces)	Length (inches)	Condition
American black bear	10–16	8	Fine, gray, downlike hair; hindquarters underdeveloped; drags self around den; 1/280 of sow's weight*
Brown bear	16	9	Lightly furred; 1/720 of sow's weight
Grizzly bear	14	8	Lightly furred; 1/625 of sow's weight
Polar bear	16–24	8–9	Pink skin; short, thin hair; no blubber; size of a house cat; 1/700 of sow's weight
Asiatic black bear	13	Information not available	Information not available
Giant panda	3–5	6	Yellowish pink skin; sparse white hair; black fuzz around eyes, on ears and shoulders at one week; squeaky voice; 1/900 of sow's weight

*Human infant is 1/25 of its mother's weight.

	Weight (ounces)	Length (inches)	Condition
Sloth bear	Information not available	Information not available	Unattractive; very strong (toes and forelegs like a sloth)
Sun bear	12	7	Skin near transparent; more hairless than other species
Spectacled bear	11–18	7	Information not available

Kodiak brown bears may have a weight increase of 1,000 times from a newborn cub to a mature adult. Humans would weigh over 6,000 pounds if they shared this increase.

Cub Characteristics at Birth (American Black Bear)

A study of American black bear cubs' characteristics at birth was conducted in Pennsylvania by research biologist Gary Alt.

	Average	Smallest/Largest	
• Weight	12.8 ounces	10.3	16.0
• Total length	9.4 inches	8.2	11.2
• Head length	2.8 inches	2.4	3.1
• Ear length	0.4 inches	0.3	0.5
• Nose width	0.4 inches	0.4	0.4
• Tail length	0.4 inches	0.3	0.6
• Hair length	0.1 inches	0.1	0.1
• Neck girth	4.3 inches	3.9	4.7
• Chest girth	6.5 inches	5.9	7.2
• Foot length (front)	0.7 inches	0.7	0.8
• Foot length (hind)	1.1 inches	0.9	1.3
• Foot width (front)	0.7 inches	0.6	0.8
• Foot width (hind)	0.6 inches	0.6	0.7
• Claw length (front foot)	0.3 inches	0.2	0.3
• Claw length (hind foot)	0.2 inches	0.2	0.2
• Umbilical cord length	1.5 feet	0.6	5.7

Cub's Eyes Open

Born unable to see, cubs' eyes generally open in a few to several days, depending on species and individuals: American black bears—28 to 40 days; brown bears—28; grizzly bears—21; polar bears—28; Asiatic black bears—7; Giant pandas—40 to 48; Sloth bears—21; Sun bears—14; and Spectacled bears—25.

Both eyes do not necessarily open at the same time. Paul Schullery, in *Yellowstone Bear Tales*, relates a story by E. E. Ogston of a young American black bear cub being transported through Yellowstone National Park. "One of his eyes had opened at Yellowstone Lake and the other at the Canyon," described Ogston.

Cub's First Walk

Unable to walk at birth (though a few are able to crawl), cubs first "walk" at varying stages depending on species and individuals. Generally, the various species, with the exception of the giant pandas, begin to walk between four and eight weeks: American black bears—5 weeks; brown bears—6; polar bears—8; Asiatic black bears—4; giant pandas—12; sloth bears—4; sun bears—2; spectacled bears—4.

Growth and Development (Cubs and Adults)

The development of cubs varies between species, and geographically and individually within a species. Some cubs are born larger and stronger than others, while litter mates

Not stranded or abandoned, but curious, these Alaskan grizzly bear cubs in Katmai National Park have their mother nearby
© *Johnny Johnson*

develop at different rates. Weight gain may be as much several pounds a day during the first year.

American Black Bear

- Six weeks: 2 pounds
- Eight weeks: 5 pounds
- Six months: 40–60 pounds
- Three years: Sexually mature
- Five years: Fully grown

Brown Bear

- Six months: 55–80 pounds
- During first year: Kodiak cubs double weight every two months
- Eighteen months: 150–200 pounds
- Three years: Eight feet long
- Four to five years: Sexually mature
- Seven to eight years: Mature
- Eight to ten years: Fully grown

Grizzly Bear

- Eight to ten weeks: 10–20 pounds
- Seven months: 50–80 pounds
- Twelve months: 150–200 pounds
- Twenty months: 200–400 pounds
- Three years: 350–425 pounds
- Four to five years: Sexually mature
- Seven to eight years: Mature
- Eight to ten years: Fully grown

Polar Bear

- Forty days: 2 pounds
- Three months: 28 pounds
- Six months: 130 pounds
- Four years: Sexually mature
- Eight to nine years: Fully grown
- Earliest maturing bear
- Females grow minimally after fourth year

Asiatic Black Bear

- Three to four years: Sexually mature

Giant Panda

- Twelve months: 77 pounds
- Thirty months: 114–121 pounds
- Forty months (female): 134 pounds
- Forty months (male): 153 pounds
- Five to seven years: Sexually mature

Sloth Bear

- Rapid growth
- Early growth is in legs
- Begin to travel sooner than other cubs
- Third year: Sexually mature

Sun Bear

- Information Unavailable

Spectacled Bear

- Information Unavailable

Cub Mortality

The first few months of a bear's life are the most perilous. There are many enemies in a cub's world, all considerably larger than this youngster who must depend upon its mother for protection.

One fourth of American black bears cubs die during their first year. A third of the first-year survivors die within the next two years, with only fifty percent of the cubs reaching three years of age. Sixty to ninety percent of brown bears survive their first one and a half years, and sixty percent to eighty percent of polar bear cubs survive their first year. Eighty-three percent of grizzly bear cubs in the Yellowstone National Park area survive their first year of life; one half reach three and only forty percent live to be five years of age.

The primary causes of cub mortality are larger bears, primarily adult males (no strange bear is a safe bear); other large enemies; and humans.

Cub Activities

Possibly the main attraction to bear cubs are their playful and comical antics. Many activities begin in the den and increase as a new world is opened to their imagination. Deceptively cuddly, cubs emerge from the den with apprehension and require considerable encouragement by the sow. Some walk and run on unsure legs (American black bears initially climb better than they walk), and giant panda cubs are carried from the den by their mother.

Their play is a near constant variety of stomping, vocalizing, exploring, and climbing, with a full display of curiosity and mischievousness. All cubs fight as the learning process begins, and will play fight up to five years of age. They share all of their mother's activities—travel, caution, feeding—as she prepares them for their life alone.

"Getting them into a sack was one of the liveliest experiences I ever had," Enos Mills writes of two orphaned cubs in *The Spell Of The Rockies*. "Though small and almost starved, these little orphans proceeded to 'chew me up' after the manner of big grizzlies, as is told of them in books."

Motherhood

The drowsy "hibernating" mother, from the moment of giving birth, begins her long effort in assuring her offspring's survival. From initial nourishment, through constant protection, to teaching them how to survive alone, she is fully and solely responsible. Her maternal behavior is paramount—she is "cubbing," without fatherly assistance.

There is a deep family bond. The mother is affectionate, devoted, protective (aggressive toward threats), sensitive, strict, and attentive to the training of her cubs. Her primary concern is for their safety and education. Considerable knowledge is necessary for the cubs to survive, and so they remain with their mother for long periods of time, learning from her during this lengthy infancy. The female cubs are the fastest learners.

A sow's most critical lessons to her cubs include:

FOOD

▲ How to find and eat specific food (a brown bear sow brings a fish to the cubs and opens its side for them to eat)

▲ How to fish

▲ How to dig

▲ How to catch prey, large and small

True motherhood is demonstrated by this grizzly bear sow in Katmai National Park, Alaska
© Johnny Johnson

NURSING CHARACTERISTICS

American black bear	Sow has three pairs of functional nipples
Brown bear	Sow has three pairs of functional nipples Cubs nurse five minutes at a time, four times a day
Polar bear	Sow has two pairs of functional nipples Cubs nurse fifteen minutes at a time, six–seven times a day
Asiatic black bear	Sow has three pairs of functional nipples
Giant panda	Sow has two pairs of functional nipples Cubs nurse: 6–14 times a day (first 1–2 days) 3–4 times a day (next 60 days) 1–2 times a day (next 150 days)
Sloth bear	Information unavailable
Sun bear	Information unavailable
Spectacled bear	Sow must assist extremely undeveloped cubs for first eight weeks

SAFETY

▲ How to recognize specific threats (enemies, hazards)

▲ The sow cuffs and sends her cubs up a tree (cubs are natural born climbers) or scurrying away to safety

▲ She spanks her cubs to make them obey (very important to their survival)

▲ She will lure an enemy away from the cubs

"Behind her were two cubs. I caught her impatient expression when she beheld me," says Enos Mills in *Wild Life On The Rockies*. "She stopped, and then, with a growl of anger, she wheeled and boxed cubs right and left like an angry mother. The bears disappeared in the direction from which they had come, the cubs urged on with spanks from behind as all vanished in the falling snow."

A sow with cubs is typically the most dangerous bear. She defends her cubs to whatever degree she believes necessary, bluffing or attacking until she has lessened the threat. She is occasionally persistent, killing and even eating the threat. The sloth bear mother is considered the most fierce defender of her cubs, though the most sensitive and patient teacher.

Motherhood is not always perfect—cub mortality is high. Sows habituated to human activity and conditioned to human foods teach their offspring these bad and often deadly habits.

Sows will occasionally abandon their young. "Picnickers disturbed a family group," explains James Cardoza in *The Black Bear in Massachusetts*. "The sow treed her three cubs and left the area, not responding even when one cub was captured and carried to a car."

Nursing

"Mammary glands are of course unique in mammals and together with hair distinguish them from all other classes," writes Jean Craighead-George in *Beasty Inventions*. "Because of the position of these glands on the warm chest and bellies, and because the infant needs the mother and the mother the infant, the most intimate relationship of all life is between the mammalian mother and child."

Nursing activities vary with the species and individual cubs. The cubs locate the nipples by sensing the sow's warmth, and individual cubs are known to dominate a specific nipple. They are demanding and nursing is often noisy with humming, trilling, and purring sounds accompanying feeding. The sow initially nurses on her side, with two nipples normally used during the den period, then sitting up, using four nipples, following emergence from the den. Nursing (lactation) is the greatest energy demand on a sow's body. Sows do not come into estrus while nursing.

Alaskan bear biologist Larry Aumiller relates an observation of two Alaskan brown bear sows with eight cubs between them. The sows would alternate caring for the cubs, and on one occasion a sow was observed nursing six of them.

Bear Milk

Bear's milk contains an average of thirty-three percent (high of forty-eight percent) fat, eleven percent to fifteen percent protein, and 0.3 to 0.6 percent carbohydrates. In comparison, human milk contains 3½ percent fat.

"Polar bear milk has the appearance and consistency of condensed milk, with a fish odor," according to Thomas Koch in *The Year Of The Polar Bear*. "The composition of

Nursing—Madonna of the wilds, an American black bear sow performing the ultimate of motherhood
Haynes Foundation Collection, Montana Historical Society, Helena, MT

polar bear milk reflects the animal's high-fat dietary requirements. Thirty per cent of the milk is fat, whereas the milk we drink contains only 4 per cent fat. The cubs receive almost the same amounts of protein and lactose from their milk as do their young cousins, the seal, the porpoise, and the whale." Barry Lopez, in *Arctic Dreams*, adds that "those who have tasted of it say it tastes like cod liver oil and smells of seals or fish."

Weaning of Cubs

Weaning is a gradual, sometimes slow, process and will vary with species of bear, and the individual family group. Lactation generally peaks in 150 days and ends in approximately 245 days, and by then the cubs will be well established on other foods. However, they may continue to nurse occasionally, some doing so until they separate from their mother.

American Black Bears   typically nurse for 30 weeks but can eliminate complete nutritional dependence in 22 weeks.

Brown Bears   can nurse for up to 82 weeks but eliminate complete nutritional dependence in 24 weeks.

Polar Bears   nurse for between 74 to 104 weeks.

Asiatic Black Bears   nurse for between 104 to 130 weeks.

Giant Pandas   nurse for between 30 to 46 weeks but usually eliminate complete nutritional dependence in seven to nine months.

Sloth Bears   nurse for between 104 to 156 weeks.

Sun Bears   usually nurse for 17 weeks.

Spectacled Bears   typically nurse for 8 weeks.

Adoption of Cubs

Sows occasionally adopt other cubs. "Adoption and interchange of cubs, though not common, has been observed in some circumstances," writes Paul Schullery in *The Bears Of Yellowstone*. "Sometimes the cubs of two sows will have the opportunity to play together . . . and actually mix, leaving with the wrong mother." "One case of this sort . . . resulted in one of the two sows assuming responsibility for all cubs."

Sows Transporting Cubs

Sows carry their cubs when necessary, normally with their mouths. "Cats grip the back of the neck and dogs take the scruffs, but grizzly and black bears take the entire head of the cub in their mouths to carry them," notes Craighead-George. In some species, the cubs routinely ride on their mothers' backs to facilitate transportation and to cement the close sow/cub relationship.

"One of the cubs . . . scrambled up to a point of vantage on some rocks and then hopped onto her [sow] back," described Frederick Drimmer in *The Animal Kingdom*. "The little fellow rode off in style, hanging on with his paws embedded in his mother's fur. The others in the family trailed along behind."

"We observed female Sloth bears transporting small young on their backs . . . one or two young up to one-third the size of the mother were carried either crosswise or with heads forward," Andrew Laurie and John Seidensticker, in *Behavioural Ecology Of The Sloth Bear*, noted during their studies at Royal Chitawan National Park, Nepal. "A young Sloth bear (age 3 to 5 months) rode on the back, hip and shoulder of the female. Usually the cub was situated on the lower back, grasping the fur if it began to slip or if the female stood up. Frequently, if the cub seemed off center, the female would shake vigorously, occasionally flipping the cub all the way over her back; if the cub was too far forward, she would elbow it back."

Social Independence of Cubs

"Siblings may remain together for up to four years even without their mother," notes David Brown in *The Grizzly of the Southwest*.

Considerable knowledge is necessary for cubs to survive; thus they remain with their mothers for lengthy periods that vary with species. They may remain with their mother longer in undernourished populations that require more time to learn critically important feeding strategies. Upon separating from the sow, siblings most often remain together for more than a year.

AMERICAN BLACK BEAR	16 to 18 months
BROWN BEAR	17 to 29 months; usually den with sow for two additional winters; males move out of mother's range; females may remain in mother's range
POLAR BEAR	16 to 17 months; often into third year
ASIATIC BLACK BEAR	24 to 36 months; sow observed with two sets of different-age cubs
GIANT PANDA	18 to 24 months

TRANSPORTATION

American black bear *Cubs rarely ride on the sow's back*

Brown bear *A few observations in Alaska of cubs riding on the sow's back*

Polar bear *Rides on sow's back on land or in the water; may hang onto sow's tail or rump hairs while walking or swimming*

Asiatic black bear *Information unavailable*

Giant panda *Carried in sow's mouth when young*
Larger young held to chest while sow travels

Sloth bear *Cub's ride on sow's back while walking, running and tree climbing*
Cubs maintain individual riding positions that do not change; fights occur to maintain the proper positions
Sow may carry cubs until they are a third her size

Sun bear *Information unavailable*

Spectacled bear *Cub's ride on sow's back if frightened and attempting to escape*
Sow may carry a cub, held against her body with a paw, as she runs on three legs

SLOTH BEAR	24 to 36 months
SUN BEAR	Until nearly fully grown
SPECTACLED BEAR	6 to 8 months

Orphaned cubs, depending on age and climate, are capable of surviving on their own. American black and grizzly bear cubs less than a year old have survived their first winter alone.

Cannibalism in Motherhood

A sow may kill and eat her cubs if she is extremely malnourished. However, a mortally wounded cub may be consumed whether the sow is malnourished or not. The author observed an American black bear sow eat one of her cubs that had just five mintues before been struck and killed by a vehicle. The remaining sibling joined its mother.

Hibernation

Hibernation is a state of dormancy and inactivity that is utilized by bears and various other animals to adapt to short winter food supplies. "Hibernation is not so much a response to extreme cold as to a seasonal shortage of food," notes Paul Schullery in *The Bears Of Yellowstone*. "The bear's warm coat is as necessary to it in the den as it would be outside."

Hibernation of bears is different from other "hibernators" such as bats, marmots, squirrels, woodchucks, and rodents that are in a deep sleep or state of torpidity, with a low metabolic rate and temperatures many degrees below normal. Several weeks are required to reach this state of dormancy.

During a bear's hibernation, its body temperature does not drop to within a few degrees of the surrounding air, its metabolic rate is comparatively high, and it may awaken during a warm period and move about outside the den, though it remains nearby.

Specific lengths of hibernation depend on climate, location, and the sex, age group, and reproductive status of the individual bear. Some bear species do not hibernate, and populations of hibernating species in areas of available foods and warm winter weather may also remain active. Bears in poor condition, with an inadequate fat reserve, may not hibernate or for only a short period.

Hibernating bears:

- ▲ Do not eat
- ▲ Do not urinate
- ▲ Do not defecate
- ▲ Curl up to conserve heat
- ▲ Change position in den
- ▲ Are sensitive to their surroundings
- ▲ Awaken and move about
- ▲ Temporarily leave den

- ▲ May be aroused and attack an intruder
- ▲ Give birth to young
- ▲ Lactate (nurse their young)
- ▲ Provide warmth for cubs
- ▲ Lick and groom cubs
- ▲ Lick self
- ▲ Slough paw pads
- ▲ Lose weight

"A bear is wiser than man," an old Abnaki Indian sage once philosophized, "because a man does not know how to live all winter without eating anything," related George Bird Grinnell in *When The Buffalo Ran* (as cited in Harold Mc-Cracken, *The Beast That Walks Like Man*).

HIBERNATION CHARACTERISTICS

AMERICAN BLACK BEAR	Hibernates; some southern populations do not during mild winters; bears of Louisiana, Florida, and Arizona sleep only a few days at a time in a den (nest in hollow tree, cave, shelter under rocks or a fallen tree, or in just a shallow excavation in a wooded area); pregnant females hibernate in southern populations; the most active bear during the winter.
BROWN BEAR	Hibernates; may den early (September) in far northern regions.
POLAR BEAR	Males and non-pregnant females do not hibernate; pregnant females hibernate.
ASIATIC BLACK BEAR	Does not hibernate over most of range; may hibernate in colder (northern) regions of habitat; some bears descend to lower elevations; nearly all pregnant females hibernate.
GIANT PANDA	Does not hibernate; experiences harsh winters; descends to lower elevations.
SLOTH BEAR	Does not hibernate.
SUN BEAR	Does not hibernate.
SPECTACLED BEAR	Does not hibernate.

Hibernation Periods

The periods of hibernation typically begin earlier and last longer in the north than in the south, and coastal bears begin hibernation later than inland bears. In North America black bears hibernate earlier than brown bears. Generally, the higher the latitude, the longer the hibernation. (The polar bear is the exception.) Pregnant females enter their dens early and, with cubs, emerge later.

Preparing to Hibernate

Preparation to hibernate—to den up—begins during late summer and early fall when bears enter hyperphagia (eating enormous quantities of food) to build up fat.

To accumulate fat, bears:

- *Eat high caloric foods*
- *Eat nuts*
- *Drink great quantities of water*

- *May eat 20,000 calories per day*
- *Eat natural sugars (fruits, berries)*

DENNING PERIODS

SPECIES	JULY	AUG	SEPT	OCT	NOV	DEC	JAN	FEB	MAR	APRIL	MAY	JUNE
American Black Bears												
Brown Bears												
Polar Bears												
Asiatic Black Bears												
Giant Pandas			DO NOT HIBERNATE									
Sloth Bears			DO NOT HIBERNATE									
Sun Bears			DO NOT HIBERNATE									
Spectacled Bears			DO NOT HIBERNATE									

PREPARATION OF DEN

HIBERNATION

Fat serves as:

- *Insulation*
- *As a food and water reserve*

Prior to hibernation:

- *American black bears add four inches of fat, gaining two to three pounds a day*

- *Brown bears add six to eight inches of fat*

- *Polar bears do not put on heavy fat for hibernation*

- *Some female bears more than double their weight*

- *Giant pandas do not hibernate due to their minimal ability to accumulate fat, resulting from the poor nutritional value of bamboo*

....

The Trigger

Bears stop eating shortly before denning. The conditions that trigger their entering the den—the beginning of hibernation—are a combination of the first inclement winter-type weather, a reduction in the supply of high-quality food, decreased mobility due to snow, and increased energy costs of keeping warm. Grizzly bear researchers John and Frank Craighead noted that a "trigger" was a snow storm (following an earlier cold snap) with drifting snow that would not thaw and would cover the bear's tracks to the den.

Bear Dens

Bear dens vary in location, aspect, elevation, size, and general construction. Dens are excavated or natural openings and holes or, in some cases, simply a ground nest. They typically have an entrance, tunnel, and chamber, and a venthole in the case of polar bears. Chamber size depends on the individual bear but invariably has good drainage. A bear may move up to a ton of material when digging a den.

Dens are prepared in a secretive manner. Hidden and secure, they provide a quick escape for a bear in danger. Some are even located high up in trees, often protected by surrounding water. Dens are relocated if the bear is disturbed.

Bedding in a den consists of grasses, moss, leaves, conifer needles, and tree branches, seven to nine inches deep. A den is partially closed with vegetation, which also serves as a camouflage. Some bears use the same den for several years; others prepare a new den each year. Still, some dens are used for decades by different bears. A pregnant sow will use a larger den.

American Black Bear Dens

Location

- Under large boulders
- Scraped-out depression under brush
- At base or in cavity of tree roots
- Caves
- Under logs
- Tree cavity, well above ground
- Under buildings
- Culverts
- Southern slope exposure
- Steep slopes; twenty percent to forty percent
- Small opening to prevent intrusion
- Half of Louisiana bears use brushpiles (fallen tree tops), ground nests, and trees
- A tree den in Louisiana was ninety-six feet above ground

Description

- Six feet deep
- 1½ feet in diameter
- Good drainage

Brown Bear Dens

Location

- Southern slope (North America and Asia)
- Eastern slope (Alaska Peninsula)
- Northern slope (Kodiak, Alaska)
- Dug in dry earth
- Dug under large boulders
- Located above valley floor
- Thirty percent slope
- Slope aspect (exposure) varies in different areas
- Under fallen trees in wet areas (Alaska)

Description

- Fifty-nine inches long
- Thirty-nine inches wide
- Twenty-five inches high

Grizzly Bear Dens

Location

- Sixty-one percent on north slope in Rocky Mountains

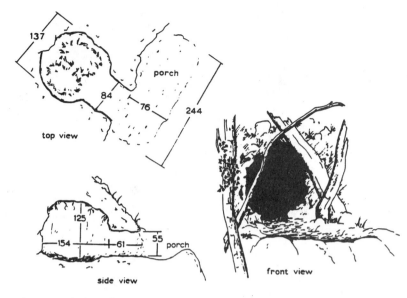

 Grizzly bear den
Courtesy IGBST

Description

- ❖ *Tunnel leads to chamber*

- ❖ *1½-foot tall × nine-foot diameter chamber*

- ❖ *Nine to twenty-seven feet into ground*

....

Polar Bear Dens Normally only the female polar bear digs a den, which is then used by all bears, especially pregnant females who remain in the den for months. A polar bear den is used as temporary winter shelter and for cooling during the summer.

Location

- ❖ *Most within five miles of coast*

- ❖ *Bear determines correct snow*

- ❖ *Dug in ice, snow, frozen ground*

- ❖ *Use deep drifted snow*

- ❖ *Snow is an excellent insulator*

- ❖ *May be sheltered snowdrift in lee of a ridge*

- ❖ *Dug through snow into earth in some areas*

- ❖ *South-facing coast*

....

Description

- ❖ *Twenty to forty percent slope*

- ❖ *Ten to fifteen-foot long tunnel, two-foot diameter*

- ❖ *Typical den chamber fifty-five to seventy-one inches in diameter, thirty-six inches high*

Polar bear den
Renee Evanoff

- Tunnel slopes upward (cold-air trap like igloo)

- Just enough room to turn around in

- Bed eight to twelve inches thick (nine to twenty inches at edge)

- Air vent (venthole) to allow fresh air

- May enlarge den after cubs are born

- Den temperature may reach forty degrees Fahrenheit, while below zero outside; den seldom below thirty-two degrees

Asiatic Black Bear Dens

Location

- Dug out in hollow tree, sixty feet above ground

- Cave or hole in ground

- Hollow log

- Steep, mountainous, sunny slope

Description

- Cave (hole) 1½-foot diameter, six feet deep

- Thick bed of branches, leaves, grass, and other vegetation

"Noticing a steamy vapor rising from a hole in the snow by protruding roots of an overturned tree," describes Enos Mills in *Wild Life On The Rockies*, "I walked to the hole to

learn the cause of it. One whiff of the vapor stiffene
and limbered my legs. I shot down a steep slope,
trees and rocks. The vapor was rank with the odo
bear." Eskimos have long hunted polar bears using t
and steam to locate dens.

A Bear's Physiology During Hibernation

Recent research has better identified the remarkable physiology that occurs in bears during hibernation. Recycling
appears to be the key to the months of inactivity without
disastrous physiological effects.

Bones of mammals, including humans, become thin and
brittle during inactivity, but bears have a capacity to build
new bone by recycling the calcium leaking into their blood.
A bear's blood calcium remains fairly constant during hibernation.

A bear also has a unique system of recycling the urea it
produces. They do not urinate during hibernation, and a
build-up of urea could be deadly, but the urine is reabsorbed
through the bladder wall back into the bear's system, where
it is processed into amino acids and protein. If the urea is
recycled faster than the bear makes it, there is a net gain of
protein during hibernation.

Researchers hope to isolate the bear' key to recycling and
apply the process to human medicine.

PHYSIOLOGICAL CHANGES IN HIBERNATING BEARS

- Do not eat, drink, defecate, or urinate during hibernation (approximately four and one-half to five months)
- Metabolism slows
- Digestive organs and kidneys shut down almost completely
- Exist on foods and fluids stored in body
- Do not dehydrate

- Lose fifteen percent to thirty percent of their body weight as fat breaks down, providing food and water
- One gram of fat produces more than a gram of water
- Use four thousand calories/day from their fat reserve during hibernation
- Blood contains "high"

levels of circulating fat including cholesterol
- Blood more concentrated to head and upper body
- Poisonous wastes, byproducts broken down and reabsorbed
- Paw pads are sloughed
- Females begin lactation

Respiration

- Requires only one half of the normal oxygen intake; breathing drops to half that of an active bear

Heart Rate

- Drops to eight to ten beats per minute (normal: ninety-eight beats per minute)
- Returns to normal over a few weeks if disturbed

Temperature

- Drops in relation to the outside and den temperatures, but has a safety mechanism preventing it from dropping below eighty-nine degrees Fahrenheit (normal: 98.5 to ninety-nine degrees)
- Ten degrees below normal is approximate minimum body temperature bears can withstand
- Polar bear's temperature drops one degree below normal
- Grizzly bear's temperature ranges, during a twenty-four hour period, from a nighttime ninety-four degrees to a daytime 96

"It appears that eighty-nine degrees Fahrenheit is about the lowest temperature the bear can safely tolerate," wrote Frank Craighead in *Track of the Grizzly*. "Below that a spontaneous arousal takes place, and metabolic processes automatically increase, this warming the bear."

A tough, fibrous plug often found in and about a den has long been identified as an anal plug, with an uncertain purpose. Two opposing theories attempt to explain the development of this blockage in a bear's lower digestive tract:

- Formed by food remnants and dead cells that occur during hibernation, and block the anus
- Formed by indigestible materials (animal hair, own hair, nut hulls, wood, dirt, moss, grass, and other plant materials) eaten during the final few days before hibernating, for the specific purpose of blocking the anus

Emergence from the Den

Early civilizations of the world, especially native Americans, considered a bear's emergence from the den a return from the dead, and a rebirth. The emergence process is typically slow with sniffing, limping, stretching, limbering stiff muscles, grooming, yawning, and scratching. The bear appears groggy but is healthy.

- ▲ Males and poorly conditioned bears emerge first; sows with cubs last
- ▲ Sow emerges ready to protect her young, remaining close to den, probably acclimating cubs to the outside
- ▲ Cubs may begin climbing the first day
- ▲ Drowsy and lethargic for several days
- ▲ Display some weakness

- ▲ Some bears extremely emaciated
- ▲ Some bears one half their pre-hibernation weight
- ▲ Some bears weigh near their pre-den weight
- ▲ Most often in good shape
- ▲ Some bears continue to lose weight for approximately two months
- ▲ Seek large quantities of water (eat snow if water unavailable)
- ▲ Not immediately interested in food
- ▲ Feed lightly
- ▲ Seek high-protein foods
- ▲ Seek roots and herbs to clear kidneys and digestive system
- ▲ Seek chaff (non-digestible) to clear system
- ▲ Seek old berries and rose hips left from the fall
- ▲ Seek new grasses, small roses, winter-kill carcasses

🐻 DAY BEDS

Located near food sources and often with a commanding view, day beds are utilized by all bears for short- or long-period resting. A bear may have several day beds throughout its range. Non-hibernating bears may use day beds as birthing beds.

"There is a dense grove of Englemann spruce and lodgepole pine nearby, in a particularly dense part of which the mother bear scoops out a cozy bowl just big enough for her and the cubs," describes Thomas McNamee in *The Grizzly Bear*. "She rips down green spruce boughs and lines the depression to form a springy, heat trapping mattress. Curled up here, concealed to perfection within defensive-charging distance of their meat cache, the bear and her young may sleep their breakfast off in watchful security."

American Black Bear	Sleeps in trees, stretched out on limbs; on ground, on grassy areas, and on conifer needles
Brown Bear	On ground, on grassy areas, and on conifer needles; in shallow depressions dug in soil or snow (lined or unlined)
Polar Bear	Dig "dens" in snow, ice, or dirt for summer cooling; digs pits at the shoreline and anywhere in the snow; sow and cubs have day beds as high as possible to detect danger; line resting sites with moss and lichens
Asiatic Black Bear	Trees, fifteen feet or higher, in sitting position; nest of branches; nest on ground; spends much of winter in day bed
Giant Panda	Bottom of trees, under stumps, crevices of ledges, under overhanging rocks, hollow trees, rock caves; bed of bamboo sticks and other vegetation; six- to nine-percent slope on eastern or southern exposure; entrance eighteen inches wide, forty-five inches high; maternity bed thirty-five to thirty-nine inches in diameter (high enough for female to sit upright) in hollow tree; rock cleft thirty-three by thirty-nine inches, seventy-eight inches high; lined with wood dust, twigs

(continued)

Sloth Bear	Anywhere; nests of broken branches in a tree or at junction of trunk and first major branch; cave during rainy season
Sun Bear	Platform (nest) of broken branches, six and one-half feet to twenty-three feet high in a tree; rests lying on belly
Spectacled bear	Platform of broken branches in a tree or at junction of tree trunk and first major limb; nest of small branches, leaves, sticks, twigs, and other plant material; rests sitting with forelegs in front of its chest

The Asiatic black bears in Japan, "have a queer habit not found among bears elsewhere," writes Phyllis Osteen in *Bears Around the World*. "They build what observers call 'basking couches.' These are oval cushions made from twigs and branches, laid on sunny slopes in front of winter lairs."

"We find a bear's nest in a hackberry—our first sign of the Asiatic black bear," writes Peter Matthiessen in *The Snow Leopard*. "The bear sits in the branches and bends them toward him as he feeds on cherry-like fruits; the broken branches make a platform which the bear may then use as a bed."

Bear Habitats

Bears have adapted to various environments, including tropical forests, swamps, tundra and tiaga, ice floes, deserts, the arctic, high mountains, and from sea level to nearly fourteen thousand feet (eighteen thousand to twenty thousand feet on some occasions).

The species, and individuals within species, have their niches of varying qualities that provide food, cover, protection, mating opportunities, and denning sites. Bears' sizes

Grizzly bears in their natural habitat of the Rocky Mountains
Courtesy Yellowstone National Park

may be influenced by habitat quality. Poor habitats normally produce relatively smaller bears, while an environment with an abundance of food with high nutritional value, such as major fish populations, produces large bears. "In the coastal areas of Alaska and British Columbia," notes Terry Domico in *Bears of the World*, "live the largest brown bears found on the North American continent."

Elevations

Individuals remain at the same general elevation, but may range between elevations during day-to-day or week-to-week searches for food. They may also range between elevations seasonally, and normally move to a different elevation to den.

AMERICAN BLACK BEARS	Sea level to 10,000 feet.
BROWN BEARS	Sea level to 10,000 feet; known to 13,000 feet; "Red Bear" of Asia is often in the yak pastures at 18,000 feet and in Bhundar at 20,000.

PRIMARY HABITATS	SPECIES							
	AMERICAN BLACK	BROWN	POLAR	ASIATIC BLACK	GIANT PANDA	SLOTH	SUN	SPECTACLED
Arctic/Alpine Tundra		■						
Arctic Coastal Regions			■					
Arctic Island			■					
Arctic Seas			■					
Bamboo Thickets					■			
Brush Savannahs								■
Coniferous Forests	■							
Damp Forests								■
Deciduous Forests	■			■				
Deciduous Monsoon Forests						■		
Desert (OPEN COUNTRY)					■			
Grasslands								■
Mixed Forests	■	■		■				
Plantations							■	
Swamps	■							
Thornbrush Forests				■				
Thornbrush Woodlands						■		■
Treeless/Scarcely Forested		■						
Tropical Rain Forests								■

Polar bear along the Manitoba coast
© Johnny Johnson

POLAR BEARS	Sea level.
ASIATIC BLACK BEARS	Rarely above 12,000 feet; to 11,480 feet during summer in Himalayas; known occasionally to 13,000 feet in Himalayas; down to 4,920 feet during winter; occasionally near sea level in Japan.
GIANT PANDAS	General range: 3,600 to 11,150 feet; known to 13,250 feet; 8,525 to 13,120 feet during summer; primary summer range: 8,900 to 10,500 feet; ranges down to 2,624 feet during winter; lower elevations limited by cultivation and habitation.
SLOTH BEARS	Sea level to base of the Himalayas.
SUN BEARS	Sea level to 9,184 feet.
SPECTACLED BEARS	600 to 13,940 feet; 1900 to 6400 feet (west, central, eastern Andes Mountains); 1,640 to 13,120 feet (Peru); a wide range of zones.

Bear Density

Bear densities vary seasonally throughout numerous habitats with food sources—such as streams congested with spawning fish and areas of poor food—significant influences. Bear densities are also influenced by human populations and activities. Bears are displaced and crowded into remaining undeveloped—and typically small—areas of inadequate quality for bear survival.

Bear Ranges

Bears have home ranges, but are not territorial. They do not defend a territory from other bears and the habitats of different species and individuals overlap. The ranges of males are normally larger than females; an adult female North American brown bear has a range two to five times as large as an adult female American black bear.

Movement of bears is in response to available food sources, and hierarchy may dictate habitat niches for sub-adults or family groups that avoid dominant male bears. The poorer a bear's habitat in relation to food, the larger its range. Ranges may increase during the fall as food becomes more scarce and bears attempt to build fat for hibernation. Stephen Herrero, in *Bear Attacks*, notes that food is the "primary determination" of where bears are found, except during breeding and denning.

Some representative ranges for each species follow:

AMERICAN BLACK BEAR	42.8 square miles (adult male); 7.6 square miles (adult female); 3.6 to 108 square miles.
BROWN BEARS	Alaskan brown bears have limited ranges due to island habitats, and concentrations of food; 2.6 to 216 square miles.
GRIZZLY BEARS	23 to 870 square miles (adult male); 10 to 642 square miles (adult female); 1,186 square miles (adult male), east side of Rocky Mountains; 642 square miles (adult female); east side of Rocky Mountains.
POLAR BEARS	More than 20,000 square miles.
ASIATIC BLACK BEARS	Small range.
GIANT PANDAS	Extremely small range due to specific food, and human encroachment; 1.6 square miles to 2.6 square miles; females share ranges with other female pandas, but appear to have 75 to 100 acres where other females are not welcome.
SLOTH BEARS	Small range.

SUN BEARS	Reliable information unavailable.
SPECTACLED BEARS	Reliable information unavailable.

"There are two factors controlling the polar bear's range: seals and ice," notes Koch. "If the ice does not break up every summer, the seals will not have the open water they require. Without seals to hunt, the polar bear must move to more productive and life-sustaining feeding grounds."

Foods and Feeding Habits of Bears

B ears have evolved from a carnivorous ancestry to be the only large omnivore. Except for the giant panda, which eats primarily bamboo, they consume virtually anything and everything. However, all species appear to have preferences and seasonal needs, though most of what they eat is controlled by the readily available and nutritious food sources of their habitat. Bears must move in response to these available sources, and originally had nearly unlimited opportunity to broaden their searches for food. Today they are limited in their movements by human activities and development.

Bears seek food from most any source, being wandering and opportunistic feeders. They scavenge; they remember size, shape, color of objects that have produced a food reward; they are generalists, diverse gluttons, and have large bodies that help them survive long periods of food shortage and poor-quality diets. Charles Feazel, in *White Bear*, relates a Pierre Berton quote from *The Arctic Grail*, "When food was available, they ate it all; when there was none, they went without, uncomplaining."

Of all bear activities, the highest percentage of time is devoted to seeking food. Diet varies with the seasons, and a bear seldom feeds very long in a single small area (except for the giant panda). North American brown bears consume considerably more foliage and roots and significantly less fruits and seeds than other groups of bears. Brown bears consume more vertebrates than Asiatic and American black bears. Carrion is special to all bears, while the brown bears, as expert fishermen and powerful swimmers, have a passion for fish. Berries are quite essential and a common food for most bears.

Alaskan grizzly bear consuming salmon in the Brooks River, Katmai National Park.
© Johnny Johnson.

Common Foods*

	SPECIES							
	American Black	Brown	Polar	Asiatic Black	Giant Panda	Sloth	Sun	Spectacled
Frogs	X	X				X		
Fish	X	X						
Ants	X			X		X		X
Insects	X	X		X			X	X
Beetle Larvae				X				
Invertebrates	X							
Crabs		X	X					
Termites				X		X	X	X
Pikas					X			
Buffalo				X				
Small Vertebrates	X						X	X
Domestic Livestock				X				X
Rodents		X			X		X	X
Birds		X	X				X	X
Bamboo Rats					X			
Hoofed Animals		X						
Clams		X						
Ringed Seals			X					
Walrus			X					
Mussels			X					
Crayfish	X							
Lizards							X	X
Grubs	X	X		X	X	X	X	X
Earthworms								X
Carcasses	X	X	X	X		X	X	
Whale Carcasses				X				
Bees	X	X		X		X	X	X
Marmots		X						
Rabbits/Hares				X				X
Llamas								X
Whales (stranded)				X				
Eggs	X	X	X	X	X	X	X	X
Human Garbage	X	X	X	X				
Berries	X	X	X	X		X	X	X
Mushrooms	X	X					X	
Grasses	X	X		X	X			
Fruits	X	X		X		X	X	X
Nuts	X	X		X				X
Seeds	X	X		X				X
Sedges		X						
Honey (including bees)	X	X		X		X	X	X
Pawpaws						X	X	
Herbs	X	X		X				
Seaweed (kelp)		X	X					
Bamboo Stalks, Leaves & Stems					X			
Bulbs		X						
Palm Nuts						X		
Mangos						X		
Lillies						X		X
Cambium (underbark)	X	X						X

(continued)

Common Foods*

	SPECIES							
	American Black	*Brown*	*Polar*	*Asiatic Black*	*Giant Panda*	*Sloth*	*Sun*	*Spectacled*
Acorns	X	X		X				
Hog's Fennel		X						
Horsetail					X			
Cherries				X				
Dogwood				X				
Fir Bark					X			
Oak Nuts				X				
Crocuses					X			
Vines					X			
Iris					X			
Palm Leaves (Unopened)								X
Sugarcane (Cultivated)						X		X
Corn (Cultivated)						X		X
Yams (Cultivated)						X		
Grain (Cultivated)					X			
Cactus								X
Orchid Pseudobulbs								X
Sprouts							X	X
Flowers of Mohwa Tree						X		
Coconut Palm Hearts							X	
Other Array of Plants	X	X		X	X	X	X	X
Figs						X		
Human Foods	X	X	X					
Gut Piles (From Hunting)	X	X						
Melons (Gardens)	X	X						
Moths (Concentrations)		X						
Vegetables (Gardens)	X	X						
Reindeer (Disabled)		X						
Muskox (Disabled)		X	X					

*Common foods are regularly consumed by the respective species, though some food items in minimal quantities. (Patricia Brown)

AMERICAN BLACK BEAR
- Not great hunters
- Use's claws, lips, tongue, and incisor teeth to remove seeds, insects, and other small morsels with dexterity
- Diet consists of 85% vegetable matter
- Uses incisors to bite grass stems

"The black bear provides a striking contrast to the panda," according to George Schaller *et al.* in *The Giant Pandas of Wolong.* "It forages on a wide variety of berries, acorns, roots, and herbs . . . foods rich in soluble carbohydrates and fats, and seasonally so abundant that the bear with little effort can consume enough extra calories daily to deposit large stores of fat."

BROWN BEAR
- North American brown bear have higher percentage of vegetation (85 to 98%) and a lower percentage of fruits than many other bears in their diet; eat more than 200 types of plants

Fishing—an Alaskan brown bear uses a waterfall in Katmai National Park
© Johnny Johnson

- Syrian brown bear almost totally vegetarian
- Kamchatka brown bear feeds principally on fish
- Feeds less than nine hours a day in some areas
- Bites grass stems with molars
- Uses claws as a specialized feeding "tool"
- Some Eurasian brown bears scoot on their haunches and butt when feeding, consuming the foods between their legs
- Uses teeth and claws to catch fish; seldom slap fish out of water
- Can catch 60 to 100 fish a day
- Can eat 35 pounds of fish in a day
- Can consume 80 to 90 pounds of fish a day during the peak of a spawning season
- Eats all of a fish except the head and gills
- Consumes more animals, prey, and carcasses than American and Asiatic black bears

Success
© Johnny Johnson

"The two combatants were fighting at close quarters, the elk fighting for his life, the bear endeavoring to kill, probably for food," described park employee Lester Abbie, in Paul Schullery's *Yellowstone Bear Tales*. "The bear [grizzly] had the elk gripped around the neck with his forepaws and was endeavoring to throw the elk, after the fashion of a rodeo performer bulldogging a steer. The elk in turn was endeavoring to get free and by so doing was shoving the bear around backward along the road."

POLAR BEAR

- Most carnivorous of the bears
- Only bear that spends more time in the water and eats more meat than the brown bear
- Stalks areas with open water and active movement of ice, and where they are most apt to find seals
- Stands to observe and locate a dark object on the ice
- Often synchronizes feeding on seals with the seal's patterns of sleeping alongside its breathing hole
- Stomach capacity is 150 pounds
- Eats skin and blubber first, then meat; eats 100 to 150 pounds of blubber per meal
- Eats mostly skin and blubber of the seal; one seal is energy for eleven days
- Typically kills and eats a seal once every four to five days.
- Digs for puffins and begs for blubber from whaling ships
- Eats berries during the summer; (butt and muzzle stained bluish)

Polar bear uses a number of feeding strategies and tools, according to Feazel. They "push ice or snow blocks ahead of them as they slither close to the breathing holes . . . build walls of snow to hide behind and they use blocks of ice to smash through the icy crust that covers a [seal's] breathing hole."

ASIATIC BLACK BEAR

- Eats a large variety of foods
- Uses domestic livestock when forced by poor natural foods

GIANT PANDA

- Has very low level of digestibility
- Must eat often and for long periods of time to gain the necessary nutrition
- Actively feeds over fourteen hours per day (65% of the day during the spring; 52% in the summer; and 62% in the winter)
- May consume 45 to 85 pounds of bamboo per day
- Sits and brings food to its mouth with paws

"It has a good sense of taste and smell which seems unnecessary for an animal that eats only bamboo," notes Clive Roots in *The Bamboo Bears*.

SLOTH BEAR

- Expert termite hunter; discovers termites by smell (termites are the year-round staple)
- Capable of locating a grub three feet deep in the ground
- Specialized snout for vacuuming termites and ants; lacks two incisor teeth; has long snout and lips that form a tube; closes nostrils by pressing down nose pad

- Noisy, with sucking sound heard more than 200 yards away
- Does not meet in feeding groups like other bears, due to even food dispersal
- Fruits are important April through June
- Rarely preys on other mammals or feeds on carrion

"To get them [termites] the bear smashes a rotten log or tears open a termite mound with its long claws," describe Paul Shepard and Barry Sanders in *The Sacred Paw*. "At the same time it alternately blows away the dirt and wood chips and sucks up termites. . . ."

SUN BEAR
- Uses exceptionally long tongue for specialized feeding
- Eats small vertebrates, invertebrates, fruits, and other vegetation

SPECTACLED BEARS
- More vegetarian than most species of bears (diet is 95% vegetable matter)
- Bromeliads make up 46.8% of diet
- Eats some plant foods that are too tough for other animals (cactus and woody plants)
- Remains in trees for several days during the trees' short fruit-ripening period (longer than other bears)

The feeding antics of a bear may be quite amusing. "A six hundred pound grizzly bear may be seen leaping about in a meadow pouncing on grasshoppers, mice, ground squirrels, or licking up a line of ants," described George Laycock in *The Wild Bears*. Some feeding situations are ludicrous but quite serious for the hungry bear. "A polar bear jumped on the back of a surfacing whale, went down with it, and came up again still trying to bite a mouthful of blubber off the forty-ton behemoth," described Frank Dufresne in *No Room For Bears*.

Other bear feeding behaviors manifest themselves in different ways. An American black bear was observed sitting in a bald eagle nest, high in a tree, in British Columbia. The actions of a pair of adult eagles nearby indicated they had lost eggs or young eaglets to the bear.

Scientists recently discovered grizzly bears in the Rocky Mountains of North America utilizing army cutworm moths. The moths are available in such numbers that bears congregate on extremely steep rocky slopes up to twelve thousand feet to eat this high-energy food.

"It was digging out mice, and now and then a ground squirrel," wrote Charles Sheldon in *The Wilderness of Denali*, describing a feeding grizzly bear. "The mice had made tunnels under the snow leading from their holes. The bear, evidently scenting a mouse in a tunnel, would plunge its nose into the snow, its snout ploughing through, often as far as ten feet, until the mouse had gone down into its hole in the ground; then the bear would dig it out and catch it with a paw."

"If there were not considerable uncertainty in ground-squirrel hunting," related Adolph Murie in *A Naturalist in Alaska*, "the bears would no doubt devote more time to it. But there is a limit to the amount of gambling they can indulge in, and even if successful they must return to foods which are available in quantity to fill their rapidly emptying paunches. The ground squirrel has been referred to as the staff of life of the grizzly, but it is only a side dish."

The graph, developed with extensive research, depicts the seasonal availability of grizzly bear foods in the Rocky Mountains. Similar seasonal food variations occur for other species worldwide.

Seasonal Availability of Foods

The different species of bears have characteristic food habits that depend in part on the environment and in part on adaptive food preferences," note Shepard and Sanders. "All bears are omnivorous, but the proportion of meat to plants in their diets varies, not only among different species but seasonally and with availability."

Food Sources

▲ Aquatic habitats

▲ Caches of other animals

▲ Dens of other animals

▲ Human sources (food, garbage; easily digested)

▲ Ranging prey animals

▲ Natural food in the ground (vegetation, animals, insects)

▲ Natural food above ground (vegetation, animals, insects)

▲ Nests

▲ Trees (fruits, birds, eggs)

Bark Stripping

The sap and cambium layer of various trees (mostly coniferous), is highly sought by bears in many areas. They grab the bark of a tree with their teeth and tear a strip, or even a sheet, down to the ground. Some bears bite large chunks from the trees. They then lick, pushing their nose and tongue up and down the exposed sapwood, enjoying the sweet sap. The major nutrient of the sap is sugar, with minor elements of minerals and nitrogen.

BEAR FEEDING BEHAVIOR BENEFITS

Prevent spread of diseases
—Eat dead animals (wild and domestic)
—Eat sick animals (wild and domestic)
• Reduce rodents and insects
• Spread seed with fecal material
• Prepare seed beds for germination by digging
• Provide other animals with foods
—Own carcass
—Scraps and remains of foods

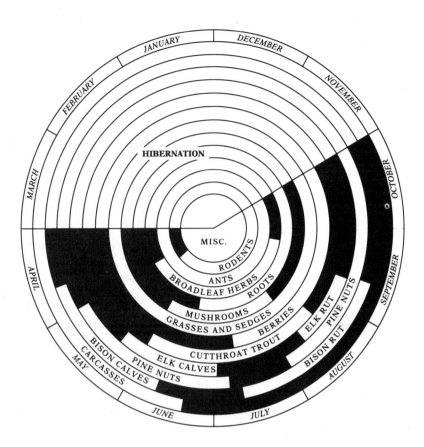

Seasonal availability of bear foods in the Yellowstone area
Courtesy Yellowstone National Park

"... the bear was lapping at the trunk as if it were a candy stick," described Roger Conter in Paul Schullery's *Yellowstone Bear Tales*.

Stripping bark for the sap is observed in the brown, American black and Asiatic black bears. This activity may girdle and kill trees, resulting in a serious economic problem (thousands of dollars lost annually) in the valuable timber forests of the Pacific Northwest and East Coast of North America, and in Asia.

In the state of Washington, the species of trees preferred by bears (in order of preference) are: Douglas fir, Western hemlock, Western red cedar, Silver fir, Sitka spruce, Lodgepole pine, and Alpine fir.

Management programs have been developed in an attempt to reduce the stripping damage. Supplemental feeding during the spring, and hunting by sportsmen and hired hunters to reduce the bear populations are major management actions.

Cannibalism

The bear possesses "a gruesome and cannibal fondness for the flesh of his own kind," noted Theodore Roosevelt in *The*

Works of Theodore Roosevelt. "A bear carcass will toll a brother bear to the ambushed hunter better than most any other bait."

Adult polar bears, not uncommonly, will resort to cannibalism to survive a summer, but an American black bear killed and consumed a smaller black bear in Yellowstone National Park during what was not necessarily a poor food year.

"During a period when heavy ice conditions made seals difficult for bears to obtain," relates Lentfer in *Wild Mammals of North America*, "an adult male [polar bear] had followed a female and two cubs approximately 3 km [1.9 miles] and then killed and nearly completely consumed both cubs."

"Black bears occasionally kill and sometime eat members of their own species," relates Cardoza. "Jonkel and Cowan ... observed that some small bears ... were killed [and eaten] by larger bears."

Accounts of bear cannibalism are common. The meat from old carcasses of bears, and those freshly killed, is consumed as bears, being omnivorous and opportunistic feeders, take advantage of the available foods. Some scientists believe cannibalism is a measure of population control among bears.

Salt Licks

Bears throughout the world use natural salt licks to supplement their mineral requirements. Bears have also been observed at domestic cattle salt blocks.

Water

Bears drink water in a sucking and vacuuming manner, rather than lapping like a cat or dog. Wading into the water is preferred if possible, so their head is near water level. There is considerable slurping and gulping, and they must stop to breath.

Bears drink several times a day, depending on the species and the individual bear's activities. However, the giant panda hardly drinks more than once a day, due to the high water content of its food. The sloth bear requires a considerable amount of water and drinks at least twice daily. In captivity, bears drink between five and fifteen gallons of water a day.

Spectacled bears obtain considerable moisture from those plants that act as natural basins to collect rain. These plants comprise most of the spectacled bear's food.

Periods of Activity

Bears are more naturally diurnal than nocturnal, their primary activity period occurring during daylight hours (though the amount of diurnal activity varies between species and individuals). They are adaptable and their activities may become more nocturnal, with some geographic and seasonal variations, when human presence and impacts (recreation, development, and hunting) increase. "Another aspect of human contact, writes Paul Schullery in *American Bears*, is that "bears became nocturnal where they were hunted. This is entirely possible (though some bears are nocturnal under natural circumstances anyway), bears being remarkably adjustable animals."

The period when bears are active may be related to food requirements. The giant panda, with a poor nutritional diet, must spend more time (day and night) seeking bamboo and eating, and therefore is active fifty-nine percent of the day.

Activity periods for some bears are affected by temperature, weather, and lunar phases. For example, a grizzly bear is active when the temperature is between seventy-two and twelve degrees Fahrenheit, being most active when the temperature is between forty-two and fifty-two. They are active in the fog and a moderate rain, least active during the period of a full moon and most active during a new moon, though seldom active on the night of the new moon.

ACTIVE PERIODS	
American Black Bear	• Diurnal • Nocturnal near human activity
Brown Bear	• Diurnal
Grizzly Bear	• Diurnal • Nocturnal near human activity
Polar Bear	• Nocturnal and diurnal
Asiatic Black Bear	• Diurnal • Nocturnal near human activity
Giant Panda	• Diurnal • Some nocturnal activity
Sloth Bear	• More nocturnal than other bears • Sows with cubs are more diurnal
Sun Bear	• Nocturnal
Spectacled Bear	• Diurnal in heavy forest habitat • Nocturnal in open country habitat

Other "Bear" Animals

Several animals throughout the world are referred to as bears due to their actions and appearance, but are in fact not bears.

Koala Bear *(Phascolarctos cinereus)* An Australian marsupial (has a pouch for its young) that originally was called a bear by the early English settlers of Australia due to its rotund, roundish, bearlike appearance. The koala has also been described as a fat bear cub and is sometimes called the Australian bear.

Wassenbear A European raccoon that is called a bear because it looks and acts like a little bear; the bear that washes its food (German *wasser*: water).

Wolverine *(Gulo luscus)*   The wolverine was called the long-tailed mud bear by Philetus Norris, the second superintendent of Yellowstone National Park, for reasons lost with time.

The wolverine is also known as the "Skunk-Bear," and has been referred to as the "bearlike weasel."

Wolverines and bears are both often labeled "gluttons" due to their eating habits.

Kinkajou, or honey bear *(Potos flavus)*   An arboreal animal of tropical America that has brownish fur and a long tail. The French word *quincajou*, from the Algonquian language, is like the Ojibwa word *quingwaage*, which means wolverine. Most likely the kinkajou, with its questionable bearlike appearance, sought bee trees and consumed the honey. Several of today's bears are referred to as honey bears.

Red Panda *(Ailurus pulgens)*   Also known as the lesser panda, this was the original "panda." The red panda is not a bear, but is closely related to the raccoon. During the 1800s, it was known as the cat-bear.

Beruang Rambai   In Jeffrey McNeely and Paul Wachtel's *Soul of the Tiger*, a biologist describes an unidentified, large primatelike animal of central Borneo. "This 'hairy bear' was neither bear nor orangutan but probably a relict species of something."

Ye Ren   Chinese researchers, according to McNeely and Wachtel, have evidence of *"ye ren,* a Bigfoot-type animal living in the mountainous jungle area of Sichuan, China, the home of the rare and reclusive giant panda."

Australian Binturong *(Arctictis binturong)*   A carnivore with poor eyesight, found in Southeast Asia rain forests, the binturong has a face of a cat, long tail of a monkey and the body of a bear.

Northern (Alaska) Fur Seal *(Callorhinums alascanus)*   Arctic explorers and hunters in the 1800s called this fur seal the sea bear.

Porcupine *(Erethizon dorsatum)*   The basic porcupine has occasionally been referred to as the prickly bear.

"The legs of this bear [grizzly] are somewhat longer than those of the black, as are its talons and tusks incompa[ ] larger and longer," recorded Merriweather Lewis in his journal. ". . . its colour is yellowish brown, the eyes smal[ ] black, and piercing; the front of the fore legs near the feet is usually black; the fur is finer thicker and deeper tha[ ] that of the black bear. These are all the particulars in which this animal appeared to me to differ from the black bear; it is a much more furious and formidable animal, and will frequently pursue the hunter when wounded."

The American black and grizzly bears are often compared, as they are the two bear species most familiar to the majority of North Americans.

FEATURE	AMERICAN BLACK BEAR	GRIZZLY BEAR
Size	Grizzly bears are relatively larger. Adult female grizzly bears weigh 1.7 to 2.3 times as much as adult female black bears.	
Skull	More pronounced forehead	Concave face profile
	Convex (Roman) face profile	
Teeth (Shape and size of the rear upper molar)	Bicuspid molar	Tricuspid molar
	Grizzly bear teeth are adapted to heavier chewing due to diet	
Paws	More hair between the toes and footpad	More skin webbing at the base of the toepad
Claws (Shape)	Short and hooked; front and hind claws similar in length; claw marks seldom visible in tracks.	Long and moderately curved; front claws much longer than hind claws.
Fur	Black bear hair overall shorter than fur of grizzly bear, and of uniform length.	
Color	Black bears rarely show the "grizzled" appearance and have a light-colored muzzle.	
Ranges	Adult female grizzly bears have ranges two to five times the size of those of adult female black bears	
Habitat	Typically forest animals, though move into open habitats	Open habitats close to forests; often found in forested areas where they use the forest meadows and other openings.
Food habits	Black bears bite grass and stems with incisor teeth; eat more green vegetation and berries.	Food comes in windfalls (large carcasses, spawning fish), so they may congregate; bite grass and stems with molars; eat more roots, corms, bulbs, and tubers.
Reproduction	Breed early in life and die young	
	Black bears reproduce more frequently than grizzly bears. There are no known incidents of black and grizzly bear interbreeding.	
Hibernation	Hibernate earlier; dens at lower elevations, in less-steep areas, and close to roads; use a natural hole or opening for their dens.	Dig and develop a more elaborate den.
Travel	Black bears wander more and their trails are not as deeply worn.	
Human Impacts	Black bears do not require as high a degree of isolation from human activity as grizzly bears, and accept environmental change better.	
Nuisance	Commonly known as the "nuisance" bear.	Not commonly perceived as a nuisance.
Digging	Grizzly bears dig better than black bears due to hump (shoulder muscles) and longer claws.	
Climbing	Generally climb trees.	Do not generally climb trees.

II

Bears in the Human World

"Bears and Indians have lived together on the continent of North America for thousands of years. Both walked the same trails, fished the same salmon streams, dug . . . the relationship was one of mutual respect. But it went well beyond that. Bears were often central to the most basic rites of many tribes. . . ."

David Rockwell
Giving Voice To Bear, 1991

The Influence of Bears on Humans

Bears in many ways remain in their world, in spite of us, who have placed them in the human world, interfering, impacting, influencing, and applying to them our anthropomorphic interpretations and attitudes.

Anthropomorphism

For as long as humans and bears have lived together the former have applied their images, perceptions, beliefs, and feelings to bears. And just possibly, the bears have thought to themselves—that "thing" (or whatever a bear considers us) acts just like a bear. Therefore, this section is compiled without the slightest worry of appearing anthropomorphic—we *are* just that!

We anthropomorphize many animals, but none as often as bears, and maybe for a good reason—there are considerable anatomical and behavioral similarities. To begin with, bears and humans share mammalian traits, but also we judge bears by our own senses, abilities, and behavior. For instance, bears stand bipedal and even occasionally walk in that manner; sit on their tails, lean back against objects to rest, and may even fold a leg across their other leg; appear human when skinned; scratch their backs against stationary objects; snore; eat the same foods as humans; enjoy sweets; eat with paws (hands); use paws and claws with dexterity; leave human-like footprints; produce similar feces; nurse and discipline their young, even spank; display moods and obvious affection during courting (petting); and are inquisitive, curious and inflexible. We describe them as intelligent, emotional, assertive, sensitive, aware, devious, and cunning, being capable of reason (more than can be said of some humans), and their teenagers (two- to three-year-olds) display the same "look out world, here I come" attitudes—all human-like characteristics. And, as Paul Schullery notes in his writings, bears may be "good" or "bad" depending on how they fit the "human plan."

"It is the bear's broad, searching, persistent openness that makes contact with us," note Paul Shepard and Barry Sanders in *The Sacred Paw*, "that flash of recognition in which men instantly perceive a fellow being whose questing provocation, whose garrulous, taciturn, lazy ways, even whose obligations and commitments to hunt, to hole up, and to dominate the space he lives in are familiar." Walt Disney and author Ernest Thompson Seton attributed human traits to bears.

Our anthropomorphic interpretations are sometimes quite dangerous as we "see" this wild animal as the amusing, bumbling Teddy, Smokey, Yogi, or "Gentle" Ben type of wonderful, lovable, and human-like creature. These are all important aspects of our childhood and adult lives, but too many people fail to recognize the difference between these cultural and fictional characterizations and real bears. This type of thinking breeds a lack of respect and appreciation for wild bears, and often results in subsequent injuries and death of bears and humans.

"Of the major carnivores that walk the wilderness trails of North America, three, the wolf, the mountain lion, and the bear, have cast an especially strong spell on human imagination and influenced substantially the lives of those who live where they are found," comments Ben East in *Bears*. "And of that somewhat mystifying trio, the bears have exercised by far the greatest influence."

Humanization terms include:

• Aggressive	• Lazy	• Cautious	• Mysterious
• Courageous	• Nasty	• Curious	• Shy
• Defiant	• Solitary	• Ferocious	• Strong
• Fun loving	• Unpredictable	• Funny	• Vicious
• Glutton	• "King of American Wilderness"	• Intelligent	

Shepard and Sanders note that the "combination of overall awareness and seeming nonchalance is among the bear's most manlike capacities: a taciturn, calculating mixture of knowing and blasé sophistication that can be unnerving to human observers."

American Indian legend relates that the grizzly bear is the ancestor of the race. "Him arms and him legs, jus like

The Eight Species in French

Ours blanc	polar bear
Ours brun	brown bear
Ours noir	black bear
Ours a lunettes	spectacled bear
Ours des cocotiers	sun bear
Ours lippu	sloth bear
Ours a collier	Asiatic black bear
Grand panda	giant panda

In Other Languages

Canadian	bear, ours (French)
Chinese	xiong
Danish	bjorn
Dutch	beer
Finnish	karhu
French	ours
Germany	bar
Greek	arctos
Hebrew	dob
Italian	orso
Japanese	kuma
Korean	kom
Latin	ursus
Nepalese	bhaalu
Norwegian	bjorn
Polish	niedz'wiedz'
Portuguese	urso
Russian	meabe'ab
Spanish	oso
Swedish	bjorn
United States	bear

Indians." The Cree Indians, according to Harold McCracken in *The Beast That Walks Like Man*, describe the grizzly bear as "him stomach . . . him heart . . . him everything all-same. Him walk like Indian too."

Bear—the Word

The word "bear" and its derivatives play an important and common part in our everyday conversations. A basic and versatile expression in the structure of our language, dictionaries devote numerous pages to the meaning of "bear" as a common noun, but most prominently as a verb. Here is a sample lexicon. . .

ARCTIC *adj*: characteristic of the North Pole, the polar regions; artik derived from *articus* (Medieval Latin); Greek *arktikos*, from *arktos*, meaning bear

ARCTURUS *noun*: 1: the brightest star in the constellation Bootes, Arcturus is approximately thirty-six light-years from earth 2: *Arktouros* (Greek): *Arcturus* is in a position behind the tail of Ursa Major, "guardian of the Bear"; *arktos*, bear plus *ouros*, a guard

BEAR *noun*: 1: the variety of normally omnivorous mammals of the Ursidae family or any of the many animals that resemble bears 2: A person who is crude, clumsy, awkward or ill-mannered 3: A hard-working, tough person of enormous endurance

BEAR *verb* (bore, bare, borne, bearing, bears): 1: to carry, support, hold up 2: to carry on one's person, convey 3: to carry as if in the mind; maintain: <bearing love for others> 4: to transmit at large <bearing clad tidings> 5: to have as a visible characteristic <bearing a scar on his right arm> 6: to carry oneself in a specific way; to conduct 7: to have a tolerance for; endure 8: to have a susceptibility to; admit to <the case will bear investigation> 9: to produce; bring forth; yield; give birth 10: to offer; render <bearing witness> 11: to move by steady pressure; to push 12: to attack with arms; wage war on <to bear arms> 13: to prove right or justified; confirm 14: to be patient or tolerant with

BEAR-BAITING *noun*: the Medieval "sport" of pitting dogs or bulls against a chained bear

BEARISH *adj*: 1: considered to be like a bear 2: the speculation of a stock market price depression

BERA *noun*: Old English bear; from Indo-European root "brown; brown animal"

BLACK BEAR *noun*: the two black bear species, *Ursus americanus* of North America or *Selenarctos thibetanus* of Asia; brown (all shades) or black in color

GRISLY *adj*: terrible; horrifying: gruesome

GRISON *noun*: the two carnivorous mammals (*Grison vittatus* or *Grison cuja*) of Central and South America, that have "grizzled" fur

GRIZZLE *verb*: to cause to be grizzly, grayish

Universal Sign Languages

Renee Evanoff

GRIZZLY *adj*: 1: grayish; streaked, interspersed or flecked with gray 2: a grizzly bear

RKSO *noun*: an Indo-European word root; bear; *ursus* (Latin—bear, ursine); *arktos* (Greek—bear, Arctic, Arcturus); *arto* (Celtic—bear, Arthur)

URSA *noun*: Latin, meaning a she-bear; feminine of *ursus* (a bear); constellations Ursa Major and Ursa Minor

URSINE *adj*: pertaining to a bear; bear family; bearlike; *Ursinus* (Latin—bear, Ursus)

URSULINE *noun*: a member of an order of nuns of the Roman Catholic Church, founded approximately 1537 and faithful to girls' education. Named after Saint Ursula

"Bear" Origins

BEAR	from the nickname bere, 'bear'
BERG	Medieval; the mountain home of the bear people
BRUIN	nickname (bruin the bear) given an animal character (beast) in a series of stories during the tenth century in France or Flanders; German word for brown
GRIZZLY	Old French word *grizel* (somewhat gray or grayish)
GRISLY	Anglo-Saxon, *grislic*, meaning horrible as in monster, demon
HORRIBILUS	how people perceived the grizzly bear

BERNARD, GILBERT, HERBERT, and **ROGER** originate from "bear"

"Bear" Slang

BEAR	a stock market term: speculate for a fall in prices
BEAR PLAY	rough and noisy behavior
BEARISH	borish; stock market bear
IF IT WERE A BEAR	it would bite; it would have bitten you (Also: if it had been a bear)
PLAY THE BEAR	to behave roughly and rudely

"Bear" in the Western United States
Vocabulary Western Slang

BEAR SIGN	doughnuts (cowboy term)
BEAR SIGN	berry jam (logger term)
BEAR TRAP	a style of saddle (cowboy term)
BEAR TRAP	a section of movable dam capable of being raised/lowered to control water flow (river-boating term)

Bear Placenames

Bear names have been used often for natural features and man-made developments, indicating the significance of bears and their impact on the early settlers of the United States. "Bear" most often became the name, or part of the name, when the animal was observed in the specific or general location such as a canyon, stream, ridge, and valley. Buildings, such as cabins, churches and schools, in those areas often adopted "bear" as a portion of their names.

State Bear Features

The United States Board on Geographic Names has officially listed features reflecting the bear in all states except Hawaii.

With each state is listed the number of recognized features (as of 1991).

Alabama 143	Louisiana 55	Ohio 62
Alaska 178	Maine 94	Oklahoma 42
Arizona 214	Maryland 36	Oregon 350
Arkansas 161	Massachusetts 75	Pennsylvania 254
California 664	Michigan 144	Rhode Island 5
Colorado 295	Minnesota 111	South Carolina 45
Connecticut 28	Mississippi 81	South Dakota 56
Delaware 5	Missouri 145	Tennessee 250
Florida 126	Montana 319	Texas 184
Georgia 93	Nebraska 7	Utah 193
Hawaii 0	Nevada 26	Vermont 27
Idaho 269	New Hampshire 49	Virginia 129
Illinois 44	New Jersey 33	Washington 167
Indiana 62	New Mexico 149	West Virginia 147
Iowa 38	New York 132	Wisconsin 115
Kansas 16	North Carolina 292	Wyoming 192
Kentucky 147	North Dakota 27	**Total 6,476**

Bear Nicknames of United States College Athletic Teams

- Alaska, University of; Fairbanks *Nanooks*
- Athens State College; Athens, Alabama *Bears*
- Baylor University; Waco, Texas *Bears*
- Bellevue College; Bellevue, Nebraska *Bruins*
- Bethany College; Scotts Valley, California *Bruins*
- Brescia College; Owensboro, Kentucky *Bearcats*
- Bridgewater State College; Bridgewater, Massachusetts *Bears*
- Brown University; Providence, Rhode Island *Bears*

- California, University of; Berkeley   *Golden Bears*
- California, University of; Los Angeles   *Bruins*
- Central Arkansas, University of; Conway   *Bears*
- Cincinnati, University of; Cincinnati, Ohio   *Bearcats*
- Franklin College; Franklin, Indiana   *Grizzlies*
- George Fox College; Newberg, Oregon   *Bruins*
- Kutztown University; Kutztown, Pennsylvania   *Golden Bears*
- Lenoir-Rhyne College; Hickory, North Carolina   *Bears*
- Livingstone College; Salisbury, North Carolina   *Blue Bears*
- Maine, University of; Orono   *Black Bears*
- McKendree College; Lebanon, Illinois   *Bearcats*
- Mercer University (Macon); Macon, Georgia   *Bears*
- Miles College; Birmingham, Alabama   *Golden Bears*
- Montana, University of; Missoula   *Grizzlies*
- Morgan State University; Baltimore, Maryland   *Golden Bears*
- New York Institute of Technology; Old Westbury   *Bears*
- New York, State University at Potsdam, College of; Potsdam   *Bears*
- Northern Colorado, University of; Greeley   *Bears*
- Northwest Missouri State University; Maryville   *Bearcats*
- Ohio Northern University; Ada   *Polar Bears*
- Pikeville College; Pikeville, Kentucky   *Bears*
- Rocky Mountain College; Billings, Montana   *Bears*
- Rust College; Holly Springs, Mississippi   *Bearcats*
- St. Vincent College; Latrobe, Pennsylvania   *Bearcats*
- Sam Houston State University; Huntsville, Texas   *Bearkats*
- Shaw University; Raleigh, North Carolina   *Bears*
- Shawnee State University; Portsmouth, Ohio   *Bears*
- Southern Christian University; Jacksonville, Florida   *Bears*
- Southwest Baptist University; Bolivar, Missouri   *Bearcats*
- Southwest Missouri State University; Springfield   *Bears*
- United States Coast Guard Academy; New London, Connecticut   *Bears*
- Ursinus College; Collegeville, Pennsylvania   *Bears*
- Washington University; St. Louis, Missouri   *Bears*
- West Virginia Institute of Technology; Montgomery, West Virginia   *Golden Bears*
- Western New England College; Springfield, Massachusetts   *Golden Bears*
- Williamette University; Salem, Oregon   *Bearcats*

United States Junior Colleges

- Brewster State JC; Fayette, Alabama   *Bears*
- Butler County CC; El Dorado, Kansas   *Grizzlies*
- Des Moines Area CC; Boone, Iowa   *Bears*
- Kellogg CC; Battle Creek, Michigan   *Bruins*
- Lon Morris College; Jacksonville, Texas   *Bearcats*
- Los Angeles City College; Los Angeles, California   *Cubs*
- Mott CC; Flint, Michigan   *Bears*
- North Central Technical Institute; Wausau, Wisconsin   *Bears*
- Phoenix College; Phoenix, Arizona   *Bears*

- Salt Lake CC; Salt Lake City, Utah   *Bruins*
- Santa Rosa JC; Santa Rosa, California   *Bear Cubs*
- Southwest Mississippi JC; Summit   *Bears*

Canadian Colleges and Universities

- Alberta, University of; Edmonton, Alberta   *Golden Bears*
- Georgian College; Barrie, Ontario   *Grizzlies*
- Lethbridge CC; Lethbridge, Alberta   *Kodiaks*
- Sheridan College (Brampton Campus); Brampton, Ontario   *Bruins/Bearcats*
- Sheridan College; Oakville, Ontario   *Bruins*

Number of Universities/Colleges with Specific Nickname

- Bear Cubs   1
- Bears   25
- Bearcats   10
- Bearkats   1
- Black Bears   1
- Blue Bears   1
- Bruins   7
- Cubs   1
- Golden Bears   7
- Grizzlies   4
- Kodiaks   1
- Nanooks   1
- Polar Bears   1

Total   61

Source: *The 1991–92 National Directory of College Athletics* (National Association of Collegiate Directors of Athletics). Cleveland: Collegiate Directories, Inc., 1991.

Bear Nicknames of Major United States Professional Teams

- Boston Bruins (National Hockey League)
- Chicago Cubs (National Baseball League)
- Chicago Bears (National Football League)

Bears and Religion

Bears have been considered spiritual; by many cultures they've been an element of religion since they first shared the earth with humans. They have been revered, feared, honored, worshipped, and sacrificed. Many myths, superstitions, and legends have followed bears through the centuries, with the performance of rites, festivals, dances, and other ceremonies centered around and within these sacred animals. Most early cultures believed them to be spirits, as well as accepting them as real animals. They were thought to be in the beginning the first Great Shaman. Bear cults, as early as the

Pleistocene epoch, and fraternal organizations have existed in many societies and cultures. "Bears, large and powerful, have been important to people since man and bears first met," writes George Laycock in *The Wild Bear*. "Many cultures have assigned the bears religious roles in their societies and credited them with super-natural powers."

Bears are associated with puberty rites, initiation of shamans, shamanism, hunting, healing and initiation of women and men into secret societies. They have been considered immortal—entering the ground in the early winter, but being reborn during the spring. Initiation rites are associated with hibernation. "The religious significance of bears stems from their association with caves and their ability to hibernate," notes Merritt in "The Sacred Paw" (magazine article). The importance of the bear in religion may be best illustrated by the Cult of the Bear. This was one of the earliest (Paleolithic) "faiths," and it survived for over twenty thousand years.

There are also many biblical references to bears in the Old and New Testaments. The Book of Mormon refers to bears.

Bears have been considered:

♦ A religious symbol

♦ To be ancestors

♦ Able to cure the sick

♦ Able to cause disease

♦ Honorable

♦ A spirit

♦ Able to impart immortality

♦ To die (hibernate) and be reborn (emerge from the den)

♦ Reincarnated family members

♦ Shamans of the animal world

♦ Messengers to the animal keeper

♦ To know the secrets of the plants

♦ To possess mystic powers

♦ Able to tell the future

♦ Half human

♦ To symbolize the ethics of maternity

♦ To determine patterns of life

♦ To determine the circumstances of death

♦ To be like people

American Indian Ceremonies

"The American Indians of the North Country respect the bear, looking upon it as a fellow citizen of the woods," explained Frederick Drimmer in *The Animal Kingdom*. "Many, when they kill a bear, are careful to apologize and to speed its spirit onward to the Happy Hunting Ground with prayers and sacrifices. In their belief, the animal's spirit is too powerful to be appeased by simple rituals—so they clean the skull and put it on top of a pole, where they hold it taboo."

> ". . . the Yavapai of Arizona said, 'Bears are like people except that they can't make fire,'"
>
> **DAVID ROCKWELL,**
> *Giving Voice to Bear.*

Group/Tribe	Ceremony/Ritual	Purpose
Acoma Pueblo	Bear with eagle plumes and a rattle painted on walls of a secret society chamber	Initiation of a boy into the society
Blackfeet	Men dressed in bear skins during a pipe-smoking ceremony	Intensified the power of the pipe
Coos (Oregon)	Bear dance	Puberty rights of girls
Cree (Eastern)	The shaman fought the bear spirit, Memekwesiw; the shaman had to win	Bear hunts would be successful
	Respected the bears they killed	The bear keepers would provide more bears
	Drew with paint on a bear skull	Brought good dreams
	Placed a bear's knee cap on a hot rock to see if it would wobble	If the knee cap wobbled, bear hunts would be successful
	Threw a pinch of tobacco into the fire	In preparation to hunt bears
Crow	Ate the bear's heart	Provided the person with the heart of a bear, with courage
Dakota	Simulated death; died like bears without fear; shared the bear's power of resurrection;	Initiations
	Fasting, and being reborn; "making a bear"	Initiations into manhood
Delaware	Bear dance and other New Year activities	Rebirth of the earth
Inuit	Polar bear killed and its bladder inflated, dried (hung) indoors and offered food and water	The bear's soul (innua) was its bladder; the bear was being honored
Neanderthals	Ate the flesh of bears with reverence	The meat of bears provided them with immortality
Ojibwa (Midewiwin)	Imitated bears; good and bad bears were present	Initiations
Ojibwa (women)	Were called and treated as bears; associated with the dangerous aspect of bears	Initiations
Ojibwa	Bear dance	Celebrated puberty; identified girls with bears
Ostyak (Western Siberia)	Successful hunter shot an unaimed arrow at the lodge	The arrow hitting an upper beam meant future bear-hunting success, a lower beam hard times
Pimi	Avoided bears	Thought they caused disease
Pomo	Dressed and imitated bears	Initiations
Pomo (eastern California)	Performed a bear dance; chased by persons dressed as bears	Initiation into manhood
Pomo (coastal California)	Grizzly bear impersonator frightened boys and girls; the "bear" dug a hole and the children collapsed into it	Initiations

◄ A polar bear on the move in the Canadian arctic near Churchill, Manitoba.
© JOHNNY JOHNSON

► Noted bear researcher Dr. Charles Jonkel with a tranquilized polar bear in the Canadian arctic.
© DAVID HISER, PHOTOGRAPHERS/ASPEN

◄ A polar bear near Churchill, Manitoba, displaying its tongue . . .
© JOHNNY JOHNSON

► . . . and shaking snow from its face.
© JOHNNY JOHNSON

▲ A polar bear sub-adult removing
snow balls from its paw.
© DANIEL J. COX

▶ A curious polar bear approaches
the photographer.
© JOHNNY JOHNSON

◀ A polar bear leaps across open water to an ice floe.
© DANIEL J. COX

▶ A cinnamon-colored black bear. The cinnamon color variation is more common among black bears of western North America.
© 1992 JOHN W. HERBST

▼ A cinnamon black bear sow
escapes up a tree with her cubs
to avoid a large male bear.
© DANIEL J. COX

◄ A black bear crosses a fallen tree
in the Tongass National Forest.
© DANIEL J. COX

◀ Black bear, standing upright.
© 1992 JOHN W. HERBST

▶ Black bear awakening from a
nap in an aspen. Black bears
frequently sleep in trees, as do
the Asiatic bears.
© DANIEL J. COX

Group/Tribe	Ceremony/Ritual	Purpose
Santa Clara Pueblo (New Mexico)	Wore bear claws on wristlet or shirt	Gave power to fight like a bear
	Hunters blackened their faces after killing a bear	Protected them from attack by a bear on the homeward journey
Yokuts (a bear clan; California)	Performed a bear dance	Honored the acorn crop
Many tribes	Sang a special song after they killed a bear	So the bears, who had control over other game animals, would allow future hunting success
Many tribes	Person brought into close contact with a bear so it was feared	Initiation; person is frightened so they would not be afraid in the future

Whu! Bear!

Whu Whu!

So you say

Whu Whu Whu!

You come.

You're a fine young man

You Grizzly Bear

You crawl out of you fur.

You come

I say Whu Whu Whu!

I throw grease in the fire.

For you

Grizzly Bear

We're one!

TLINGIT INDIANS
Grizzly bear song

The Shaman

Shamans were North American Indian medicine men. They sought to control bear magic and were messengers to the animal keeper. "An important role of the shaman was to assist in the hunt, especially when times were hard," relates Rockwell. "When hunters were unsuccessful and famine threatened, the shaman, in a trance, visited an Owner Of the Animals to ask for release of food animals."

Bears and shamans were thought to possess similar powers, and the shamans impersonated the bear and practiced its healing forces. "Shamans who had the bear as a spirit helper wrapped themselves in the skins of bears, wore necklaces of bear claws, painted bear signs on their faces and bodies, and smoked pipes carved in the shapes of bears," describes Rockwell. "In their medicine bundles they kept bear claws and teeth and other parts of the animal. They used bear claws and gall and bear grease in their ceremonies. They ate the plants bears ate and used them as their medicines. They danced as they thought bears danced, and they sang power songs to the animal. . . . a grizzly bear song of the Tlingit [Indians of the Pacific Northwest area of North America], in which the shaman expresses sense of oneness with the bear."

Hon Kachina   The bear Kachina (Katchina, Katcina) of the Hopi Indians, in the southwest United States, is of such great strength that it is felt he can cure the sick. He appears in the Kachina return, or Soyal of First Mesa, as the watchman or side dancer for the Chakwaina.

Bears and the Bible

The bear is often spoken of in the Bible, less often only than the lion, and has been considered a symbol of God's vengeance. In Lamentations, Jeremiah sees God in His anger as a bear lying in wait and in The Revelation the dragon gave power to a beast with the feet of a bear. Possibly the most well-remembered bear episode is in the Old Testament, 2 Kings, when the prophet Elisha is mocked for his baldness by some children. He curses them, whereupon two "she bears" rush out of the woods and kill forty-two of them. The bears of the bible are Syrian brown bears.

Biblical References

Old Testament

1 Sam. 17.34 And David said unto Saul, Thy servant kept his father's sheep, and there came a lion, and a bear, and took a lamb out of the flock:

1 Sam. 17.36 Thy servant slew both the lion and the bear:

1 Sam. 17.37 David said moreover, The Lord that delivered me out of the paw of the lion, and out of the paw of the bear, he will deliver me out of the hand of the Philistine.

2 Sam. 17.8 For, said Hushai, thou knowest thy father and his men, that they be mighty men, and they be chafed in their minds, as a bear robbed of her whelps in the field:

2 Kings 2.24 And he turned back, and looked on them, and cursed them in the name of the Lord. And there came forth two she bears out of the wood, and tare forty and two children of them.

Prov. 17.12 Let a bear robbed of her whelps meet a man, rather than a fool in his folly.

Prov. 28.15 As a roaring lion, and a ranging bear; so is a wicked ruler over the poor people.

Isa. 11.7 And the cow and the bear shall feed; their young ones shall lie down together: and the lion shall eat straw like the ox.

Isa. 59.11 We roar all like bears, and mourn sore like doves:

Lam. 3.10 He was unto me as a bear lying in wait, and as a lion in secret places.

Dan. 7.5 And behold another beast, a second, like to a bear, and it raised up itself on one side, and it had three ribs in the mouth of it between the teeth of it: and they said this unto it, Arise, devour much flesh.

Hos. 13.8 I will meet them as a bear that is bereaved of her whelps, and will rend the caul of their heart, and there will I devour them like a lion: the wild beast shall tear them.

| Amos 5.19 | As if a man did flee from a lion, and a bear met him; or went into the house, and leaned his hand on the wall, and a serpent bit him. |

New Testament

| Rev. 13.2 | And the beast which I saw was like unto a leopard, and his feet were as the feet of a bear, and his mouth as the mouth of a lion. |

Bears and the Book of Mormon

| 2 Nephi 21:7 (2 Nephi 30:13) | And the cow and the bear shall feed; their young ones shall lie down together; and the lion shall eat straw like the ox. |

Bears and Saints

 Numerous saints had strong associations and influences with bears, with some deriving their name from *Ursus*.

Saint Augustine	Recommended eating the testicles of bears as a cure for epilepsy ("famous against the falling sickness").
Saint Blaise	Represents a pagan myth where Orpheus (most common example) appears as a bear.
Saint Bonaventure	Described a monk who prayed for aid and a bear appeared, to serve this man of God.
Saint Bridget	Celtic fire goddess; Christian saint; the name "Bridget" is a stem word for the word "bear."
Saint Columba	Depicted with a palm branch and a bear on a chain.
Saint Gall	Exchanged bread with a wild bear for wood to build his house.
Saint Korbinian	Depicted with a tame bear. While traveling to Rome, a bear killed his packhorse, thereupon, he forced the bear to carry his load.
Saint Peter Damian	Described a Pope being transformed into a bear in the afterlife.
Saint Sergius of Radonezh	Lived in a forest and shared his bread with a bear cub.
Saint Ursula	A legendary British princess of the Christian faith who received her "bear" name when she reputedly died defending her 11,000 virgin maidens against the bear's onslaught. A variation of the legend claims the attack upon Ursula and her maidens was by the Huns in the fourth to fifth centuries A.D.

Saint Valentine   His twin brother was raised by a bear, and when later domesticated by Valentine, named Orson (meaning bear).

Bear Goddess

Callisto was the Greek bear goddess and called a "she-bear." Bears in pre-classical Greek were closely related to water-springs. Callisto was considered a river nymph, and her tomb was near a spring.

Bear Festivals and Holidays

ears are honored during annual holidays and festivals around the world. All of the events are festive, some religious, and bears are the focus of the majority.

Ainu Bear Festival (Holiday—Japan)

The Festival of the Slain Bear is the bear feast of the Ainu, practiced in Japan each December to honor the bear, The Divine One Who Rules the Mountains. The Ainu annually capture and raise a bear cub (Asiatic black bear) as an honored guest, being nursed by the Ainu women. The bear is sacrificed during the festival, with its soul returning home. "The Ainu believed that the manlike gods were garbed as animals only in the land of man, that meat and fur were gifts to men from them," wrote Shepard and Sanders, "and that the slain bear returned to its divine form. It is sent to the spirit world with festival dancing and feasting."

Bear Creek Folklore Festival (Mississippi)

The annual one-day festival in early June consists of pioneer arts, crafts, and music, in Tishomingo.

Bears of the Blue River Festival (Indiana)

An annual nine-day festival in late August and early September, with arts and entertainment, in Shelbyville.

Bear's Day

February second is Candlemas, the date of the Sacred Marriage. Called Ground Hog Day in America, it is considered Bear's Day in Austria, Hungary, and Poland, the day when bears emerge from their dens to look for their shadows.

The Candlemas Bear Hunt (Holiday—France)

A celebration of the presentation of Jesus at the temple.

Celebrations in Oruro (Holiday—Bolivia)

A carnival in Oruro where individuals costumed as condors and bears walk among dancers as they recall the days of worship and feast.

Festival of the Nine Imperial Gods (Holiday—Singapore)

An annual festival occurring during the first nine days of the ninth month (September). It is based on a century-old Chinese belief that the Nine Imperial Gods reside in the northern heavens. Seven Gods are in each of the seven stars of Ursa Major, the Big Dipper; the other two are in two nearby stars visible only to immortals. The festival includes processions that seek the Gods, inviting them to descend.

McCleary Second Growth and Bear Festival (Washington)

The City of McCleary's annual bear festival began in 1958, when an argument occurred as to whether Skamania County or Grays Harbor County had the tastiest bears. A tasting contest was held later that year in McCleary and the Annual Bear Festival was born. Each year during the third weekend of July, four to five thousand attend this two-day celebration.

The American black bear is celebrated with art and crafts shows, baseball, the world-famous bear stew contest and feast, bingo, children's play day, dances, a pancake breakfast, queen's coronation, musical entertainment, parades, 10k Run (Ursa major), two-mile run (Ursa minor), and a salmon barbecue.

The festival is officially known as the Second Growth and Bear Festival. When the festival began, young trees, planted to replace the old growth trees cut down for timber, were growing in the area surrounding McCleary (hence the second growth). Bears caused serious damage to the young forest, utilizing the bark as food. They were killed to protect the trees, and a bear hunt became an important aspect of the festival. Today, a more effective system is in place—the bears are fed during the spring to protect the trees.

Swiss Bear Festival (North Carolina)

The annual two-day bear festival (Swiss performances and attractions) in October celebrates the Swiss heritage of the town of New Bern.

Teddy Bear Picnic (Colorado)

The annual Teddy Bear Picnic, in Estes Park, is an event for all ages that features a drawing whose proceeds benefit the national organization Good Bears of the World. Musical entertainment and contests are included in this one-day function, including a contest rewarding the family that brings the most teddy bears. The eighth annual picnic was held in 1992.

Tori-No-Ichi (Japan)

The "bird fair" is a Shinto celebration that includes an activity involving influential members of this sect and wealthy merchants. The participants have a market mascot—a "Kumade" (bear hand), which is an ordinary bamboo rake resembling the clutching claws of a bear paw. The lore of the Kumade is that the possessor will have magic power to pull (rake) all desired treasure.

Ute Tribal Bear Dance (Utah)

An annual three-day festival in early April (in Ouray) welcomes spring with ancient and ceremonial dancing.

Vagabonds' New Years (Poland)

A New Years festival with costumes, pantomime and improvisations where the devil and the bear frolic in the snow.

Bears in the Heavens

Polaris, the North Star, which we are taught to locate when very young and which was for so long the navigational monument of the Northern Hemisphere, is also known as alpha Ursae Minoris. Two constellations, Ursa Major (the Great Bear) and Ursa Minor (the Little Bear), move counterclockwise around the North Star. The first two stars in Ursa Major are pointing to Polaris, at the tip of Ursa Minor's tail.

The "bear constellations" never set, and since at least the beginning of recorded history the Great Bear and the Little Bear, with the North Star, have guided explorers, travelers and navigators in the north.

Ursa Major

The Big Dipper, an asterism consisting of seven bright stars (six shine with extreme brightness) and seven fainter stars, forms only the hips (the cup) and the tail (the handle), but is the most conspicuous part of the Great Bear.

The British have long believed the Big Dipper to be the Plow, the Wain, or the Wagon. Some people believe the Great Bear more resembles a mouse, not a lumbering bear.

Arabians considered the four stars of the Big Dipper bowl a coffin and the handle stars the mourners marching behind the coffin.

The stars of the Big Dipper are continually and very slowly changing position. The "dipper" will be a "frying pan" in 100,000 years.

Ursa Minor

The Little Bear is a constellation consisting of seven stars, with the Little Dipper comprising the major portion. Early peoples thought the Little Dipper resembled a dog's tail and called it Cynosure; others referred to it as a jackal or jewels. Today it is considered to appear as an old-fashioned cream ladle or gravy spoon.

The North Star, alpha Ursae Minoris, is the brightest star in Ursus minora and is at the end of the Little Dipper's handle (tail).

Many beliefs existed among ancient peoples as to the origin and influences of the Great Bear and the Little Bear. Some remain in a few of today's cultures and societies.

Origins of Ursa Major and Ursa Minor

Greek mythology: Jupiter fell in love with the nymph Callisto, and his jealous wife turned her into a bear. When Callisto approached her son, he did not recognize her and raised his spear to kill the "bear." Jupiter saved

Little dipper (Ursa minor)
Renee Evanoff

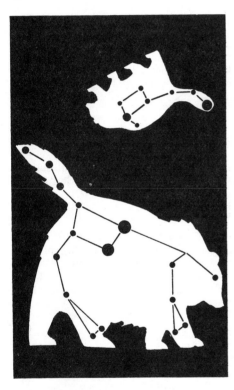

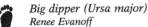

Big dipper (Ursa major)
Renee Evanoff

Bowl of the Dipper

Dubhe (Alpha; the Bear), pointer star

Merak (Beta; loins of the Bear), pointer star

Phecda (Gamma; thigh of the Bear)

Megrez (Delta; root of the tail)

Handle of the Dipper

Alioth (Epsilon)

Mizar (Zeta): Mizar has a companion star, Alcor, that has long been considered "The Test" of eyesight

Alkaid (Eta; end of the tail; also called Benetnash)

Paws of the Great Bear

Talitha (front paws)

Tania Borealis (hind paws)

Tania Australis (hind paws)

PROMINENT STARS
OF URSA MINOR

Bowl of the Dipper

Kochab (Beta)

Pherkad (Kochab and Pherkad are the guardians, or guards, of the pole)

Handle of the Dipper

Yildun; the Surpassing Star

Polaris (Alpha); the North Star, the Pole Star

her by changing her son into a bear, and then placed them both in the sky. (Some writings relate similar origins, but with Zeus placing the bears in the heavens.)

Eskimo: A woman betrays the "Bear" men, and a bear kills her. Dogs attack the bear, and both rise into the sky, therefore the bear and light become a constellation.

Finns and Voguls: The bear of the earth originated of a cloud near the Great Bear.

Ostyaks (Siberians): The bear of the earth originated in the heavens, a combining of the Big Bear, the sun and the moon, and descended to earth.

One legend describes the bears as causing trouble on earth and Hercules swinging them by their tails into the sky.

Beliefs

The constellations have been integral entities in the beliefs and religions of many peoples. In mythology, both constellations were combined and called the Great Bear, and their turning has led to traditional symbols such as the "cross," "swastika," and the "spiral."

Hindus: Called Ursa major, the Seven Bears, or Seven Wisemen. They placed red spirals on structures where a child was about to be born to aid the newborn into life.

Iroquois and Micmac Indians: The Great Bear was four stars with seven hunters, the second hunter (Mizar) with a pot (the tiny companion star Alcor) to cook the bear. The bear's den was a group of stars above the bear. The hunters were seven birds (blue jay, Canada jay, chickadee, owl, pigeon, robin, saw-whet).

North American Indians: These peoples knew bears did not have long tails, therefore the "tail" stars were hunters pursuing the bears. The Great Bear rides low in the sky during the fall, therefore it is looking for a place to bed down, preparing for winter (hibernation). Mizar and Alcor were horse and rider.

Greeks: The Hunter, (Bootes) was pursuing the Great Bear and the Little Bear around Polaris—a celestial hunt.

Siberians: The Great Bear and the Little Bear together were the sacred elk Kheglen, and were being chased by Mangi the bear spirit (Bootes).

The early watchers of the heavens found the bears to have long tails, which is probably based on their association or knowledge of the cave bear, *Ursus spelaeus*, which became extinct approximately 10,000 years ago.

During the early history of Western civilization the arctic was thought to lie beneath the constellations. The Arktik'os, as it was referred to by the Greeks, was considered the country of the great bear.

The constellation Bootes (Bo oteas), known as the bear driver, bear keeper or herdsman, appears to be chasing the Great Bear. The star Arcturus (arctos-bear; ouros-keeper) is the left knee of Bootes.

Early cultures believed the constellations influenced many aspects of life and the environment, such as good health, strength and childbirth, climate, seasons and the weather, crop diseases, and animal behavior.

Bear Myths and Tales

Many misconceptions and fallacies surround bears. Some are amusing tales, often obviously untrue, and several quite dangerous if taken as fact.

Black bears are not dangerous: All bears are wild, unpredictable and potentially dangerous animals.

Bears are poor swimmers: Bears are excellent swimmers, often swimming as play and to cool off. They will swim across lakes and strong rivers to reach a food source, mate, or just to cross.

Grizzly bears can't climb trees: Mature grizzly bears normally do not climb like American black and other bears due to the structure of their claws and their weight as adults. They do not have the sharply curved claws necessary to dig into tree bark, but are quite capable of "laddering" up a tree utilizing available limbs to climb (as a person would). There are even a few observations of grizzly bears climbing in the same manner as black bears. Grizzly bear cubs, and other small bears of the species, climb quite well.

Bears are large, cumbersome, and slow: Bears are large, and appear cumbersome, but most are fast (some capable of running thirty-five miles per hour for short distances), agile, able to leap long distances, and capable of climbing trees and scaling cliffs.

 BEARS IN WITCHCRAFT

Bears are found in the writings of witchcraft throughout the world. Ursus ('orsus') in witchcraft was considered "a beginning." A sow produced a formless creature (fetus) and sculptured her brood with her mouth, her licking shaping legs, head and body.

Witches had the skill and ability to change shape and become a bear by means of the devil, a curse, or by magic. A witch became the bear for a specific period of time and the bear was occasionally a "familiar" spirit. They also transformed humans into beasts, including bears.

Centuries ago, in Northern Europe, humans were thought to become bears by wearing a bear skin, or by anointing with a magic salve. Witches murdered, crippled, or harmed persons with "image magic." They sometimes used a bear that would be tortured and killed, believing that the actions would be transferred and a person would also suffer and die.

A bear was the disguise of the devil, the Grand Devil of the celebration, the God, the Grand Master.

A companion dog keeps bears away while in bear country: Dogs may be of assistance in keeping bears away from a camp or providing a mutual warning of the bear's and your nearby presence. However, on many occasions, a dog has chased a bear, found too great an adversary and retreated back to its master with the bear in hot pursuit.

Bears can't run well downhill: You can not outrun a bear downhill. Bears run uphill, sidehill and definitely downhill nearly as well, always with speed, and are not known to stumble.

Bears do not eat human flesh: Bears do not normally prey on humans. However, when they do, or if they kill in a defensive action, their victims are often consumed.

Bears will not attack sleeping people: Bears have attacked people sleeping in tents and out in the open. More than once they have clawed or bitten a head protruding from a sleeping bag as the individual slept "under the stars."

Bears that approach or come in close contact with people are tame: Bears that are willing to be close to people are either conditioned to a nearby food source or are habituated to human activity. These bears are wild and dangerous animals—maybe more dangerous than the normally shy, retreating bears.

A repellent is protection from an aggressive bear: A repellent is "false security," often replacing good sense and important precautionary actions necessary in bear country.

Bears hug their enemies to death (bearhug): A bear often appears to be hugging its prey, when actually it is standing to hold the victim and gain better advantage while using its powerful paws and jaws.

Grizzly bears always charge at first sight: Grizzly bears are normally shy and will retreat if at all possible. During the settling of North America bears may have nearly always charged, but probably not at first sight. The early explorers and pioneers were often aggressive and the bear was threatened, often wounded. Today, many of those early "charges" would be considered defensive aggression.

Bears are hard to kill: Bears have thick skulls and considerable endurance, and many tales of difficulties in killing bears have saturated our early bear literature. However, the

Bear stories "are like fine wine, they improve with age."

UNKNOWN

major problem the early explorers and pioneers had was inadequate firearms.

Bears hibernate: Bears are not true hibernators as are bats, squirrels, and woodchucks, though we normally utilize the word in describing the winter activity of many bears, as they do become quite lethargic and fall into a deep sleep.

Humans and bears have been crossed (interbred): There have been many reports of bears being crossed with humans. However, all scientific investigations have found the reports of this interbreeding to be untrue.

Bears mate just before hibernation: The time between the beginning of hibernation and the birth of cubs is approximately the appropriate gestation period. However, bears mate several months before hibernation; the process of delayed implantation defers the development of the embryo until hibernation.

Bears suck their paws for sustenance: Early observers believed bears sucked nourishment from their paws during the long "fast of hibernation." The misconception was based on the fact bears do on occasions suck their paws, and during the spring as bears emerge from their dens they slough the pads of their paws (a natural "shedding" of the skin).

Bears use the left front paw to eat honey: "The meat of the bear's left front paw is said to be the sweetest and most tender part of the animal," relate Judy Mills and Chris Servheen in *The Asian Trade in Bears and Bear Parts*, "because, according to myth, this is the paw used to [collect] honey from bees' nests." Actually, bears have been observed using either front paw while collecting and eating the contents of a bee hive or nest.

Bears attack telegraph poles and wires: Bears have climbed and damaged telegraph poles and wires in Siberia, and telephone poles in Los Padres National Forest, California. It is theorized that the purpose for climbing the poles is the humming wires sound like the buzzing of bees, and the bears are merely seeking bees and honey.

Bears have poor eyesight: This is a misleading belief. A bear's eyesight is not good—it is nearsighted—but it can detect form and movement at long distances.

Ancient Myths

The ancient saying "lick into shape" appears to be based on the belief that a bear gave birth to an unformed, shapeless "ball of fur" that the sow licked into the proper shape of a bear. According to Aristotle there would be no mature bears without the sow's primal, maternal intervention, relate Shepard and Sanders. "Having produced them [cubs], by licking them with her tongue she completes their warming and concocts them, matures them." *Ours mal leche* (a badly licked bear) is a still-used French phrase and describes an incorrigible, ill-behaved child.

"A bear is much subject to blindness of the eyes, and for that cause they desire the Hives of Bees, not only for the Hony," writes Edward Topsell in *The History of Four-Footed Beasts* (1607), "but by the stinging of the Bees, their eyes are cured." Why Topsell believed this is uncertain, but it certainly is no more than a tale.

YETI/SASQUATCH BEARS

Myths and reality most often include bears in the long-contested debate: What are the Abominable Snowman (Yeti) of Asia and Big Foot (Sasquatch) of northwestern North America? Are they beings in themselves—an unknown, humanlike animal? Apes? Or bears?

Local residents, Sasquatch "watchers," and scientists have for many years identified and weighed the evidence.

PRO-BEAR EVIDENCE

Tracks

❖ *Yeti dimensions are similar to bears; 6"–7" long, 4" wide*

❖ *Dimensions are often similar to grizzly bears; 14" × 8"*

❖ *Some Yeti dimensions are 16"–24" long (typical 10"–12") in the snow*

❖ *Distinct toes and insteps*

❖ *Heels are indistinct*

❖ *Short "claw" marks*

❖ *Forepaws turn inward*

❖ *Hindpaws are generally straight in tracks*

❖ *Proportionally, tracks are more bear-like than human*

❖ *Generally, tracks are bear-like*

❖ *Outline of tracks bear-like, not ape-like*

❖ *A single set of tracks (followed) in shade were small, with claw marks; large with the claw marks appearing as toe marks in sun*

Bipedal Track

- *Bears walk bipedally*
- *Bears, when walking*

quadpedally, superimpose hindpaw track into forepaw track (only two tracks)

Location

- *Asiatic black bear habitat*
- *Brown bear habitat*
- *American black bear habitat*

- *Elevations frequented by Asiatic black bear*
- *Ranges overlap with bears*

Activities

- *Cross swift streams; more bear-like than ape-like*

Diet

- *Bears are omnivorous; necessary for "Yeti habitat"*

Size

- *Bears approximately same height as a Yeti*

Color

- *Bears are similar in coloration; reddish or brown*

General

- *No hard evidence (skulls, bones, captives, perfect photographs) of a true Yeti or Sasquatch*

- *Many European naturalists claim that abominable snowman tracks often lead to excavations dug into the burrows of pikas, an important bear food*

PRO-HUMAN, APE EVIDENCE

Tracks

- *Sasquatch track length averages 16 to 17 inches long; sometimes 22 inches*

- *Sasquatch tracks are too large to be bear's*

- *Largest tracks are usually in snow; enlarged with melting of snow*

- *Some tracks depict toes on heels; apes walk on bent knuckles of hands, fingers pointing back*

Stride

- *Long at times, unbear-like*
- *Walks too great a distance for bears*

....

Bipedal

- *Walks upright like a human; bears walk slowly and clumsily upright (bipedally)*

....

Size

- *Sasquatch is too large to be a bear*

....

Activities

- *Slides down snow on rump; not bear-like (bears slide on their chests, or schuss on forepaws)*
- *Sasquatch sightings are during all months; bears are hibernating during the winter*

....

General

- *Soft evidence is available such as footprints, scalp, hairs, mummified droppings, eyewitness accounts*

....

There appear to be habits and traditions of claiming Yeti is, and is not, "a bear." Some Yeti and Sasquatch sightings are without doubt actually sightings of bears, as well as humans and other wild animals. Bears may not have initiated the legends, but definitely have perpetuated the stories.

The Legend of Yosemite

"One morning a young chief of the tribe [Ah-wah-nee-chees], while on his way to Ah-wei-ya (Mirror Lake), where he intended spearing some fish, was suddenly confronted by an immense grizzly bear. The bear resented this intrusion upon his domain and made a fierce attack upon the young chief. The chief, who was weaponless, armed himself with the dead limb of a tree, which was lying near, and, after being sorely wounded, succeeded in killing the bear. Bleeding and exhausted he dragged himself back to the camp where he told his story to the admiring members of the tribe, who in acknowledgment of his bravery and skill, called him Yo-sem-i-te, their word for the fearless monarch of the forest, the grizzly bear. This name was transmitted to his children, and in time, because of their fearless and warlike natures, the entire tribe came to be known as the Yo-sem-i-tes." (Wilson, *The Lore and Lure of Yosemite*.)

Bears in North American Art

The bears of North America have been creatively and realistically captured by numerous artists of the nineteenth and twentieth centuries. The reader should visit art galleries and libraries to study these "stories" of natural history and human/bear interactions. The following list of paintings is only an example, as bears are represented in many forms of art.

1800s, Early 1900s

Adams and Ben Franklin
(grizzly bear)
Henry Hinkel, mid-1800s; Library of Congress, Washington, D.C.

The Bear Dance of the Sioux
(Indian bear dancers)
George Catlin; Glenbow Museum, Calgary, Alberta

Cautious Encounter
(grizzly bear)
Olaf Seltzer; Fenn Galleries, Ltd., Santa Fe, New Mexico

Death Battle of Buffalo and Grizzly Bear
Charles Russell; circa 1903

The Fight with Old Slewfoot
(American black bear)
N.C. Wyeth, circa 1939;

The Frightened Grizzly
(grizzly bear)
Henry Hinkel, mid-1800s; Library of Congress, Washington, D.C.

The Great American Hunter & Trapper (grizzly bear)

S.E. Hollister, 1903; Amon Carter Museum, Fort Worth, Texas

Grizzly at Bay
William R. Leigh, 1915; Buffalo Bill Historical Center, Cody, Wyoming

Grizzly Bear
Carl Rungius; Shelburne Museum, Shelburne, Vermont

Grizzly Bear and Mouse
George Catlin; National Gallery of Art, Washington, D.C.

Grizzly Bears Attacking Buffalo
George Catlin, 1830s/1840s; National Gallery of Art, Washington, D.C.

The Grizzly King
Frank B. Hoffman, circa 1911; William Doyle Galleries, New York, New York

His Last Stand (grizzly bear)
Frederick Remington, 1895; Sid W. Richardson Foundation Collection

Hunting of the Grizzly Bear
Karl Dodmer, 1830s; Library of
Congress, Washington, D.C.

**Indians on Horseback with
Lances** (grizzly bear)
George Catlin; National Gallery
of Art, Washington, D.C.

Kodiak with Sockeye
John Scheonherr; Kings Gallery,
New York, New York

**Native Californians Lassoing a
Bear** (grizzly bear)
F.O.C. Darley; Library of
Congress, Washington, D.C.

Polar Bear
John Woodhouse Audubon, circa
1852

Roping a Grizzly
Charles M. Russell; 1903; Buffalo

Bill Historical Center, Cody,
Wyoming

Roping the Bear (grizzly bear)
J. Walker; California Historical
Society, Sacramento, California

Timberline (grizzly bear)
W. Herbert Dunton, circa 1920;
Gerald Peters Gallery, Santa Fe,
New Mexico

An Unequal Combat (grizzly
bear)
H.H. Cross; Library of Congress,
Washington, D.C.

**The White Cloud, Head Chief of
the Iowas**
George Catlin; National Gallery
of Art, Washington, D.C.

A Wounded Grizzly
Charles M. Russell, 1906; Buffalo
Bill Historical Center, Cody,
Wyoming

1980s and 1990s

Along the Ice Floe—Polar Bears
John Seerey-Lester, 1986

Bad Water Bear (grizzly bear)
Morten E. Solberg, 1987

Bear and Blossoms
(American black bear)
Stephen E. Lyman, 1980s

Black and Blue (American black
bear)
John C. Pitcher

Black Bears/Tower Creek
Michael Coleman

Close to Mom (grizzly bear sow
with three cubs)
Carl Brenders

Cloud Drift/Logan Pass
(grizzly bear)
Lee Stroncek

Doubled Back (grizzly bear)
Bev Doolittle

End of Season—Grizzly
Robert Bateman, 1986

The First Season (grizzly sow
with two cubs)
John Seerey-Lester, 1990

Grizzly Country
Paul Kraft

Heavy Going—Grizzly
John Seerey-Lester, 1987

Into the Wind (grizzly bear)
Morten Solberg, 1985

The Invaders (polar bear)
Fred Machetanz, 1986

**Keeping Pace—Grizzly with
Cubs**
John Seerey-Lester, 1992

Lone Wanderers of the Arctic
(polar bears)
David Shepherd, 1988

McNeil River Fishermen
(grizzly bears)
Morten Solberg

Mighty Intruder (American black
bear)
Carl Brenders, 1985

Monarch of the North (grizzly
bear)
Rod Frederick, circa 1985

November Light—Grizzly
Terry A. Isaac, 1990

Out of the Mist—Grizzly
John Seerey-Lester

Passing Shower (American black bear sow with two cubs in a Yellowstone National Park geyser basin)
Michael Coleman

The Stillness (grizzly bear sow with two cubs)
Bonnie Marris, circa 1990

Tense Moment (two polar bears)
Fred Machetanz, 1986

Treading Water—Polar Bear
Audrey Casey, 1991

Uzumati—the Great Bear of Yosemite (grizzly bear)
Stephen Lyman, 1988

Waiting for the Freeze (polar bear)
Bonnie Marris, late 1980s

Washburn Grizzly
Gary Carter, 1988

When Predators Meet (grizzly bear sow with two cubs)
Gary Carter

When Winter Warms (polar bear)
Morten E. Solberg, 1989

Zero (polar bear)
Bradley J. Parrish, 1991

Bears in Literature

T he earliest writings about bears may have occurred approximately three thousand to four thousand years ago, in China.

Literature has long been saturated with books containing bear stories or publications devoted entirely to the animal. They have addressed bears in folklore, fables, epics, in technical writings and mythical tales. Ballads, romances, fairy tales, poetry, religion, comedy, and historical narratives have all described bears and their behavior. They have been described as evil, friendly, heroes, and are accounted for in the classics, comic books, textbooks, and in the bible. Writings have been for all ages, though mostly directed to children.

"In literature it [the bear] is both smart and naive, forgiving and vicious," describe Shepard and Sanders.

Some early authors who utilized the bear were William Shakespeare, the Grimm brothers, Aesop, and Charles Dickens.

Some Early Bear Writings

Aesop's Fables. Aesop, a Greek slave
Beauty and the Beast. W.R.S. Ralston
Goldilocks and the Three Bears. Robert Southey
The History of Four-Footed Beasts. Edward Topsell (1607)
Jungle Book. Rudyard Kipling
Mother Goose's Fairy Tales of 1878
Roman de Renart. Evolved from Aesop's Fables between 1170 and 1250
Snow White and Rose Red. Grimm Brothers
The Willow-Wren and the Bear (*The Bear and the Kingbird*), Grimm Brothers

Sherlock Holmes and Bears

Sir Arthur Conan Doyle included a reference to a bearskin hearthrug in "The Adventure of the Priory School" (*The Return Of Sherlock Holmes*). Dr. Thorneycroft Huxtable, M.A., Ph.D. entered Holmes' Baker Street home, staggered against a table, slipped to the floor and came to rest prostrate on a bearskin hearthrug.

Doyle's "A Study In Scarlet" refers to a large and savage grizzly bear, on the Great Alkali Plain, a repulsive desert of North America (near the Great Salt Lake, Utah).

And Sir Arthur wrote of polar bears during the late 1800s, though without Sherlock Holmes. In *Life On A Greenland Whaler*, he refers to polar bears as ". . . poor harmless creatures, with the lurch and roll of a deep-sea mariner."

A "LIST" OF BEAR BOOKS

The bibliography (see page 306) is extensive, and much of it might be deemed uninteresting "reading." However, it includes several books considered by bear authorities, enthusiasts, authors, and readers as excellent writings—interesting, educational, practical, entertaining, and enjoyable. Some may be entirely about bears, while a few only address them as a part of the story. Below are listed some of these publications—plus a few others.

American Bears. Theodore Roosevelt (Paul Schullery, Editor)

The Bamboo Bears. Clive Roots

Bears of the World. Terry Domico and Mark Newman

The Bear Hunter's Century. Paul Schullery

The Bear Who Wanted to be a Bear. Jorg Steiner

The Bears of Yellowstone. Paul Schullery

Ben Lilly Legend. Frank J. Dobie

The Biography of a Grizzly. Ernest Thompson Seton

Bully Bear books. Peter Bull

The Cave Bear Story. Bjorn Kurten

The Everywhere Bear. Sandra Chisholm Robinson

Giving Voice to Bears. David Rockwell

Grizzly Bears. Candace Savage

Grizzly Cub. Rick McIntyre

The Grizzly. Enos Mills

The Grizzlies of Mount McKinley. Adolph Murie

The Grizzly Bear. Thomas McNamee

The House at Pooh Corner. A.A. Milne

The Last Grizzly. David Brown and John Murray, editors

Meet Mr. Grizzly. Montague Stevens

No Room for Bears. Frank Dufresne

The Only Good Bear is a Dead Bear. Jeanette Prodgers

Polar Bears. Ian Sterling

Arctic Dreams. Barry Lopez

Bear Attacks: Their Causes and Avoidance. Stephen Herrero

The Bear. William Faulkner

The Bear Who Slept Through Christmas. John M. Barrett

The Bears of Alaska in Life & Legend. Jeff Rennicke

The Beast that Walks Like Man. Harold McCracken

The Berenstain Bears Series. Jan and Stan Berenstain

Black Bear. Daniel J. Cox

California Grizzly. Tracy Storer and Lloyd Tevis, Jr.

The Clan of the Cave Bear. Jean M. Auel

The Giant Pandas of Wolong. George Schaller

Goldilocks and the Three Bears. Robert Southey

Grizzly Country. Andy Russell

Grizzly Years. Doug Peacock

The Grizzly in the Southwest. David Brown

The Grizzly Bear. Bessie and Edgar Haynes

The Grizzly Bear. William H. Wright

The Last Bit-Bear. Sandra Chisholm Robinson

Little Bear series. Else Holmelund Minarik

Mountain Man & Grizzly. Fred Gowans

Now We are Six. A.A. Milne

Paddington Bear series. Michael Bond

Pooh Bear series. A.A. Milne

(continued)

TEDDY BEAR

O Teddy Bear! with your
head awry
And your comical twisted
smile,
You rub your eyes—do you
wonder why
You've slept such a long, long
while?
As you lay so still in the
cupboard dim,
And you heard on the roof
the rain,
Were you thinking . . . what
has become of him?

ROBERT SERVICE

Poetry

Bears have been included in poetry for centuries. Real and fictional bears have appeared in more than a hundred modern items of poetry.

Robert Service, in *Ballads Of A Bohemian*, penned "Teddy Bear"—a tale not unusually sad for Service, and the background of which he describes. "There was one jolly little chap who used to play with a large white Teddy Bear," he explained. "He was always with his mother, a sweet-faced woman, who followed his every movement with delight. I used to watch them both, and often spoke a few words. Then [after a month or more] this morning I saw the mother in the rue D'Assas. She was alone and in deep black. I wanted to ask after the boy, but there was a look in her face that stopped me."

Cartoon Bears

BARNSTABLE is the bear in the syndicated comic strip "Walt Kelly's Pogo," by Doyle & Sternecky.

WOODRUFF is the grizzly bear of "The Simple Beasts," by Doug Hall.

PARK BEARS are the primary subjects of Phil Frank's "Travels with Farley."

POLAR BEARS are found in "Mukluk," by Robin Heller.

BEARS are not uncommon subjects of "The Far Side" cartoons by Gary Larson, and are often the characters of the political cartoons of other journalists.

Textbooks

The California State Department of Education, in 1966, published *Arctos the Grizzly*, by Rhoda Leonard (illustrations: Joseph Capozio). This book was utilized throughout the California school systems.

The Financial World and Bears

As stock markets bound and rebound, there is a common and often frequent reference to the bear: "a bear market," or the opposite, a bull market.

"In stock market parlance," according to Charles Funk in *A Hog On Ice*, "a bear is a speculator who sells a stock that he does not own in the belief that before he must deliver the stock to its purchaser its price will have dropped so that he may make a profit on the transaction. A bull, on the other hand, is optimistic of future rises in the value of a stock. . . ."

The term "bear market" is based on Old English definitions:

- "To sell the bear skin before the bear is caught"

- To sell a bear: "To sell what one hath not"

- The stock sold: "A bear skin"

- The dealer: "The bear-skin jobber"

- The dealer (more recent): "The bear"

Stock market bear
Courtesy D.A. Davidson & Co., Great Falls, Montana

Honey, Bees, and Bears

There was reported by Demetrius Ambassador at Rome, from the King of Musco, that a neighbour of his going to seek Hony, fell into a hollow tree up to the brest in Hony, where he lay two days, being not heard by any man to complain;" describes Edward Topsell in *The History of Four-Footed Beasts* (1607), "at length came a great Bear to this Hony; and putting his head into the tree, the poor man took hold there-of, whereat the Bear suddenly affrighted, drew the man out of that deadly danger, and so ran away for fear of a worse creature."

Honey is undoubtedly attractive to bears since they and bees share the same habitats. Often fantasized as the only food of bears, honey is quite popular wherever a bear may find a natural beehive or commercial apiary. In reality, the bears are more interested in the brood (bee larvae) than the honey.

The sloth and sun bears are each known as the "honey bear"; however, all bears will take advantage of a bee hive or swarms of bees. They will rip open bee trees, climbing to the highest limbs, or seek and destroy a commercial apiarist's hives. During their honey (and larvae) collection endeavors, the bears are incessantly stung. They whine and squeal as their eyes and ears are stung and the bees are deep in their fur. However, they are not deterred.

"Like all other bears, the black bear is fond of honey. An experienced old bear will get the honey out of a tree with only a few stings;" explains Frederick Drimmer in *The Animal Kingdom*, "the youngsters, more greedy than wise, get badly stung and bawl with pain—but they do not stop until they have eaten all the honey."

Bears, primarily the American black bear, inflict serious and costly damage to the broods as well as to the hives of commercial apiaries in North America, and eat the honey that was destined for the market. Annual loss of income from damaged equipment and lost honey production in some states and provinces today reaches between $270,000 and $310,000, and hundreds of American black bears are removed (mostly shot) due to their conflicts with the apiarists.

Many apiarists attempt to discourage determined bears with a variety of methods, but once a bear obtains a reward of honey—or any food, for that matter—it will persist to the source. Honey farmers place costly electric fences around their hives, and place the hives on roof tops or on poles.

Bears are relocated but, like any food-conditioned bear, they return. Unfortunately, the only truly successful deterrent is to kill the bear.

A few states and provinces, including Pennsylvania, Vermont, New Hampshire, and Minnesota provide compensation to the apiarist for bear damages.

The bears' special interest in bee hives has not changed over time, for as Topsell wrote nearly four centuries ago, "... and will break into Bee-hives sucking out the Hony."

War and Bears

Like other wild animals, bears have paid a price during civil and international wars fought in their habitats. They have died by direct mortality (shot, exploding mines, artillery), as a result of displacement from their habitat or habitat destruction, and by being used as food during war-related economic decline. During World War I and World War II, bears were targets for soldiers behind the front lines as well as in battle, and displacement from their habitat caused significant indirect mortality. Bear research, protection, and other necessary management is minimal, if not non-existent, during war. Wars and revolutions provide firearms for civilians who later use them to kill bears.

During the 1800s, the Indian Army and Indian Civil Service slaughtered great numbers of sloth bears, which had been extremely numerous prior to that period. The soldiers were "trigger-happy," killing them for target practice and to pass the time.

War struck captive bears in 1940, when Albert Rix's entire bear act was destroyed by British RAF bombers that attacked the train on which it was traveling in southern Germany.

Bears have been shot in recent conflicts and, according to a Yugoslavian biologist, at least six brown bears are known to have been killed by mines during the recent Crotia-Serbia war. Bears (and other animals) in the former Yugoslavian zoos have also died from starvation.

The drug wars of South America have resulted in indirect mortality of spectacled bears, as their habitat is impacted when the drug cartel seeks more remote business locations, and by the government's program of forest defoliation to locate and counter the cartel.

Wildfire and Bears

Bears have evolved with fire of various origins (volcanic, lightning, spontaneous combustion, and human). Fire (also flood, insects, disease, and drought) has altered the landscape, displaced bears, rejuvenated and improved habitats and food sources, created other foods, caused death, and triggered curiosity, fear, and flight. Wildfire has minimal negative impact on bears and is generally beneficial.

Twenty-one grizzly bears were monitored before, during, and following the Yellowstone fires of 1988. Of this group, thirteen moved into burned areas after the fire front passed, three remained within actively burning areas, three remained outside burning and burned areas, two may have perished in fire storms, and five bears denned within and eight outside burned areas (den sites of eight bears were not located, which is not unusual).

"The most important immediate effect of the fires on grizzly bears was the increased availability of ungulate carcasses during a fall otherwise offering few foraging opportunities," note Bonnie Blanchard and Richard Knight in "Reactions of Grizzly Bears to Wildfire in Yellowstone National Park." "The fires had no apparent effects on overall choice of den sites, annual range sizes, or . . . [normal] movement."

"Bears were the most matter-of-fact fellows in the exodus," notes Enos Mills in *The Spell of the Rockies*. "Each loitered in the grass and occasionally looked toward the oncoming danger. Their actions showed curiosity and anger, but not alarm."

Other Bears

Automobiles and Boats

Stutz Bearcat   Harry C. Stutz, inventor, and owner of the Stutz Motor Company of Indianapolis, Indiana, produced a series of "Bearcats," considered one of the greatest American sports cars, a true champion of the race course as well as the road. First built in 1919, the automobile was a technical anomaly for the time, the chassis and body light and quick, the engine with only four cylinders and side valves. It was considered the sportscar of the jazz age, usually red, yellow, or blue.

Great Bear (Christie)   The Christie, produced in the early 1900s, and entered in the second Vanderbilt Cup race in

1905, was the first front-wheel-drive racer. It moved in a zig-zag manner due to a transversly mounted engine and a complex transmission system, therefore was deemed the "Great Bear."

Polar Bear   A trading schooner in the early 1900s, later served as a whaling ship in the Arctic Ocean. Purchased by Vilhjalmur Stefansson in 1915 for arctic exploration.

Bear   A wooden-hull steam vessel, built for the United States Navy and launched in 1874, the *Bear* was a 198-foot cutter, displacing 1,700 tons. Acquired by the United States Revenue Cutter Service in April 1885, it served in the arctic, providing passenger service and transporting reindeer purchased from Siberia by the United States. A rugged ship, it handled the rough arctic seas and ice well. In 1929, the *Bear* became a merchant vessel, the *Bear Of Oakland*, prior to returning to the Navy for service from 1939 to 1948.

U.S.R.C. Bear (Nome, Alaska)
The Charles Bunnell Collection, Accession #58-1026-1103. Archives of Alaska and Polar Regions Department, University of Alaska, Fairbanks

Brown Bear A patrol boat for the Aleutian Island Wildlife Refuge during the 1930s, the *Brown Bear* was lost during World War II.

Hvidbjornen (Polar Bear) A Danish navy patrol boat assigned to serve in the coastal waters of Greenland, the *Hvidbjornen* enforces fishing regulations and protects the polar bear population.

Teddy Bear A ship of the early 1900s used in Siberian trading, the *Teddy Bear* carried oil prospectors and passengers.

Stamps

The United States Postal Service has on occasion issued sheets, booklets, and blocks of wildlife postage stamps depicting bears.

WILDLIFE BOOKLET, MAY 14, 1981
* *Wildlife, 18 cents—brown bear and polar bear*

The brown bear and polar bear stamps are from a booklet of ten wildlife stamps engraved from photographs by Jim Brandenburg of Minnesota, contract photographer for *National Geographic*.

PRESERVATION OF WILDLIFE HABITATS, JUNE 26, 1981
* *Save Mountain Habitats, 18 cents—grizzly bear*

A grizzly bear approaching an evergreen forest with snow-covered mountains in the background. The stamp is from a block of four commemorative stamps designed by Chuck Ripper, noted wildlife illustrator and author from Huntington, West Virginia. They were issued to enhance public awareness of the necessity of the preservation of the environment of native wildlife.

Save Mountain Habitats

NORTH AMERICAN WILDLIFE, JUNE 13, 1987
* *Biological Diversity, 22 cents—brown bear, American black bear*

An Alaskan brown bear standing in the fall colors of dwarf birch, and an American black bear climbing a tree. The stamps are from a sheet of fifty commemorative wildlife stamps also designed by Chuck Ripper. They were issued to depict the geographic and biological diversity of wildlife native to North America.

 © 1987 Reproduced with permission of the U.S. Postal Service

"BEAR" PLANTS

Bears have notably influenced the taxonomy of plants. The flora that have been named primarily because they are utilized by bears for food and healing include:

bearbane	bear grape
bearberry, alpine	bear grass
	bear huckleberry
bearberry, evergreen	bear-mat
	bear moss
bearberry, red	bear oak
bearberry honeysuckle	bear's breech
	bear's ear
bearbine	bear's foot
bearfoot	bear's garlic
bearroot	bear's head
bearwood	bear's paw
bear brush	bear's tail
bear cabbage	bear's toes
bear clover (mountain misery)	bear's weed
	bear's wort
	bear tongue
bear corn	

Bears in Heraldry

Heraldry is the profession or systematic use of an arrangement of charges or devices on a shield. Beginning with the crusades, bears have long been significant constituents of heraldry, including: the symbol of Mother Russia; the heraldic figures of Berne, Switzerland; Buskerud County, Norway; and Berlin, Germany; the arms of Lander in Germany; and the seal of California.

Swiss cantons favored the bear with heraldric honor in Berne (canton), Appenzell Ausser-Rhoden, and Appenzell Inner-Rhoden.

"The Swiss canton and town of St. Gallen are named for St. Gallus, who, according to legend, tamed a bear to help him build a house," notes Marvin Grosswirth in *The Heraldry Book*. "It is not surprising therefore, that a bear appears in the arms of St. Gallen."

There was, however, a problem with the use of bears in heraldry. In Switzerland, the male organ of the bear had to be painted bright red, or the heraldist would be mocked for use of a she-bear. Such mockery led to a war in 1579 between St. Gallen and the canton of Appenzell.

Bear Flags

The states of Alaska, California, and Missouri portray bears on their state flags. The Alaskan flag is the most mythical, but the California flag is the most famous, being the symbol of an armed revolt.

Alaska State Flag The Big Dipper (Ursa Major—the Great Bear).

Missouri State Flag Two grizzly bears, representing power and courage, support the state seal, which depicts a grizzly bear.

California State Flag: The Bear Flag Revolt. On June 14, 1846, a group of Americans in central California rose in an armed rebellion to secure California for the United States and prevent colonization by the British Empire. They seized the Sonoma garrison of Colonel Mariano Vallejo, the military commandant of the northern Mexican forces. The California Republic was formed as the Bear Flag was raised above the garrison at dawn the next day.

Original "state" flag
Courtesy California State Library

(Reproduction; the original Bear Flag was in the possession of the Society of California Pioneers, and was destroyed during the 1906 San Francisco earthquake and fire.)

The flag had been hastily made of material from a bolt of cotton. A star was placed on the flag in the tradition of Texas. A red stripe was added at the bottom and then William Todd, nephew of Mary Todd Lincoln (wife of Abraham Lincoln), drew a California grizzly bear. Todd was a poor artist and the bear better resembled a pig. The lettering "California Republic" was added below the "bear."

Within a few days Edward Kern, an artist and map drawer, was deployed by Captain John Fremont to Sonoma, where he made the flag's "pig" look like the appropriate and intended California grizzly bear. The bear adorning the present flag is from a painting by Charles Nahn and represents one of Grizzly Adams' bears.

Present state flag
Courtesy Old Sacramento Stamp Company, California

 Courtesy Northwest Territories, Transportation

Berne, its name a corruption of the German word *baren* (bears), was founded in AD 1191 by German Duke Berchtold von Zahringen at a location where he had previously hunted and killed numerous brown bears.

Berne (Bern) is the capital of both Switzerland and the canton of Berne. The image of the bear adorned the city's first coat of arms as early as 1224, and today the city landmark is the Zeitglockenturm (clock tower built in 1530) where a dancing bear, with other animals, appears as the clock strikes the hour. The "bear" is a decorative feature of the city, with figures on door knockers, fountains, gates, and lampposts, and bear images adorn pastries, candies, pipes, and toilet articles.

The Berne Bear Pits have been well known exhibits since 1441, and during the French Revolution bears were "captured" at the pits and taken to Paris as prisoners. Today, in Berne, twelve or more bears exist in a thirty-nine foot wide and 11-1/2 foot deep fortified pit next to the Nydegg Bridge along the Aare River.

An ancient statue of the Celtic bear goddess Dea Artio was unearthed in the city during 1832, another indication of the bear's longtime significance and association with Berne—"the city of the bear."

The Bear License Plate

A bear has historically and infrequently adorned the license plates of a few states and provinces, including the present Alaska plate, which displays the Alaska flag with the Big Dipper (Ursus major). However, the Northwest Territories has the most imposing "bear" license plate. First issued in 1970, the plate characterizes the polar bear.

Beartrap Saddle

The "Beartrap" saddle is exactly that—a trap for the rider. The saddle has a high upright pommel, and the cantle, also high and upright, often hooks back toward the rider's thighs. Considered by many as a killer, it is good for breaking horses due to the tightness that keeps the rider "in the saddle." If the horse falls, the rider is normally injured. A few beartrap saddles remain in use in the United States.

THE BEAR AS A STATE AND PROVINCIAL ANIMAL

Many states and provinces of North America have officially designated various wildlife as "state" or "provincial" animals, including the American black and the grizzly bear. The states of Mexico do not have "state animals."

State/Bear		State/Bear	
• Arkansas	black bear (considered the bear state in pioneer days; now the state of opportunity)	• Texas	black bear
• California	grizzly bear	• West Virginia	black bear
• Kentucky	black bear (considered the bear state)	• New Brunswick	black bear
• Montana	grizzly bear	• Nova Scotia	black bear
• New Mexico	black bear	• Quebec	black bear

Bears as Pets

Bears have been harbored as pets in many different settings for centuries. Winnie the Pooh was patterned after Winnipeg, the pet American black bear cub of Captain Harry Colebourn of the British military, who had the bear as a pet in his brigades' camp. Theodore Roosevelt wrote of pet black bears in Yellowstone National Park during 1903 (Paul Schullery: *Yellowstone Bear Tales*). "Bears are tamed until they will feed out of the hand, and will come at once if called. Not only have some of the soldiers and scouts tamed bears in this fashion, but occasionally a chambermaid or waiter girl at one of the hotels has thus developed a bear as a pet." Grizzly Adams may well have had the most famous "pet" bears (See Grizzly Adams, page 231).

"Pet" is defined as an object of affection, an animal kept for companionship. The long history of bears as pets has seen a variety of interpretations of the word—from playful companions inside the home to an animal caged outside for occasional viewing, a novelty to show guests. These interesting, delightful, and sometimes tragic relationships are normally quite short-lived. "A sun bear is easily tamed and makes an amusing household pet," notes Drimmer. "However, with age it is likely to grow bad tempered and become dangerous." This transition is also true with other bear species—they become undisciplined and dangerous as they grow older.

Bears are wild animals born with wild traits. Unlike dogs, cats, and possibly some birds that have been domesticated during centuries of conditioning, a pet bear is a captured, conditioned wild animal that is extremely dangerous. Too often, "pet" and "tamed" become synonymous, which is unfortunate. Tame may mean conditioned to food, and when the edible reward is unavailable, wildness replaces tameness. Early behavioral adjustments may have occurred, but the bear remains a "wild" animal.

Bears definitely are amusing, especially as cubs when they are small and many of their actions and antics are done with minimal strength and power. However, as they grow older, like humans they appear to become more irritable and, combined with enormous strength, are quite capable of serious damage and harm to whomever and whatever they direct this attitude and power. A playful pet is capable of serious harm if it only rolls its three hundred-plus pounds on a person.

When a bear is no longer wanted as a pet, it is nearly impossible to return to the wild, and is most often destroyed.

Around the world bears are captured as orphans, or taken from their mothers, and become pets. The sale of bears as pets in southeast Asia is a major business.

Though it may display wild traits and behavior, it has not been raised to fear humans, and possibly did not learn to locate wild foods while it was with its mother. Returned to the wild, it would most likely seek foods from human sources, resulting in major conflict with people. In Asia, bears are sold for their parts when they are no longer desired as pets.

There are positive "pet" stories. Montana author Ben Mikaelsen (*Rescue Josh McGuire*) has an American black bear (acquired from a research laboratory) he considers more a friend than a pet. However, Ben is quick to explain Buffy, all six hundred-plus pounds of him, is not tame and is dangerous, unintentionally or otherwise, and would without doubt kill anyone other than himself entering the bear's enclosure. He and Buffy have developed a trusting and total relationship—an understanding that includes closely followed rules has been established between the two. The bear responds to specific demands and Ben respects and meets the bear's requirements.

Ben identifies Buffy's displays of trust, honor, remorse, very high level of pride (not to be laughed at), and emotions similar to humans. The bear expresses loneliness, jealousy, and an indication of being grief stricken when left alone. Buffy actually laughs (using lips and chest). And he understands a sense of justice and is protective of his friend Ben.

Bears in Entertainment

Bears have long been utilized as performers in circuses, bear gardens, street acts, vaudeville, movies, and television.

The Romans considered bears a symbol of power and strength and included them in "circus" performances, with chariot races and warrior contests. The bears fought bloody battles with dogs, prisoners or gladiators, performing in large outdoor arenas such as the Circus Maximus, which held 150,000 spectators.

Roman Emperor Caligula, AD 37 to 41, one of the most depraved and monstrous rulers of all time, used four hundred bears during a single "games," and Emperor Gordian, AD 238, used one thousand bears in a single event. The fights were to the death with the men, alone or as a group, using bow and arrow, sword, or spear.

Competition was not always important, as there is evidence of a person with a spear facing six "snarling" bears, and prisoners were sometimes unarmed during the encounters. The disregard for fairness was at times reversed, as in the case of Emperor Commodus, AD 180 to 192, who shot one hundred bears with arrows in a single "event," while remaining out of their reach.

The bears performing in these activities were brown bears from the "known" world, and they often fought dogs, usually mastiffs often joined by Irish wolfhounds. Sometimes herds of bears fought packs of dogs. Roman circus battles also included polar bears that were placed in a flooded arena with seals.

Bearbaiting

Bear gardens, with bearbaiting, occurred as popular entertainment from the time of the Norman Conquest, AD 1066 into the eighteenth century, approximately 700 years.

The bear garden facilities consisted of a round building with three levels of seating (galleries) surrounding a fifty-five-foot diameter ring. The gardens eventually contained several rings, and private and public playhouses with a variety of performances, such as gorillas riding on horses' backs.

"The primary activity," explain Lavahn Hoh and William Rough in *Step Right Up!*, "involved chaining a large bear, or perhaps a feisty young bull, to a stake in the center of a ring (by their neck or hind leg) where large mastiff dogs were encouraged to attack it. The dogs were particularly courageous, and they would continue to attack over and over again until they were too weak from the loss of blood to stand. Bets were taken on how many dogs would be killed before the bear or bull died."

Bulls were "pitted" against bears. A German playbill announced: "And lastly, a furious and hungry bear, which has had no food for eight days, will attack a wild bull and eat him alive on the spot; and if he is unable to complete the task, a wolf will be in readiness to help him." (*Harper's New Monthly Magazine*, October, 1855.)

Bear gardens (bearbaiting) helped develop several major social innovations:

▲ they gathered an enormous variety of performers in one place

▲ they established the tradition of audiences closely seated around a central arena (ring)

▲ they reestablished the tradition of audiences gathering at a fixed location for entertainment

Similar to the Roman circus, the London bear gardens were not "family entertainment," not only due to the brutal and gory scene, but because the spectators were vulgar and unruly at best. According to Hoh and Rough, the bear gardens, "were extremely popular with Londoners struggling through the filth of daily existence."

The gardens were notorious for noise and riotous disorder. There was chaos, tumult, confusion and, in today's terms, disorderly conduct. Bearbaiting was also enjoyed by royalty, with one such event using thirteen bears for the entertainment of Queen Elizabeth I.

The gardens have been considered the beginning of the circus and "theaters," including the Elizabethan theater.

Street Bears and Vaudeville

Bears have entertained in the streets for centuries. They were trained and led around on chains for public amusement during the middle ages, AD 476 to AD 1453. In Egypt during the thirteenth century, marketplace entertainment displayed trained animals, including bears that "danced" or went to sleep when instructed.

Bears were utilized to amuse nobility and attract audiences to traveling musicians and jugglers. During the eighteenth and nineteenth centuries, itinerant musicians wandered throughout the countries of Eurasia, playing a musical instrument while exhibiting bears dressed in costumes. Brown bears from the Pyrenees Mountains were famous dancing performers. Vaudeville acts were using bears in the United States at the end of the nineteenth century.

Today's wandering musicians in Eurasia continue to use bears. Bears are associated with beggars, traveling shows, and street merchants. Wrestling matches are held between humans and bears, and they play basketball. In India, bears that ride bicycles and sit up are utilized by wandering beggars. Some Asian gypsies and other itinerant entertainers wander with dancing bears that are seldom trained, but forced by torture to perform.

A bear has been on a radio program in the United States, where it exchanged grunts with a comedian.

These performing bears are normally obtained as cubs to be trained at an early age. Bear schools (academies) have existed for decades; there, these performers learn tricks and are trained to "act."

The brown and Asiatic black bears are trained for a variety of "performances," while the sloth bear is often used as a dancing bear. The American black bear is used in United States exhibitions. The bears are usually muzzled while performing and are often declawed.

Bear and Bull Fights

Fights pitting a bear against a bull occured in Calif between 1816 and the early 1880s. These extremely popular fights were festive occasions normally reserved for holidays, Sundays, and special religious days, and were widely advertised with posters. The idea for these staged fights may have originated as ranchers and vaqueros observed violent fights out on the range between wild bulls and grizzly bears.

The fights were held in arenas, where spectators could witness the entire battle between the large California grizzly bear and the Spanish bull, which had no fear, retreated from no enemy, and appeared to be born to fight.

The combatants were tied together, with a cord of approximately twenty yards in length, the front hoof of the bull to the rear paw of the bear. The bull would charge, attempting to gore the bear, and the grizzly would counter with paws and teeth. The grizzly often grasped the bull's snout with its teeth and would be in control and could break the bull's neck. "If the bull won, triumph usually came early in the struggle," describe Tracy Storer and Lloyd Tevis in *California Grizzly*, "only with full fresh strength could he plunge his long, curving horns into the bear's body, toss his adversary high in the air, and then gore him to death as the bear lay prostrate on the ground."

The fights were viscious with the bear the normal victor, but both fighters generally were injured, and the victor occasionally later died.

Fights between Bears and Lions

Storer and Tevis relate the story of a staged mountain lion/grizzly bear fight in California in 1865. "The lion, which seemed to have no fear, leaped onto the bear's back and while clinging there and facing forward scratched the grizzly's eyes and nose with its claws. The bear repeatedly rolled over onto the ground to rid himself of his adversary; but as soon as the bear was upright, the cat would leap onto his back again. This agility finally decided the struggle in favor of the lion."

A fight was staged in Monterrey, Mexico between a large California grizzly bear and a "man-killing" African lion. The grizzly bear, according to Storer and Tevis, handled the African king as a cat would a rat. The conflict was over so quickly that the spectators hardly realized how it was accomplished.

Circus Bears

The modern circus with bears originated in England during the mid- to late 1700s. Though bears appear to have given the early impetus to circus-type acts, they were "late" arriving in the more modern circus.

"A bear had been introduced into plays at Astley's (Philip) in 1822," according to George Speaight in *A History of the Circus*, "but it proved incapable of performing the feats intended for it. Another appeared at Usher's benefit in 1837, but it was not until nearly the end of the century that there was much development in the training of these genial-looking but dangerous and untrustworthy animals."

CIRCUS BEARS—A CHRONOLOGY

1888	Polar bears perform with Krone in Germany
1889	A bear rides a horse, leaps through a balloon, plays with an English mastiff (a reversal from the Elizabethan bear gardens)
1890	Permane's Siberian bears were at a table and drink out of bottles, walk on a globe, and swing on a swing. "Bears have a good sense of balance," notes Speaight
1904	Polar bears perform in England as part of Wombell's menagerie
1909	Seventy polar bears, trained by Hagenbeck, perform at the London Hippodrome
1911	The Hagenbeck bears perform at the Blackpool Tower Circus, where 40 polar bears are in the water occupying a ring only 42 feet in diameter.

Disposition, Temperament and Training of Circus Bears   Circus bears of today most commonly consist of Siberian and European (Syrian) brown bears, polar bears, and Asiatic and American black bears. Some giant pandas and sloth bears are also performing. The polar bear is considered the most "eye-catching," while Syrian brown bears are the quickest to learn and the cleverest.

The Asiatic black bears are the comedians of the performing bears. They appear to appreciate applause and will intentionally move into their prescribed position late to attain laughter and attention.

Bears are ideal for training because of their personalities. They have human-like mannerisms, are highly intelligent and curious, and will develop a very close rapport with their trainer. Physically they have excellent balance and eye/paw

BARNUM & BAILEY GREATEST SHOW ON EARTH

PALLENBERG
MOST FAMOUS OF ALL ANIMAL TRAINERS

BEARS THAT DANCE SKATE, PLAY MUSICAL INSTRUMENTS, WALK THE TIGHT-ROPE, RIDE BICYCLES AND ARE ACTUAL COMIC ACTORS.

Circus World Museum, Baraboo, Wisconsin (Reproduced by permission of Ringling Brothers—Barnum & Bailey Combined Shows, Inc.)

coordination. However, their most important trait in being highly responsive to training and learning specific functions may be that they enjoy playing.

David Jamieson and Sandy Davidson, in *The Colorful World of the Circus*, relate a wonderful example of rapport. "One evening when James Clubb was presenting his brown bears on Chipperfield's circus, the generator failed and the lights went out, leaving the ring in pitch darkness. One bear immediately rushed to James and hugged him. To begin with, he thought he was being attacked but then he noticed the bear was shaking with fright and he realized she had run to her trainer for reassurance."

Circus bear handlers have found that bears should never be taken for granted during training and performance. According to Hoh, bears "look much more harmless and cuddly than they really are." They show no emotion or facial expressions, are not affectionate, will hold a grudge, and will attack out of instinct with no warning or obvious provocation. They must perform in cages, on leads, or muzzled, and be handled by rewards, loving care, and infinite patience. The bears must recognize the trainer as the master. Performances are better if their required action has meaning to them, is a "natural" role, not a new and difficult skill.

There is an ominous saying in the circus world, according to Hoh, "that bear trainers never retire." The "armless wonder" Jack Hubert lost one arm to a bear and the other to a lion; Chubby Guilfoyle was maimed by his bears. One trainer suffered a seriously broken leg when a bear fell on him. Polar bears, though the most versatile, are also the most dangerous of circus bears. Trainer Captain Jack Bonavita (né John F. Gentner) was killed in 1917 while working with a group of polar bears.

Through the years nearly all trainers have found that reward, not punishment, is the only effective way to train a bear for performance. Gentle methods of wild animal training are favored over the threat.

Mixed Animal Acts   Bears have been occasionally mixed with other animals in various acts, though these performances are difficult and extremely dangerous. A bear's expression is poorly developed, therefore there is suspicion and a lack of rapport between the bears and other animals.

Herman Weedon, in 1903, mixed two lionesses, a tiger, a leopard, a puma, two striped hyenas, a polar bear, a brown bear, and two white mastiff dogs.

Alfred Court, in the Blackpool Tower Circus during the 1930s, mixed eight lions, three polar bears, two black bears, two leopards, two tigers, and a jaguar.

One circus act, Peace in the Jungle, had eighteen different species of animals, including bears, in a single ring. Another act placed lions, tigers, leopards, pumas, jaguars, cougars, panthers, hyenas, and brown and polar bears peacefully together in the ring.

BEAR ACTS

Historically, bear performances have included:

- Riding a bicycle

- Pulling a rickshaw or wagon with another bear on the seat

- Standing on and rolling a ball

- Foot-juggling a burning pole

- *Walking on its fore-feet round the ring*
- *Performing a handstand on another bear's back*
- *Balancing on the rola bola*
- *Dancing the* pas de quatre *from Swan Lake*
- *Sitting in a chair at a table*
- *Pedaling a small car*
- *Roller skating*
- *Skipping rope*
- *Riding motorcycles*
- *Balancing on a tightrope*
- *Playing the harmonica*
- *Wrestling with each other*
- *Playing the concertina (accordian)*
- *Somersaulting*
- *Eating with knife and fork*
- *Dunking a basketball*
- *Pushing a cart with another bear as a passenger*
- *Boxing with a human*

- *Marching to band music*
- *Performing handstands on wooden tubs*
- *Making a hoop with their body and tumbling*
- *Juggling items*
- *Sliding down slide into water*
- *Rolling*
- *Diving*
- *Riding horseback*
- *Walking bipedal on two tightropes*
- *Wrestling with people*
- *Dancing in a set with a woman*
- *Falling dead when "shot"*
- *Simulating the pursuit of an enemy*
- *Playing the drums*
- *Going through the manual exercise of a soldier with a musket*
- *Ringing bells*

Bear Troupes and Handlers Bear acts are relatively rare today, with circuses generally not owning their own acts. Troupes and handlers work under contracts with the various circuses.

Troupes and handlers no longer performing include:

- Charlie Allen
- The Bauers on the Tarzan Zerbini Circus
- Clyde Beatty
- Beljakow Bears
- Eloise Berchtold
- The Berouseks on the Ringling Red Unit

- George Berrota, Sr.
- Captain Jack Bonavita
- Jimmy Chipperfield
- James Clubb
- Alfred Court
- Vladimir Filatov

- John C. "Chubby" Guilfoyle
- Karl Hagenbeck
- Wilhelm Hagenbeck Troupe
- Hengler
- Jack Hubert
- Terrell Jacobs

- Kasseev

- Benta Klauser

- Walter Klauser Bear Troupe, Ringling Brothers and Barnum and Bailey Circus

- Wally Knotten

- The Lilovs with their Siberians on the Ringling Blue Unit

- Emil and Catherine Pallenberg

- Permane's Siberian Bear

- Bucky Steele

- The Steeples on the Great American Circus

- Herman Weedon

- The Weldes

- Bill Yates

Troups and handlers presently performing include:

- Jackie Althoff

- William Althoff

- Ursula Boettcher, State Circus of East Germany; considered the most celebrated polar bear troup of the present; kisses and feeds bears meat by hand

- Bill Burgess (wrestling bears)

- Jim and Teppa Hall (Castle Bears)

- Rex and Ingrid Horton, Horton's Performing Bears

- Lilov Family Russian Bears

- Renee (George Carden)

- David Rickman

- Albert Rix

- Jeanette Rix (polar bears)

- Dan Roberts (wrestling bears)

- Bobby Steele, Jr., Steele's Performing Bears

- Eddie Steeples

- Johnny and Monica Welde

BODYGUARD BEARS

Roman Emperor Valentinian I (AD 321 to 375; became emperor in AD 364) used two quite large brown bears in the capacity of "bodyguards," chaining them nightly in front of his sleeping chamber. His bodyguards were apparently effective at their home post, as the emperor died during a battle in Moravia.

Bears in the Movies

Movies with a bear as the "star" have been relatively few. Many short animated cartoons have highlighted bears, but little more than a dozen full-length films featuring a bear have been in the nation's movie theaters.

THE SONG OF THE SOUTH, 1947, Disney, animated; featured Brer Bear

THE TWO LITTLE BEARS, 1961

HEY THERE, IT'S YOGI BEAR, 1964, animated

NIGHT OF THE GRIZZLY, 1966

BEAR COUNTRY, Walt Disney

THE JUNGLE BOOK, 1967, Disney, animated; featured Baloo, the only bear to sing an Oscar-nominated song, "Bare Necessities"—vocalist, Phil Harris; in Rudyard Kipling's book, *Jungle Tales*, Baloo is a sloth bear

GENTLE GIANT, 1967; black bear; from novel, *Gentle Ben*

KING OF THE GRIZZLIES, 1970, Disney

MAN IN THE WILDERNESS, 1971

THE BEARS AND I, 1974, Disney

GRIZZLY, 1976

THE LIFE AND TIMES OF GRIZZLY ADAMS, 1976

DAY OF THE ANIMALS, 1977

PROPHECY, 1979; a mutant animal, most likely a bear

THE BEAR, 1989

Bears in Zoos

Bears were the first zoo animals, probably due to being the easiest to keep. The Queen of Egypt, Hatshepsut, had a facility in 1500 BC that possibly could be considered the earliest zoo. Early Chinese rulers also had zoos, and King Ptolemy II of Egypt (285 to 246 BC) had a polar bear in a private zoo in Alexandria.

Menageries—small traveling exhibits—became popular and were the forerunner of the present-day zoo. The first United States zoo was established in Philadelphia during 1859, with a polar bear as the first North American "zoo bear."

The sources of today's zoo and wildlife park bears are those that are problems and must be removed from conflicts with people, bred and raised in zoos, or bears captured specifically—legally and illegally—for sale to zoos. Zoos have paid thousands of dollars for bears, and in one purchase over $28,000 was paid for a giant panda.

Zoos serve as laboratories, and much knowledge of certain species has been learned only from zoo animals. Zoos offer visitors an opportunity for a better understanding of bears. The Denver Zoo describes a visit to the zoo as "serious fun."

Humans often, in their anthropomorphic manner, interpret a zoo bear's actions to be unhappiness. However, zoologists claim zoo bears are "happier" than wild bears. Life is without question easier and many bears, having been born in captivity, know no other life than the zoo or wildlife park. Present-day zoos are improving the "environment" for bears, with caves, streams, trees, and boulders, and wildlife parks offer larger, more diverse, and interesting habitats. Bears are offered an opportunity for enrichment. Food is hidden and they must "work" for it. There is "furniture" (trees, rocks, logs, pools, areas to dig) for their exploration and play. They have objects to handle.

Children, adults, and families visiting the Denver Zoo's Asiatic black bears
© *Gary Brown*

Zoo Food

Foods are not what would be considered "wild," but are carefully regulated for the nutrition of the zoo bear. "Omnivore" food is specifically prepared by dietitians—vegetables, chicken and other meat, fruits, vitamins, and minerals. Bears are fed one to four times daily, usually with a main evening meal and "snacks" during the day. In wildlife parks, the morning snack is often hidden outside where they must search as if in the wild.

DAILY CALORIE REQUIREMENT

▲ American black bear, juvenile, 155 pounds: 3,876

▲ Grizzly bear, adult, 704 pounds: 10,592

▲ Grizzly bear, adult, 374 pounds 6,591

▲ Grizzly bear, cub, 110 pounds 4,611

The daily diet for American black bears and grizzly bears consists of:

- ▲ Omnivore chow (UNIZOO, commercially prepared)
- ▲ Dry dog food (commercially prepared)
- ▲ Apples
- ▲ Carrots
- ▲ Bread, white
- ▲ Chicken heads, fresh
- ▲ Eggs, hard boiled
- ▲ Fish, substituted for dog food

Zoo bears often develop "cage fat," and are fatter and heavier than wild bears. A thirty-month-old giant panda at a zoo weighed 176 pounds, while wild thirty to thirty-three-month-olds are 110 to 121 pounds.

Bear "habitats" are cleaned daily, and the bears have regular preventive and responsive veterinarian health care. The cost of feeding and maintaining a bear for a year is $500 to $1,000. Security must be maintained at the bear facilities to protect the bears, visitors, and bear keepers. The escape of a bear *must* be prevented. Feeding and habitat maintenance is accomplished with the bears in auxiliary compounds, as bear keepers must be continually alert to avoid conflicts, injury, or death. Visitors must be prevented from feeding bears or gaining access to the bear habitat. Recently an intoxicated youth, having sneaked into a New York zoo during the night, entered a polar bear area and was killed by the bears. The polar bear is considered by many zoo keepers as the most dangerous zoo bear. (The Denver Zoo staff considers elephants and leopards the most dangerous "zoo" animals.)

Zoos with Bears

The table information is from the International Species Information System (as of July 31, 1991), Apple Valley, Minnesota, and includes only zoos participating in the system (there are other zoos with bears). Some zoos list bears by subspecies: they are grouped below by species, except for grizzly, brown, and Kodiak bears. Bears are transferred between zoos by loan and sale, and cubs are occasionally born, so numbers and species often change. Unknowns are cubs with sex not yet identified.

Bears in Zoos

	Male	Female	Unknown
Australia			
ADELAIDE ZOOLOGICAL GARDENS			
• polar	1	1	—
MELBOURNE ZOOLOGICAL GARDENS (Parkville, Victoria)			
• brown	2	1	—
SYDNEY'S TARONGA ZOO			
• Kodiak	1	2	—
• American black	2	—	—
British Isles			
JERSEY WILDLIFE PRESERVATION TRUST (Jersey, Channel Islands)			
• spectacled	3	1	—
Canada			
CALGARY ZOO (Alberta)			
• American black	1	3	—
• Asiatic black	1	1	—
• grizzly	1	3	—
• polar	—	3	—
• spectacled	2	1	—
GRANDBY ZOO (Quebec)			
• Asiatic black	—	2	—
• brown	1	1	—
• grizzly	—	1	—
• polar	1	1	—
METROPOLITAN TORONTO ZOO (Ontario)			
• grizzly	1	1	—
• polar	1	2	—
QUEBEC-JARDIN ZOOLOGIQUE (Charlesbourg, Quebec)			
• American black	3	4	—
• grizzly	1	2	—
• Kodiak	—	1	—
• polar	1	3	—
ST. FELICIEN ZOO (Quebec)			
• American black	9	4	1
STANLEY PARK ZOO (Vancouver, British Columbia)			
• polar	1	1	—
China			
TAIPEI ZOO (Taiwan)			
• sun	—	1	—
Colombia			
CALI ZOOLOGICAL GARDEN			
• American black	—	2	—
• Asiatic black	2	2	—
• grizzly	—	1	—
• spectacled	1	1	—

	Male	Female	Unknown
MEDELLIN-PARQUE ZOOLOGICAL SANTE FE (Medellin)			
• spectacled	3	2	—
Commonwealth (Former Soviet Union)			
MOSKOVSKII ZOOLOGICHESKI PARK (Moscow)			
• brown	2	1	—
• polar	1	1	—
• spectacled	2	3	—
Czechoslovakia			
PRAGUE ZOO			
• Kodiak	—	1	—
• polar	1	1	—
Denmark			
AALBORG ZOO			
• Asiatic black	1	2	—
• brown	1	2	5
• polar	1	3	—
COPENHAGEN ZOOLOGISK HAVE			
• Asiatic black	1	1	2
• brown	2	4	—
• polar	1	2	—
Finland			
HELSINKI ZOO			
• brown	1	3	—
• Kodiak	2	—	—
• sun	—	1	—
France			
VINCENNES-PARC ZOOLOGIQUE DE PARIS			
• Asiatic black	2	2	2
• brown	1	—	—
• giant panda	1	—	—
• polar	1	1	—
• spectacled	1	—	—
• sun	1	1	—
LA PALMYRE ZOO (Royan)			
• polar	1	2	—
MULHOUSE ZOOLOGIQUE BOTANIQUE PARC			
• brown	1	2	—
• polar	1	2	—
MENAGERIE DU JARDIN DES PLANTES (Paris)			
• brown	1	1	—
TOUROPARC-ROMANECHE (Thorins)			
• sun	1	2	—

Bears in Zoos

	Male	Female	Unknown
Germany			
AUGSBURG ZOOLOGISCHER GARTEN			
• Asiatic black	1	1	2
• brown	2	4	—
DUISBURG ZOO			
• Kodiak	1	2	—
• polar	1	4	—
FRANKFURT ZOOLOGISCHER GARTEN			
• spectacled	1	1	—
HANNOVER ZOOLOGICAL GARTEN			
• American black	1	2	—
• brown	1	2	—
• polar	1	2	—
HELLABRUNN MUNCHENER TIERPARK (Munchen)			
• brown	1	2	—
• polar	1	4	—
KARLSRUHE ZOOLGISCHER GARTEN			
• brown	2	1	—
• polar	1	6	—
KOLN ZOO			
• Asiatic	2	2	—
• spectacled	2	2	1
• sun	1	2	—
SAARBRUCKEN ZOOLOGICAL GARDEN			
• sun	1	1	—
STUTTGART-WILHELMA ZOO			
• brown	1	1	—
• polar	2	2	—
India			
KANPUR ZOOLOGICAL PARK (Azadnagar, Kanpur)			
• Asiatic black	2	1	—
• sloth	1	1	—
MYSORE ZOO (Karnataka, South India)			
• Asiatic black	1	1	—
• sloth	2	4	—
SHRI SAYAJI BAUG ZOO (Baroda, Gujarat)			
• Asiatic black	1	3	—
Ireland			
BELFAST ZOOLOGICAL GARDENS			
• brown	2	1	—
• polar	1	2	—
• spectacled	2	1	—
Israel			
JERUSALEM BIBLICAL ZOOLOGICAL GARDENS (Romena)			
• brown	2	1	—

	Male	Female	Unknown
TEL-AVIV/RAMAT GAN ZOOLOGICAL CENTER (Ramat Gan)			
• Asiatic black	1	3	—
• brown	1	1	—
Mexico			
GUADALAJARA ZOO			
• American black	1	1	—
• sloth	1	1	—
New Zealand			
AUCKLAND ZOOLOGICAL PARK			
• American black	—	1	—
• polar	1	1	—
WELLINGTON ZOOLOGICAL GARDENS			
• American black	1	—	—
Poland			
WARSZAWA-MIEJSKI OGROD ZOOLOGICZNY (Warsaw)			
• Asiatic black	2	1	—
• brown	3	3	—
• polar	2	2	—
• sloth	1	1	—
Puerto Rico			
MAYAQUEZ ZOOLOGICAL GARDENS			
• Asiatic black	2	—	—
• brown	1	—	—
• sun	1	2	—
Scotland			
EDINBURGH ZOO-SCOTTISH NATIONAL ZOO			
• polar	1	1	—
GLASGOW ZOO			
• Asiatic black	1	4	—
South Africa			
PRETORIA NATIONAL ZOO GARDENS			
• Asiatic black	1	1	2
• brown	1	2	—
Spain			
BARCELONA ZOO			
• American black	1	1	—
• Asiatic black	1	1	—
• brown	2	4	—
• Kodiak	1	—	—
• polar	1	1	—
MADRID-ZOO DE LA CASA DE CAMPO			
• American black	—	2	—
• Asiatic black	—	1	—
• brown	5	3	—
• giant panda	2	—	—

Bears in Zoos

	Male	Female	Unknown
• polar	—	2	—
• sun	—	2	—

Switzerland
ZURICH ZOOLOGISCHER GARTEN

	Male	Female	Unknown
• polar	1	2	—
• spectacled	1	4	—

The Netherlands
AMERSFOORT DIERENPARK

	Male	Female	Unknown
• Asiatic black	—	2	—

AMSTERDAM-ARTIS ZOO

	Male	Female	Unknown
• sloth	2	2	—

BURGER'S ZOO EN SAFARI (Arnhem)

	Male	Female	Unknown
• polar	2	1	—

OUWEHAND ZOO (Rhenen)

	Male	Female	Unknown
• polar	1	1	—

ROTTERDAM ZOO

	Male	Female	Unknown
• polar	—	1	5

SAFARIPARK BEEKSE BERGEN (Hilvarenbeek)

	Male	Female	Unknown
• sun	1	3	—

United Kingdom
BRISTOL, CLIFTON, WEST ZOOLOGICAL SOCIETY

	Male	Female	Unknown
• polar	2	1	—

CHESTER ZOO (Cheshire)

	Male	Female	Unknown
• brown	1	1	—
• polar	—	1	—

COLCHESTER ZOO

	Male	Female	Unknown
• Asiatic black	1	1	—
• brown	—	1	—

DUDLEY & WEST MIDLANDS ZOOLOGICAL SOCIETY LTD.

	Male	Female	Unknown
• Asiatic black	1	5	—

WELSH MOUNTAIN ZOO (Colwyn Bay, Clwyd-North Wales)

	Male	Female	Unknown
• brown	1	1	—

WHIPSNADE ZOOLOGICAL PARK (London)

	Male	Female	Unknown
• brown	1	3	2

UNITED STATES

Alabama
BIRMINGHAM ZOO

	Male	Female	Unknown
• Asiatic black	1	2	—
• grizzly	—	2	1
• polar	—	2	—

MONTGOMERY ZOO

	Male	Female	Unknown
• American black	3	2	—

Arizona
REID PARK ZOO (Tucson)

	Male	Female	Unknown
• polar	1	2	—
• sun	1	2	—

ARIZONA-SONORA DESERT MUSEUM

	Male	Female	Unknown
• American black	1	1	—

Arkansas
LITTLE ROCK ZOOLOGICAL GARDENS

	Male	Female	Unknown
• Asiatic black	1	3	—
• polar	1	1	—
• sloth	2	2	—
• sun	1	2	—

California
CHAFFEE ZOOLOGICAL GARDENS

	Male	Female	Unknown
• grizzly	1	1	—
• sun	1	1	—

CHARLES PADDOCK ZOO (Atascadero)

	Male	Female	Unknown
• Asiatic black	—	1	—
• sun	—	1	—

FOLSOM CITY ZOO

	Male	Female	Unknown
• American black	1	1	—

HAPPY HOLLOW ZOO (San Jose)

	Male	Female	Unknown
• American black	1	—	—

LOS ANGELES ZOO

	Male	Female	Unknown
• polar	1	1	—
• sloth	1	1	—
• spectacled	2	2	—

MICKE GROVE ZOOLOGICAL GARDENS (Lodi)

	Male	Female	Unknown
• American black	1	1	—
• polar	—	1	—

MOORPARK COLLEGE (Exotic Animal Program)

	Male	Female	Unknown
• American black	—	2	—

OAKLAND ZOO IN KNOWLAND PARK

	Male	Female	Unknown
• sun	—	2	—

SACRAMENTO ZOO

	Male	Female	Unknown
• grizzly	1	—	—
• polar	1	1	—
• sloth	1	1	—

SAN DIEGO ZOOLOGICAL GARDEN

	Male	Female	Unknown
• brown	4	3	4
• polar	1	2	—
• sloth	1	3	—
• spectacled	2	1	—
• sun	4	4	—

SAN FRANCISCO ZOOLOGICAL GARDENS

	Male	Female	Unknown
• Kodiak	3	—	—

Bears in Zoos

	Male	Female	Unknown
• polar	1	3	—
• spectacled	1	1	—
• sun	1	1	—
SEQUOIA PARK ZOO (Eureka)			
• American black	—	2	—

Colorado
CHEYENNE MOUNTAIN
ZOOLOGICAL PARK
(Colorado Springs)

	Male	Female	Unknown
• Kodiak	1	1	—
• polar	1	—	—
DENVER ZOOLOGICAL GARDENS			
• Asiatic black	1	2	—
• grizzly	1	2	—
• polar	3	5	—
PUEBLO ZOO			
• sun	—	1	—

Connecticut
BEARDSLEY ZOOLOGICAL
GARDENS (Bridgeport)

	Male	Female	Unknown
• American black	1	1	—

Delaware
BRANDYWINE ZOO
(Wilmington)

	Male	Female	Unknown
• American black	1	—	—

District of Columbia
NATIONAL ZOOLOGICAL PARK

	Male	Female	Unknown
• giant panda	1	1	—
• Kodiak	—	1	—
• sloth	1	1	1
• spectacled	1	2	—

Florida
CENTRAL FLORIDA
ZOOLOGICAL PARK
(Lake Monroe)

	Male	Female	Unknown
• American black	—	2	—
DREHER PARK ZOO (West Palm Beach)			
• American black	—	1	—
• sun	1	1	—
FLORIDA STATE UNIVERSITY (Tallahassee)			
• American black	2	1	—
LOWRY PARK ZOOLOGICAL GARDEN (Tampa)			
• American black	1	1	—
• sloth	1	2	—
MIAMI METROZOO			
• Asiatic black	1	1	—

	Male	Female	Unknown
• sloth	1	1	—
• sun	1	3	—

Georgia
CHEHAW WILD ANIMAL PARK
(Albany)

	Male	Female	Unknown
• American black	1	3	—
ZOO ATLANTA			
• Asiatic black	1	—	—
• Kodiak	1	—	—
• polar	—	1	—

Hawaii
HONOLULU ZOO

	Male	Female	Unknown
• sun	1	3	—

Idaho
ROSS PARK ZOO
(Pocatello)

	Male	Female	Unknown
• American black	2	2	—
• grizzly	1	2	—

Illinois
CHICAGO ZOOLOGICAL PARK
(Brookfield)

	Male	Female	Unknown
• Kodiak	3	—	—
• polar	2	1	—
• sloth	1	1	—
• spectacled	2	1	—
HENSON ROBINSON ZOO (Springfield)			
• Asiatic black	1	1	—
LINCOLN PARK ZOOLOGICAL GARDENS (Chicago)			
• polar	1	1	—
• spectacled	2	3	—
NIABI ZOO (Coal Valley)			
• American black	1	—	—

Indiana
INDIANAPOLIS ZOO

	Male	Female	Unknown
• Kodiak	2	—	—
• polar	2	2	—
MESKER PARK ZOO (Evansville)			
• American black	1	1	—
POTAWATOMI ZOO (South Bend)			
• Asiatic black	1	1	—
• brown	1	1	—

Kansas
LEE RICHARDSON ZOO
(Garden City)

	Male	Female	Unknown
• Asiatic black	1	1	—
RALPH MITCHELL ZOO (Independence)			
• American black	2	1	—
• sun	1	1	—

Bears in Zoos

	Male	Female	Unknown
SEDGWICK COUNTY ZOOLOGICAL & BOTANICAL GARDEN (Wichita)			
• spectacled	1	1	—
SUNSET ZOO (Manhattan)			
• grizzly	1	—	—
• sloth	2	—	—
• spectacled	1	—	—
Kentucky			
LOUISVILLE ZOOLOGICAL GARDEN			
• American black	1	—	—
• polar	1	2	—
Louisiana			
AUDUBON PARK ZOOLOGICAL GARDEN			
• American black	1	1	—
• sun	1	2	1
GREATER BATON ROUGE ZOO (Baker)			
• Asiatic black	1	3	—
• brown	3	3	—
• polar	1	1	—
Maryland			
BALTIMORE ZOO			
• American black	1	1	—
• Kodiak	1	1	—
• polar	1	1	—
• sloth	—	1	—
• spectacled	1	1	—
• sun	1	1	—
CATOCTIN MOUNTAIN ZOOLOGICAL PARK (Thurmont)			
• grizzly	1	—	—
• sun	—	1	—
SALISBURY ZOOLOGICAL PARK			
• spectacled	1	1	—
Massachusetts			
BOSTON METROPARKS ZOOS			
• polar	1	—	—
NEW ENGLAND SCIENCE CENTER (Worcester)			
• polar	—	2	—
Michigan			
DETROIT ZOOLOGICAL GARDENS			
• grizzly	1	1	—
• polar	2	8	—
• spectacled	1	1	—

	Male	Female	Unknown
POTTER PARK ZOOLOGICAL GARDENS (Lansing)			
• American black	1	—	—
Minnesota			
JOHN BALL ZOOLOGICAL GARDENS (Grand Rapids)			
• Asiatic black	1	1	—
LAKE SUPERIOR ZOOLOGICAL GARDENS (Duluth)			
• Kodiak	1	1	—
• polar	1	1	—
MINNESOTA ZOOLOGICAL GARDEN (Apple Valley)			
• sloth	1	1	—
ST. PAUL'S COMO ZOO			
• grizzly	1	—	—
• Kodiak	1	1	—
• polar	1	1	—
Mississippi			
JACKSON ZOOLOGICAL PARK			
• grizzly	1	1	—
• sloth	1	1	—
• sun	1	2	—
Missouri			
DICKERSON PARK ZOO (Springfield)			
• American black	1	2	—
• Asiatic black	1	1	—
ST. LOUIS ZOOLOGICAL PARK			
• American black	1	3	—
• brown	1	2	—
• grizzly	2	—	—
• polar	1	2	—
• sloth	1	1	2
• spectacled	1	1	—
• sun	1	1	—
Nebraska			
FOLSOM CHILDRENS ZOO (Lincoln)			
• spectacled	1	1	—
• sun	1	—	—
GRAND ISLE HERITAGE ZOO (Grand Island)			
• sun	—	1	—
OMAHA'S HENRY DOORLY ZOO			
• grizzly	—	2	—
• polar	2	3	—
• sun	2	1	—

Bears in Zoos

	Male	Female	Unknown
New Jersey			
CAPE MAY PARK ZOO	1	2	—
• American black			
COHANZICK ZOO			
(Bridgeton)			
• American black	—	1	—
New Mexico			
RIO GRANDE ZOOLOGICAL			
PARK (Albuquerque)			
• polar	1	2	—
New York			
BUFFALO ZOOLOGICAL			
GARDENS			
• Kodiak	1	1	—
• polar	4	2	—
• spectacled	3	1	1
BURNET PARK ZOO			
(Syracuse)			
• grizzly	1	1	—
• brown	1	1	—
CENTRAL PARK ZOO			
(New York)			
• polar	1	2	—
NEW YORK ZOOLOGICAL			
PARK (Bronx)			
• Kodiak	2	2	—
• polar	2	1	—
ROSS PARK ZOO			
(Binghamton)			
• spectacled	1	1	—
SENECA PARK ZOO			
(Rochester)			
• polar	1	1	—
UTICA ZOO			
• grizzly	1	1	—
North Carolina			
CARNIVORE PRESERVATION			
TRUST (Pittsboro)			
• sun	—	1	—
North Dakota			
DAKOTA ZOO (Bismarck)			
• American black	1	1	—
• brown	1	1	—
• Kodiak	—	1	—
ROOSEVELT PARK ZOO			
(Minot)			
• Kodiak	1	2	—
Ohio			
CINCINNATI ZOO &			
BOTANICAL GARDEN			
• polar	2	1	—
• sloth	1	1	—
• spectacled	1	1	3

	Male	Female	Unknown
CLEVELAND METROPARKS			
ZOOLOGICAL PARK			
• brown	1	—	—
• grizzly	3	—	—
• Kodiak	—	2	—
• polar	2	2	—
• sloth	—	1	1
• spectacled	1	2	—
• sun	—	1	—
COLUMBUS ZOOLOGICAL			
GARDENS (Powell)			
• American black	1	1	—
• grizzly	2	1	—
• polar	1	2	—
TOLEDO ZOOLOGICAL			
GARDENS			
• American black	1	1	—
• Asiatic black	1	2	—
• polar	1	1	2
Oklahoma			
OKLAHOMA CITY ZOOLOGICAL			
PARK			
• grizzly	1	1	—
• sloth	1	3	2
• spectacled	2	1	—
TULSA ZOOLOGICAL PARK			
• American black	1	—	—
• Kodiak	1	1	—
• polar	1	2	—
• spectacled	1	1	—
Oregon			
WASHINGTON PARK ZOO			
(Portland)			
• American black	—	3	—
• Asiatic black	1	1	—
• grizzly	2	—	—
• Kodiak	—	2	—
• polar	2	2	—
• spectacled	—	2	—
• sun	1	1	—
WILDLIFE SAFARI, INC.			
(Winston)			
• American black	4	3	—
• brown	3	2	—
Pennsylvania			
ERIE ZOOLOGICAL GARDENS			
• Kodiak	1	1	—
• polar	1	1	—
PHILADELPHIA ZOOLOGICAL			
GARDENS			
• polar	—	2	—
• sloth	1	—	—
• spectacled	1	—	—

Bears in Zoos

	Male	Female	Unknown
PITTSBURGH ZOO			
• American black	1	1	—
• Kodiak	1	2	—
• polar	—	3	—
• sun	—	1	—
ZOOAMERICA NORTH AMERICAN WILDLIFE PARK (Hershey)			
• American black	1	1	—

Rhode Island
	Male	Female	Unknown
ROGER WILLIAMS PARK ZOO (Providence)			
• polar	1	1	—

South Carolina
	Male	Female	Unknown
RIVERBANKS ZOOLOGICAL PARK (Columbia)			
• polar	1	1	—
• spectacled	3	1	—

South Dakota
	Male	Female	Unknown
GREAT PLAINS ZOO (Sioux Falls)			
• grizzly	1	1	—

Tennessee
	Male	Female	Unknown
GRASSMERE WILDLIFE PARK (Nashville)			
• American black	1	1	—
KNOXVILLE ZOOLOGICAL PARK			
• American black	1	2	—
• polar	1	3	—
MEMPHIS ZOOLOGICAL GARDEN & AQUARIUM			
• grizzly	—	3	—
• polar	1	2	—
• spectacled	1	—	—
• sun	1	2	—

Texas
	Male	Female	Unknown
ABILENE ZOOLOGICAL GARDENS			
• polar	—	2	—
CENTRAL TEXAS ZOO (Waco)			
• American black	2	1	—
EL PASO ZOO			
• American black	1	1	—
• Kodiak	1	—	—
• sun	—	1	—
ELLEN TROUT ZOO (Lufkin)			
• American black	1	—	—
• Asiatic black	2	—	—
FORT WORTH ZOOLOGICAL PARK			
• sun	1	2	—

	Male	Female	Unknown
GLADYS PORTER ZOO (Brownsville)			
• polar	1	2	—
• sloth	1	1	—
• spectacled	1	1	—
• sun	1	4	—
HOUSTON ZOOLOGICAL GARDENS			
• Asiatic black	1	1	—
• grizzly	1	—	—
• spectacled	1	1	—
SAN ANTONIO ZOOLOGICAL GARDEN & AQUARIUM			
• Asiatic black	1	3	2
• grizzly	—	2	—
• polar	1	1	—
TEXAS ZOO (Victoria)			
• American black	1	1	—

Utah
	Male	Female	Unknown
HOGLE ZOOLOGICAL GARDENS (Salt Lake City)			
• Kodiak	1	1	—
• polar	2	2	—

Washington
	Male	Female	Unknown
NORTHWEST TREK WILDLIFE PARK (Eastonville)			
• American black	1	—	—
POINT DEFIANCE ZOO (Tacoma)			
• polar	1	2	—
WOODLAND PARK ZOOLOGICAL GARDENS (Seattle)			
• Kodiak	1	1	—
• sun	3	2	—

West Virginia
	Male	Female	Unknown
OGLEBAY'S GOOD CHILDREN'S ZOO (Wheeling)			
• American black	1	1	—

Wisconsin
	Male	Female	Unknown
HENRY VILAS ZOO (Madison)			
• grizzly	—	2	—
• polar	1	1	—
• spectacled	—	1	1
MILWAUKEE COUNTY ZOOLOGICAL GARDENS (Milwaukee)			
• American black	1	1	—
• Asiatic black	2	2	2
• brown	—	2	—
• grizzly	3	3	—
• polar	2	2	—
RACINE ZOOLOGICAL GARDEN			
• Kodiak	1	1	—

Bears Etc.

Grizzly Adams

Born John Capen Adams, on October 22, 1812 in Medway, Massachusetts, "Grizzly" Adams became one of the most colorful characters in bear fact and fiction.

He worked as a circus hand (where he was mauled by a tiger he was handling), shoemaker, farmer, rancher, and trapper, as well as attempting several other businesses. The gold rush lured him to California in 1849, where he became a mountain man.

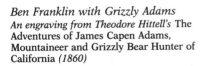

Ben Franklin with Grizzly Adams
An engraving from Theodore Hittell's The Adventures of James Capen Adams, Mountaineer and Grizzly Bear Hunter of California *(1860)*

While hunting and exploring the Oregon and Washington country, he captured a grizzly bear cub whom he named "Lady Washington." She was the first of his "trained" captive grizzly bears that accompanied him on the streets of San Francisco. Ben Franklin, captured as a cub, became Lady Washington's companion. Samson was taken as an adult and, being "unreliable," was kept caged. Adams captured other bears, and established a Mountaineer's Museum in San Francisco where he displayed his bears with a jaguar, deer, mountain lion, and other small animals. Lady Washington and Ben Franklin were more than displayed—they wandered freely through the museum.

Grizzly Adams was extremely knowledgeable about bears, but often unreliable in relating the facts. He did not keep a journal and his memory often did him injustice. More of a hunter and trapper than a scientist, but also a naturalist, he was a keen observer. He was aware, in the 1860s, that rings are added to the bears teeth each year; growth rings have much more recently become a valid indication of a bear's age.

He loved bears, but hunted and captured them relentlessly and may have been the most famous California bear hunter. Naturalist A. Starker Leopold claimed Grizzly Adams to be one of the persons most responsible for the elimination of the grizzly bear in California.

Adams died in Massachusetts in 1860. His many skirmishes with grizzly bears, a tiger, and the mountains of the West had finally cashed-in.

The Teddy Bear

This lovable bear has been a most popular American and international "toy" since the early 1900s, loved by adults and children alike. Based on a cartoon drawing of a bear, Morris Michtom, of Brooklyn, New York created the Teddy Bear as a Christmas item. Patterned after the koala bear, the toy bear with shoe-button eyes was originally named "Teddy" after and with the permission of Theodore Roosevelt.

Michtom had observed the 1902 "Drawing the Line" cartoon by Clifford Berryman of the *Washington Post*. The cartoonist was expressing President Theodore Roosevelt's reaction to a request to shoot a "roped" bear provided for him so his Mississippi bear hunt would be successful. The cartoon was not only about drawing the line between good and bad sportsmanship, but was thought to also reflect a sensitive racial issue (the "color line") and a boundary dispute between Mississippi and Louisiana. Though the cartoon depicts a cub, the Louisiana black bear in the actual occurrence was an adult weighing 230 pounds.

Theodore Roosevelt drawing the line in the 1902 Clifford Berryman cartoon that led to the "Teddy Bear" From The Teddy Bear Book, *by Peter Bull, New York: Random House, 1970.*

The Teddy Bear has evolved during its ninety years, becoming more portly, and though other toy bears have come onto the scene Michtom's remains a fixture of American childhood.

Winnie-The-Pooh

In 1914, during World War I, Captian Harry Colebourn was leaving his Winnipeg, Manitoba, Canada home by train to join his military regiment at Eal Cardier, Quebec. During a stop at the White River in Ontario, he bought an American black bear cub for $20 from a hunter who had killed the mother.

Colebourn, who loved animals and provided them with affection and care, named the cub "Winnipeg" (Winnie). The "tame" bear became his companion and would sleep under the Canadian soldier's cot.

Colebourn was a veterinarian caring for army horses. When his brigade began preparing to ship out from England to the bloody battlefields of France, he realized his bear could not accompany him to the frontline. Therefore, he donated Winnie to the London Zoo where she became one of its most popular attractions. Being tame and gentle—even eating out of a person's hand—she would give youngsters rides around the zoo grounds.

Author A. A. Milne, creator of the honey-loving bear Winnie-The-Pooh, regularly visited Winnie at the zoo. She was the inspiration that in 1926 gave the world Winnie-the-Pooh, a bear of very little brain that has enchanted children around the globe.

Milne's books, *Winnie-the-Pooh* and *House at Pooh Corner*, have been translated into more than twenty languages, including Latin, Esperanto and Scerbo-Croat.

Winnie is the subject of a feature-length animated film by Walt Disney, and in the Commonwealth of Independent Nations, Winnie-The-Pooh is a popular children's character known as Vinni Pukh.

When Winnipeg died at the zoo in 1934, her popularity prompted a London newspaper to run an obituary as though she were prominent royalty.

Smokey Bear

The famous guardian of the forests for nearly sixty years is an American black bear. In August 1944, the United States Forest Service developed their forest fire prevention symbol—Smokey Bear—issuing posters of the now-famous bear pouring water from a bucket onto a campfire. Smokey's popularity rapidly spread and in 1947 he began to use his equally famous fire prevention slogan "Remember, Only YOU Can Prevent Forest Fires."

Firefighters in the Lincoln National Forest of New Mexico, during the spring of 1950, observed a bear cub along the firelines. Later, following a blowup of the fire, the cub was found with seriously burned paws and hind legs. Rescued by the firefighters and assisted by a local rancher and a New Mexico Game and Fish ranger, the cub was flown to Santa Fe for veterinary aid.

The young bear recovered and the New Mexico State Game Warden presented it to the United States Forest Service to be utilized in its fire prevention program; thus the living symbol of Smokey Bear. "Smokey" lived his life at the National Zoo in the nation's capitol. He passed away on November 9, 1976, but the symbol—the bear dressed in blue jeans with a belt, carrying a shovel—continues to remind us to "prevent forest fires."

MARYLAND STATE POLICE
MARYLAND TROOPERS ASSOCIATION, INC.

 Courtesy Governor's Drug & Alcohol Commission, State of Maryland

Bears Against Drugs

The State of Maryland, Governor's Drug & Alcohol Abuse Commission, in conjunction with the Maryland Troopers Association, has utilized the bear in its fight against drugs. An intensive education program uses the theme BAD (Bears Against Drugs).

6 Bear Hunting

Hunting

Bear hunting has occurred since early "humans" and bears shared the same areas of the Eurasian continent. Bears were sources of food and clothing—and they were enemies. In the days of chivalry, the Spanish kings held the bear hunt in high order, pursuing the quarry with select hounds and their finest horses. The Norsemen of Norway, Denmark, and Finland would seek no advantage in a hunt, meeting the bear alone, fighting and killing with only a sword or spear.

"When the Indians hunt it [grizzly bear] they generally go six or eight in a band" observed John Long, Indian interpreter and trader, in 1778 (Fred Gowans, *Mountain Man & Grizzly*). "The instant they see one, they endeavour to surround it, by forming a large circle: if it is on the march they fire at it." Gowans also relates that Lewis and Clark were told by the Mandan Indians that "they 'hunted [the grizzly] in parties of eight to ten men,' and that 'the warriors wore war paint as they would when going to war against enemies.' "

Bears are hunted today, as they were historically, for a myriad of cultural, personal, and economic purposes that include:

- ❖ *Bring the bear to justice*
- ❖ *Defense of property*
- ❖ *Eliminate "vermin"*
- ❖ *Family tradition*
- ❖ *Food*
- ❖ *Hired for another person's reasons*
- ❖ *Manhood rites*

- ❖ Parts for the market
- ❖ Pleasure
- ❖ Practice for war
- ❖ Record book
- ❖ Religious
- ❖ Self-defense
- ❖ Sport
- ❖ Status in the community
- ❖ The thrill of the hunt
- ❖ Trophies

....

"The Eskimo who brings down a polar bear is respected by his folk as a master hunter," wrote Frederick Drimmer in *The Animal Kingdom*.

When early explorers reached North America they began killing bears, and hunting became an important element in colonial settlement. Hunting to bring the bear to justice, without a conservation ethic, colonists and pioneers killed enormous numbers of bears and populations quickly diminished. A Pennsylvania hunter killed four hundred in his lifetime, and a New York settler ninety-six in three years. Fur companies sold eighteen thousand skins a year in the early years of North American settlement. During one three-year period, over eight thousand bear skins were shipped from Ohio alone. There are no bears in Ohio today.

Hunting for bears provided entertainment, as well as sport, for the New England colonists during the 1700s. They conducted bear and turkey shoots where a bear was pursued and killed, with the carcass going to the best marksman.

Weapons

Weapons were crude, and hunters lacked an advantage, until about one hundred years ago. "Traditionally, the Eskimo has hunted the polar bear with a lance," according to Thomas Koch in *The Year of the Polar Bear*. "It was not until recently that guns were introduced to the Eskimo's culture."

"During the days of muzzle-loading rifles, its [the grizzly bear's] name and fame inspired terror throughout the mountains and foothills of the wild western domain which constituted its home," writes zoologist William Hornaday in *The American Natural History*. "For many years it held the old-fashioned Kentucky rifle of the pioneer in profound contempt, and frequently when it was used to annoy him, the user met a tragic fate. I believe that Grizzlies have killed and maimed a larger number of hunters than all other bears of the world combined."

"It took six to ten warriors to kill a single bear, and even then the risks were so great that the same ceremonial preceded a grizzly hunt that preceded the setting forth of a war party."

JOHN BAKELESS, 1966

Hunters have killed or captured bears with an assortment of weapons and "tools," from various firearms and traps to arrows, knives, rocks, and poisons. Weapons have ranged in size from pocket knives to whaling (harpoon) guns.

The Spaniards and Indians in the early 1800s killed bears with a box trap, "a large, strong box made of rails and having a doorway," as Tracy Storer and Lloyd Tevis describe in *California Grizzly*. "A riata was coiled on the floor round a hunk of meat. When a grizzly stepped within, the rope was yanked to snare him and the door was slammed shut. Then the Indians attacked with spears."

An illustration from a nineteenth-century magazine depicting a Russian Hunter with an espatoon and a brown bear

Spanish gentleman lassoing a grizzly bear in Old California
Painting by Stanley Walker

Spear-traps were popular in Eurasia. They were constructed of "a spear with an iron head wedged horizontally in the ground between two upright sticks," describe Desmond Morris and Ramona Morris in *Men and Pandas*, "the tip of the weapons being set at an appropriate height to pierce the heart region." The trap was automatic, with a sapling as a spring, and a cord attached to a trigger that was sprung by the bear.

Set guns consisted of an anchored double-barreled shotgun directed at a bait, with trigger wires or strings attached to the bait. When the bear pulled the bait, the wires pulled the trigger, firing the gun. Pistols were also used in this fashion.

One aggressive, or foolish, hunter sat in a baited pit with logs over it and shot the bear on the logs overhead.

Innovative methods were resorted to by those without a firearm or willingness to build a "trap." Bait was laid in the path of a bear. A bent sapling was anchored and a knife was attached to the loose end of the sapling. The bait and sapling were "set" with a figure-four trigger. When the bait was moved, the sapling drove the knife at the bear.

In California, one of the most noble and thrilling means of taking a bear was with the riata, or the lariat. "The vaqueros would never dream of hunting a grizzly with a gun, but solely with their rawhide reatas, which were between sixty and eighty feet in length," notes Thomas McIntyre in *American History—Grizzly*. According to "Bears and Bear Hunting," in *Harper's New Monthly Magazine*, 1855, "The native population . . . Mexicans, are excellent horsemen, and throw the lasso with the precision of the rifle-ball." And Storer and

Tevis, in *California Grizzly*, quote the common saying, *"La reata es el rifle del ranchero"*—the lasso is the rifle of the rancher. They also relate a description of this exciting method. "The animals were lassoed by the throat and also by the hind leg, a horseman at each end, and the two pulling in opposite directions till the poor beast succumbed." (W.H. Davis, *Sixty Years In California*, 1889).

Bear hunters around the world have pursued bears by numerous means, including on foot, horseback, snowmachine, and elephantback; in trucks, cars, boats, dugout canoes, airplanes, and helicopters (and in armor during the Medieval period); from roads, trees, scaffolds, trails, and blinds; with dogs, other bears; in wilderness areas, developments, the ocean, and on ice floes; and they have hunted and trapped alone, in groups, and in masses. The quarry has been taken by the hundreds, and the hunter has also, at times, returned empty-handed.

Present-Day Bear Hunting

Bear hunting in North America today is in many respects a different activity. There are improvements in firearms, ammunition, and transportation. Hunting philosophies are somewhat different, as is the need to kill bears. The distribution of bears has drastically changed and there are fewer. They have been eliminated in some regions. Today bears are hunted by game wardens and other government hunters for management purposes (population control and reduction of nuisance bears), and by sport and trophy hunters. Bear hunting licenses and tags are a major revenue source for states and provinces. Sport hunting occurs mostly during weekends and special vacations, and the day to day, relentless pursuit of bears by an individual is rare if not nonexistent. However, "the thrill of the hunt" remains for those seeking a bear.

Professional bear hunter Bernard Paque, in a 1991 *Wall Street Journal* article, perhaps best describes present-day bear hunts. "Hunting with friends, two rigs and CB radios is fun, but when I'm chasing through the woods, just me and the bear and the dogs, now that's a bear hunt."

Firearms

The early firearms used to hunt bears were without question inadequate. Theodore Roosevelt describes them in *American Bears* (Paul Schullery) as "the long-barrelled, small-bored pea-rifle, whose bullets ran seventy to the pound, the amount of powder and lead being a little less than that contained in the cartridge of a thirty-two calibre Winches-

ANNUAL BEAR HUNTING HARVESTS (NORTH AMERICA)

United States	American Black Bear	Grizzly Bear	Polar Bear
Alaska	1,470	1,200	*
Arizona	245	—	—
Arkansas	30	—	—
California	1,190	—	—
Colorado	640	—	—
Florida	50	—	—
Georgia	115	—	—
Idaho	2,300	—	—
Kentucky	1	—	—
Maine	2,500	—	—
Massachusetts	18	—	—
Michigan	800	—	—
Minnesota	2,350	—	—
Montana	1,490	*	—
New Hampshire	390	—	—
New Mexico	270	—	—
New York	660	—	—
North Carolina	770	—	—
Oregon	1,000	—	—
Pennsylvania	1,560	—	—
South Carolina	10	—	—
Tennessee	100	—	—
Utah	44	—	—
Vermont	275	—	—
Virginia	500	—	—
Washington	1,300	—	—
West Virginia	400	—	—
Wisconsin	1,250	—	—
Wyoming	250	—	—

Canada	American Black Bear	Grizzly Bear	Polar Bear
Alberta	1,700	40	—
British Columbia	4,000	300	—
Manitoba	2,000	—	*
New Brunswick	1,100	—	—
Newfoundland	150	—	4*
Northwest Territories	**	30	692*
Nova Scotia	100	—	—
Ontario	6,800	—	*
Quebec	2,800	—	*
Saskatchewan	2,200	—	—
Yukon Territory	95	10	1*

*Some exceptions to general hunting law are·
Alaska   No sport hunting; polar bears may be taken by Native Americans; no limit; salvage of the bear is required; annual harvest information unavailable.
Manitoba   No sport hunting; treaty Indians may hunt for own use, but sale of hides prohibited; quota thirty-five.
Montana   Mortality of fourteen bears (maximum of six females) is allowed, due to any cause (hunting, accidental, management action etc.); annual hunter harvest average 2.6 bears.
New Foundland   No harvest; quota of four maintained for nuisance bears.
Northwest Territories and Yukon (including Beaufort Sea)   Harvest primarily by Inuvialuit Native Americans; sport hunters use approximately fifteen percent of the hunting tags in Northwest Territories and must take their bear by dog team under the supervision of a local Inuit guide; harvest quota determined annually; October 1 to May 31.
Ontario   No sport hunting; "treaty Indians" may hunt; quota thirty.
Quebec   No sport hunting; the taking of polar bears is exclusively reserved for the Native Americans of Northern Quebec (Inuit and Indians).
**Information unavailable

BROWN BEAR

22 of the 33 largest from Kodiak Island, Alaska
31 of the 50 largest from Kodiak Island, Alaska

POLAR BEAR

6 of the 10 largest from Kotzebue, Alaska
24 of the 45 largest from Kotzebue, Alaska

GRIZZLY BEAR

All of the 5 largest from British Columbia
8 of the 11 largest from British Columbia
3 of the 11 largest from Alaska
22 of the 39 largest from British Columbia
13 of the 39 largest from Alaska
4 of the 39 largest from Alberta

AMERICAN BLACK BEAR

6 of the 14 largest from Arizona
4 of the 14 largest from Utah
2 of the 14 largest from Colorado
2 of the 14 largest from Saskatchewan

ter." Some old advice was that in order to gain an advantage, you should hunt "close-um," meaning to hunt at close range, saving ammunition and being more accurate. Nothing was mentioned about being more vulnerable to an attack.

Roosevelt also subscribed to the fact that if you had a "thoroughly trustworthy weapon and a fairly cool head," you could follow a bear "into its own haunts and slay grim Old Ephraim."

Bear hunting is and always has been life threatening, but the firearms of today provide the killing power hunters lacked during prehistoric times and the periods of continental settlement.

The "best firearm" to hunt bears is continually debated, but may be best described by Clyde Ormand in *Complete Book of Hunting*. "The 'best' grizzly rifle is the most powerful rifle the hunter can shoot well." He further comments that for the Alaskan brown bear "the right rifle-cartridge combination is the most powerful the hunter can handle within reason."

Trophy and Record Bears

Trophies are an important product of bear hunting, with a full mount or head, skull, and hide popular with the individual hunter. "The black bear is among the most coveted trophies in the United States," relates hunting authority Ben East in *The Ben East Hunting Book*.

The largest is important to many trophy bear hunters. However, "largest" is normally difficult to determine. An official scoring system meant to record skull size is managed by the Boone and Crockett Club. The club, started by Theodore Roosevelt in 1887, ascribes to strong ethical hunting, such as fair chase, and many of its standards have been adopted by states and provinces.

Official Boone and Crockett Scoring System

Recorded skulls normally originate from a fair-chase hunt, though a few were "picked up." The recorded score is the total (inches) of the skull length and width. Records are maintained by species of bear.

Bear Hunters

The author finds it tempting to categorize th hunters as "great," "famous," "an incidental hunter," or whatever. However, the criteria for great, or any category, is debatable. The hunters killed by bears may be considered famous—or were they just foolish and careless? The hunters who eliminated all bears from an area—are they famous or notorious? The hunters of the 1800s, a wide-ranging type of people, were famous due to their strange personalities or, in the case of Theodore Roosevelt, because they were prominent individuals (or President of the United States). David Brown notes in *The Grizzly of the Southwest* that you must be "fanatical" to be a famous hunter.

"Famous" Bear Hunters

The list of "famous" hunters is compiled from historical and present-day literature. Few hunters of today make the list,

BOONE AND CROCKETT CLUB BEAR RECORDS (NORTH AMERICA)

SPECIES	SCORE	SEX	YEAR	LOCATION
Brown bear	30 12/16	M	1952	Kodiak Island, Alaska
Polar bear	29 15/16	M	1963	Kotzebue, Alaska
Grizzly bear	27 2/16	Unknown	1970	Bella Coola Valley, British Columbia
Grizzly bear	27 2/16	M	1982	Dean River, British Columbia
American black bear	23 10/16	Unknown	1975	San Pete County, Utah

SPECIES	SKULL LENGTH	SEX	YEAR	LOCATION
Polar bear	18 8/16	M	1963	Kotzebue, Alaska
Brown bear	17 15/16	M	1961	Kodiak Island, Alaska
Grizzly bear	17 6/16	Unknown	1970	Bella Coola Valley, British Columbia
American black bear	14 12/16	Unknown	1975	San Pete County, Utah

SPECIES	SKULL WIDTH	SEX	YEAR	LOCATION
Brown bear	12 13/16	M	1952	Kodiak Island, Alaska
Polar bear	11 7/16	M	1963	Kotzebue, Alaska
Grizzly bear	10 5/16	M	1983	Ungalik River, Alaska
American black bear	8 14/16	Unknown	1975	San Pete County, Utah

probably being considerably more rational than early hunters, but they are also better equipped, have less necessity to hunt and minimal opportunity for notoriety—today's North American hunter lives in a considerably different world.

The list provides considerable information about some, with little about others, but they were all "bear hunters"—notorious, legendary, famous across the continent or in their community. They hunted as a profession, for subsistence, to help a friend, incidental to another occupation, for sport, or shot a bear only at an opportune moment, and even occasionally "in self-defense." Some could be considered infamous, as they eliminated all bears from a specific area while others, such as Ben Lilly, hunted with an obsession.

Benjamin "Ben" Vernon Lilly

- *Occupation:* blacksmith, farmer, cowboy, logger; a fanatical bear hunter (markethunter, hunt master, government hunter)

- Late 1800s to early 1900s
- *Location:* Louisiana, Mississippi, Texas, Mexico, New Mexico
- *Species hunted:* grizzly bear, black bear
- *Number of bears killed:* 300 to 400; used up to twenty-five dogs at times

- In the 1880s, according to David Brown in *The Grizzly in the Southwest*, Lilly was "about five feet nine inches tall . . . about 180 pounds of muscle and sinew . . . and a reputation for endurance that was already legendary." He was a remarkable tracker and possessed a fabled ability to unfailingly travel through any area, familiar or otherwise, and know his whereabouts. His persistence and eccentric nature were well displayed in the early 1900s when he tracked a grizzly bear, as Brown notes, "through three states [Chihuahua, Sonora, New Mexico] in two countries [Mexico and the United States]."

John Adams (James Capen Adams; Grizzly Adams)

- *Occupation:* wilderness traveler, hunter/trapper, mountaineer, shoemaker, frontiersman
- Mid-1800s
- *Species hunted:* grizzly bear, black bear

Robert Eager Bobo

- *Occupation:* soldier, farmer
- Late 1800s
- *Location:* Mississippi
- *Species hunted:* black bear
- *Number of bears killed:* 150 to 300/season (27 on a single day)
- *Largest bear killed:* 711 pounds

Jake Borah

- *Occupation:* hunter, guide
- *Location:* Colorado
- *Species hunted:* black bear, grizzly bear
- Borah and partner John Goff were considered by Theodore Roosevelt as two of the best at hunting bears with dogs in the mountains.

Amos Boorn

- Early to mid-1800s
- *Location:* Massachusetts
- *Species hunted:* black bear
- *Number of bears killed:* Total unknown, but he, was according to W. Bassett in *Town of Richmond, Cheshire County, New Hampshire*, "A bear hunter especially successful in ridding the country of these pests."

James Bridger

- *Occupation:* hunter, trapper, guide
- Early to mid-1800s

- *Location:* Rocky Mountains
- *Species hunted:* grizzly bear, some black bear
- One of the greatest American frontiersmen, referred to as "Old Gabe," he was the legendary mountain man who faced bears without fear.

Holt Collier
- *Occupation:* slave, valet, Confederate soldier
- Mid-1800s to early 1900s
- *Location:* Louisiana, Mississippi
- *Species hunted:* black bear
- *Number of bears killed:* Directly responsible or assisted in killing over 3000 bears

Don Jose Ramon Carrillo
- A California aristocrat of the late 1800s who is referred to by Tracy Storer and Lloyd Tevis in *California Grizzly* as the "most dauntless of the Californians who pursued the grizzly."
- *Location:* throughout California
- *Species hunted:* grizzly bear
- Hunting for sport only, he was famous for dueling with bears using a light-handled sword.

David (Davy) Crockett
- *Occupation:* soldier, scout, Congressman, pipe-stave maker, hunter
- Late 1700s to mid-1800s
- *Location:* Tennessee
- *Species hunted:* black bear
- *Number of bears killed:* Total unknown; 105 during winter of 1825–1826 (6 months)
- *Largest bear killed:* 617 pounds

W. H. (William) Eddy
- A member of the ill-fated Donner Party, snowbound in the Sierra Nevada mountains of California in November 1846. Faint from starvation, Eddy found the tracks of a large grizzly bear and followed them. He wounded the bear and it charged. Impeded by its wound, the bear could not catch Eddy, who shot it a second time. Having used his only two bullets, he finally killed the bear by striking it in the head with a club.

Grancel Fitz
- *Occupation:* hunter, writer, photographer
- *Species hunted:* black bear, Alaskan brown bear, grizzly bear, polar bear
- Hunting from 1923 to 1955, he was the first to hunt all classes of North American big-game animals.

Edwin Grimes
- *Occupation:* hunter
- *Location:* Pennsylvania
- *Species hunted:* black bear
- *Number of bears killed:* Over 200; killed his 200th on his 80th birthday

Wade Hampton III
- *Occupation:* soldier/patriot, Confederate general, Governor of South Carolina, U.S. Senator (South Carolina)
- 1800s
- *Location:* eastern Tennessee, western North Carolina, South Carolina, Mississippi to eastern Texas
- *Species hunted:* black bear
- *Number of bears killed:* involved with killing 500 (directly responsible for two thirds of those); once killed 4 bears in a day, once 3 bears in a day, and frequently 2 bears in a day; killed 68 in five months; killed 30 to 40 with a knife
- *Largest bears killed:* 408 pounds and 410 pounds
- Used 40 dogs at times

Allen Hasselborg
- *Occupation:* hunter
- Early 1900s
- *Location:* Admiralty Island, Alaska
- *Species hunted:* brown bear
- *Number of bears killed:* Total unknown, but considered numerous
- Collected specimens for C. Hart Merriam, U.S. Bureau of Biological Survey, in 1912; seriously mauled by a brown bear

"Bear" Howard
- *Occupation:* hunter, rancher (horses), farmer (tobacco), soldier in Mexican War
- 1800s
- *Location:* Arizona
- *Species hunted:* grizzly bear
- Named in part for his 6'8" height, Howard hunted bears to market the meat and sell the gall bladders to Chinese apothecary shops.

"Old Ike"
- Late 1800s
- *Species hunted:* grizzly bear
- *Number of bears killed:* nearly 100
- Theodore Roosevelt considered him one of the most successful bear hunters
- Killed by a grizzly bear

Moses Leonard
- Late 1700s to late 1800s
- *Location:* Massachusetts
- *Species hunted:* American black bear
- *Number of bears killed:* 150 during his lifetime (also 300 wolves)

Tom Locke
- Early to mid-1800s
- *Location:* Massachusetts
- *Species hunted:* black bear
- *Number of bears killed:* 16 in one fall alone

Walter Metrokin
- Early 1900s
- *Species hunted:* Kodiak and Alaskan brown bear
- The one-handed bear hunter of Kodiak, Alaska, Metrokin was a hero among his fellows because of his many exploits as a bear hunter. A strong character of Russian heritage who stood out among his fellows, he lost his right hand in a hunting accident as a youth. Metrokin could tie knots and roll cigarettes, and rowed a boat with an oar lashed to his stub.

James A. "Bear" Moore
- *Occupation:* hunter, farmer
- Late 1800s to early 1900s
- *Location:* New Mexico
- *Species hunted:* grizzly bear
- Badly mauled in 1883, Moore tortured bears thereafter; killed a wounded grizzly bear with a knife

George Nidever
- Early to mid 1800s
- *Location:* San Luis Obispo County, California
- *Species hunted:* grizzly bear
- *Number of bears killed:* Up to 200; 45 in 1837

Ramon Ortega
- Late 1800s
- *Location:* mountainous Ventura County of California
- *Species hunted:* grizzly bear
- *Number of bears killed:* over 200; 70 in five years; 15 in a day; killed 40 in just over a month
- Considered by some to be the greatest California bear hunter

Bernard Paque
- *Occupation:* hunter for the Washington Forest Protection Association
- Late 1960s to early 1990s (23 years)
- *Location:* Washington
- *Species hunted:* Black bear
- *Number of bears killed:* Over 2,300

William Pickett
- *Occupation:* soldier, civil engineer, Wyoming representative of the Boone and Crockett Club, artist, rancher (subject in Ernest Thompson Seton's *Biography of a Grizzly*)
- *Location:* Wyoming, Yellowstone National Park (legal at that time)
- *Species hunted:* grizzly bear
- *Number of bears killed:* more than seventy

Samuel Pope
- *Occupation:* hunter
- *Location:* southern Ohio
- *Species hunted:* black bear
- *Number of bears killed:* total unknown; killed three in a single day

- Killed a wounded bear with a tomahawk
- Locally famous as a bear hunter

Colin Preston
- *Occupation:* lawyer, hunter
- Mid 1800s
- *Location:* California
- *Species hunted:* black bear and grizzly bear
- *Number of bears killed:* total unknown; over 200 one year
- Baited bears with rum and molasses

Theodore Roosevelt
- *Occupation:* rancher, soldier, writer, President of the United States
- Mid- to late 1800s to early 1900s
- *Location:* Colorado, Idaho, Louisiana, Mississippi, Montana, North Dakota, Wyoming
- *Species hunted:* grizzly bear (his favorite big-game animal), black bear

Andy Sublette
- *Occupation:* guide, mountain man, miner, fought in Mexican War
- Mid-1800s
- *Location:* across the United States
- *Species hunted:* grizzly bear, black bear
- *Number of bears killed:* many
- Had two grizzly bear cubs as pets
- Killed by a grizzly bear

Wilburn Waters
- *Occupation:* apprentice saddler, sheriff, artist, hunter (often known as "the hunter of White Top," the mountain on which he lived)
- Mid-1800s
- *Location:* southwestern Virginia, east Tennessee
- *Species hunted:* black bear
- Often killed bears with dogs and knife

James St. Clair Willburn
- *Occupation:* school principal, meat hunter
- *Location:* Trinity County, California, 1857
- *Species hunted:* black bear, grizzly bear
- *Number of bears killed:* unknown

- Killed a wounded grizzly bear with a knife
- Lost an arm to a bear

Tazewell Woody
- *Occupation:* hunter
- *Location:* Rocky Mountains and Great Plains
- *Species hunted:* black bear, grizzly bear
- *Number of bears killed:* total unknown, but "very many grizzlies," according to Theodore Roosevelt in *American Bears*, edited by Paul Schullery

Dick "Uncle" Wootton
- *Occupation:* trapper, scout, Indian fighter, rancher, buffalo hunter, innkeeper, infamous mountain man in the pre-Civil War West
- Mid-1800s
- *Location:* Kentucky, Colorado
- *Species hunted:* black bear, grizzly bear
- *Number of bears killed:* total unknown, but he was considered to have "killed his share"

William Wright
- *Occupation:* blacksmith, mailman, carpenter, hunter, naturalist
- Late 1800s to early 1900s
- *Location:* Idaho, Montana, Washington, British Columbia, Alberta
- *Species hunted:* grizzly bear, black bear; used a 12-pound, single-shot .45-100 Winchester
- *Number of bears killed:* total unknown; once killed five grizzly bears with five shots in five minutes
- A noted hunter in the western United States; wrote *The Grizzly Bear: The Narrative of a Hunter-Naturalist*, in 1909, with some of the earliest grizzly bear photos.

George Yount
- One of the first pioneers in California, arriving at Napa Valley in February 1831
- *Species hunted:* grizzly bear, black bear
- *Number of bears killed:* total unknown; claimed to have often killed five or six in a day
- Considered a famous bear hunter; bas-relief bear on his gravestone

Hunters Who Killed Bears
With a Knife

A frontiersman might occasionally be without a firearm but never without a knife, and too often it came forth as the weapon of the moment. Bears were killed by knives out of necessity when a gun failed, or for sport or excitement. The use of the knife to kill a bear was described by one frontiersman as "cold steel, with blade as slick as silk."

Theodore Roosevelt's description of Wade Hampton's method of hunting with a knife is related by George Laycock in *The Wild Bears*. "Hampton always had the help of a pack of hounds," wrote Roosevelt, "sometimes forty in number. When he heard the dogs holding a bear at bay, he rode up and urged them to close with the animal. Then as the dogs worried the bear, Hampton ran in close, reached across the animal and stabbed it behind the shoulder on the opposite side. This hazardous system worked so well that Hampton, in killing between thirty and forty bears with his knife, was injured by only one of them which managed to rip open the general's arm."

A few of the knife-wielding hunters:

JIM BAKER	Attacked and killed a grizzly bear, with minimal injury to himself; then a second grizzly (wounded) attacked him, all within a few minutes; he also killed the second bear, though he was badly mauled
ROBERT EAGER BOBO	Black bear
COLONEL WILLIAM BUTTS	Wounded grizzly bear in San Louis Obispo County, California, March 29, 1853; badly mauled but survived; later editor of the newspaper *Southern Californian*
DAVY CROCKETT	Black bear
JOHN HUGH GLASS	Trapper; wounded grizzly bear. (There is an infamous story of Glass being left for dead, and his subsequent tracking-down of those who left him behind)
TIM GOODALE	Grizzly bear
WADE HAMPTON III	Black bear
GENERAL STONEWALL JACKSON	Grizzly bear, in the Southwest
BEN LILLY	Wounded (intentionally) black bear, and other bears, to protect his dogs when a shot might hit a dog
RICHARD MILLER	Grizzly bear in the Southwest, 1935
JAMES A. "BEAR" MOORE	Wounded grizzly bear

JAMES ST. CLAIR WILLBURN	Wounded grizzly bear
DICK WOOTTON	Grizzly bear; awakened with the bear standing over him
WILLIAM WRIGHT	Killed a wounded grizzly bear with a pocket knife

Hunters Who Killed Bears With Other Weapons

Bears were killed with a variety of other weapons, for sport and out of necessity. "In 1754 [in Connecticut] . . . Israel Putnam, later a famed Revolutionary soldier," according to James Cardoza in *The Black Bear in Massachusetts*, "lost a hog to a hungry bear. Tracking the bear to its den, Putnam reputedly entered the lair and dispatched the bear and its two cubs with a club, and recovered the carcass of his pig."

DON JOSE RAMON CARRILLO	Dueled grizzly bears with a light-handled sword.
W. E. (WILLIAM) EDDY	Clubbed a grizzly bear while stranded in California in 1846 with the Donner Party. Wounding the bear with his only bullets, he killed it with a club.
GENERAL "RED" JACKSON	Sabre; grizzly bear; while on horseback.
JOSEPH LAPOINT	Bayonet fixed on gun; grizzly bear; death by bayonet uncertain; possibly shot as well.
JOSEPH MEEK	Tomahawk; wounded grizzly bear with cubs.
SAME POPE	Tomahawk; wounded grizzly bear.
ED WISEMAN	Arrow; killed possibly the last grizzly bear in Colorado, with a hand-held arrow, as he was being mauled.

Frontiersmen Killed by Bears

Most fatalities involved a combination of being inadequately armed or unarmed, using inadequate caution, and meeting a wounded bear.

Jim Boggs One story of Boggs' death tells us that while hunting in the Russian River country of California in 1850, Boggs approached within 12 feet of a lair where a grizzly sow with cubs attacked and killed him. Another account of the incident says that while hunting, a companion roped a large grizzly bear and was attacked. Boggs approached and shot the bear, who released the companion. The wounded bear then attacked and killed Boggs.

Fred Fritz A rancher in eastern Arizona around the turn of the century, Fritz surprised a grizzly bear while on horseback and armed only with a pistol. The bear attacked him and, during the mauling, he shot the bear six times, broke the pistol over its head and attempted to use his pocket knife. His dogs chased the bear away. Badly mauled, he became an "authority" on how it feels to be attacked by a bear. Though he survived for about five years afterward, the primary cause of his death was considered to be the mauling.

Dr. Monroe Hamberlin A physician, Hamberlin was hunting at the Mound on Lake George near Vicksburg, Mississippi. After commenting that, "I never saw one [bear] that I was afraid to tackle," he shot at a 640-pound black bear, and the ball glanced off the bear's head. Attacked by the bear, Hamberlin fought with his knife. His dogs pulled the bear from him, but they were beaten and the bear returned to the doctor. Subsequently his companions shot the bear, but Hamberlin died after three days of suffering.

Peter Lebec Killed by a grizzly bear on October 17, 1837 at the site that became Fort Tejon, Kern County, California. The Indians of the area related a story during the late 1800s of a person (assumed to be Lebec) who pursued a grizzly bear, shot it and, believing it to be dead, approached and was killed by the bear. His companions buried him at the site.

Hyrum Naegle Naegle and his brother George were following a grizzly bear they had wounded, near Colonia Pacheco, Chihuahua, Mexico, around 1885. "They had been briefly separated while George repaired a malfunctioning rifle," relates David Brown in *The Grizzly in the Southwest*. "Then George heard a shot and went to investigate. He found Hyrum under the bear's forefeet, the animal 'tearing at his head.' On seeing George, the bear released his victim, only to be felled by George's repaired rifle." His brother managed to get Hyrum on his horse, tied to the saddle and home alive, but he died of his dreadful wounds after two days.

Andy Sublette A mountaineer, trapper, and guide who was badly mauled by a grizzly bear in 1853, but later had two grizzly cubs as pets. While separated from his party, on December 18 (or 19), 1854, in Malibu Canyon near the present-day area of Santa Monica, California, Sublette shot and wounded a grizzly bear. Apparently he was then attacked and fought the bear with his knife and the aid of his dog. The bear died. His dog survived, but after several days Sublette died, at the age of 46.

Isaac Slover A trapper and hunter who was considered durable and stubborn and had a great ambition to kill grizzly bears, Slover shot one on October 14, 1854, on Mount San Antonio, California. The large wounded bear crawled into the brush and Slover reloaded and followed, where he was attacked, torn to pieces and died. He was approximately 81.

"Old Ike" An experienced bear hunter, but considered somewhat careless, Old Ike was killed by a grizzly bear in the spring or early summer of 1886 at the headwaters of the Salmon River, Idaho. He was hurriedly following the bear, and pursued it to a dense stand of trees where it charged him. "He fired one hasty shot, evidently wounding the animal, but not seriously enough to stop or cripple it; and as his two companions ran forward they saw the bear seize him with its wide-spread jaws, forcing him to the ground," describes Theodore Roosevelt in *American Bears* (edited by Paul Schullery). "They shouted and fired, and the beast abandoned the fallen man on the instant and sullenly retreated into the spruce thicket, wither they dared not follow it. Their friend was at his last gasp; for the whole side of the chest had been crushed in by the one bite."

Name Unknown Ernest Thompson Seton, in *Lives Of Game Animals*, describes a trapper who was killed in Ontario, Canada in November, 1929, by a "monstrous" black bear with face and neck laden with festering porcupine quills.

Names Unknown Three New Mexicans, shortly before 1850, "attacked" two grizzly bears. The encounter resulted in one dead bear, two dead hunters, with the other hunter badly mauled.

Name Unknown A man was killed in the "early days" by a grizzly bear in Strawberry Canyon, now part of the University of California campus, Berkeley, California, according to M.T. Carleton in *The Byrnes of Berkeley*.

Name Unknown "Near Bodega, Sonoma County [California, mid-1800s], a young man armed only with pistols, followed a mortally wounded bear into a thicket and was literally torn to pieces," according to Tracy Storer and Lloyd Tevis in *California Grizzly*.

Richard Wilson A hunter, and partner of Bear Howard, Wilson shot a grizzly bear with an inadequate rifle in Oak Creek Canyon, Sedona, Arizona, during mid-1885. Alone, he followed the wounded bear into a thicket, where he was attacked. He attempted to climb a small tree, but was dragged down and killed.

The Use of Bears and Bear Parts

Bear Parts

Since early "man" shared his habitat with bears, there have been tangible and material uses of the bear, as well as spiritual and ceremonial influences. Food, clothing, medicine, heat, light, shelter, ornaments, and tools have been provided from all species and used by many different cultures including native inhabitants, explorers, pioneers, and early settlers. Parts were not only for individual uses but were traded, used as gifts, bartered, and sold. Many of these traditional uses continue today.

The meat of a bear was considered an excellent food. In 1784, one colonist noted, according to Cardoza, that "all who have tasted the flesh of this animal say that it is most delicious eating; a young Bear, fattened with the autumnal fruits, is a dish fit for the nicest epicure. It is wholesome and nourishing, and resembles pork more than any other meat." The meat was prepared like ham, as bears in some situations were used in place of hogs. The light oil of the fat was pure white. "All of the Indians of the Upper Missouri," relates Fred Gowans in *Mountain Man & Grizzly*, describing Prince Maximilian's story, "often wear the handsome necklace made of the claws of the grizzly bear. These claws are very large in the spring, frequently three inches long, and the points are tinged of a white colour, which is much esteemed; only the claws of the fore feet are used for necklaces, which are fastened to a strip of otter skin, lined with red cloth, and embroidered with glass beads, which hangs down the back like a long tail."

A mark of distinction. *An Indian chief with a claw necklace—a symbol of the bear's power*

Traditional Uses

Baculum   magic potency and aphrodisiac

Bones   ceremonial; hand tools (many were carved); weapons (dagger)

Claws

- Belts
- Bracelets
- Headbands
- Jewelry
- Necklaces (sometimes 40 claws)
- Ornaments
- Wristlets

Fat

- Cooking (pies, cakes, biscuits, doughnuts)
- In place of butter
- Fry fish
- Hair pomades
- Hair restorer
- Healing salve
- Lamp oil
- Leather softener
- Medicine (rheumatism and other infirmities)
- Miracle drug
- Ointment
- Olive oil substitute
- Perfume
- Salad oil
- Salves for human and animal wounds
- Source of dietary fat
- Tonic
- Waterproofing (shoes, boots)

The fat of bears was used as a medicine for a variety of ailments. Cardoza quotes a colonist's story: "One Mr. Purchase cured himself of the Sciatica with Bear-grease, keeping some of it continually in his groine. It is good too for Swell'd Cheeks upon cold, for Rupture of the hands in winter, for limbs taken suddenly with Sciatica, Gout, or other diseases that cannot stand upright nor go, bedrid. . . ." And another colonist claimed it quite popular against baldness.

Not only was the fat a home remedy, but Cardoza quotes physician John Josselyn, who recorded in the 1800s that "Grease is very good for Aches and Cold Swellings, the Indians anoint themselves wherewith from top to toe, which hardens them against the cold weather." Cardoza also relates an individual's story that the Canadian Indians smeared their bodies with bear oil "when they are excessively cold, tired with labour, hurt and in other cases. They believe it softens the skin, and makes the body more pliant, and is very serviceable to old age."

Feces   Cure for constipation (taken when frozen)

Hides

- Alter coverings
- Bedding
- Boot bottoms
- Boot covers
- Boot laces
- Burial robes
- Busbies (towering caps like those worn by the royal guard at Buckingham Palace)

- Caps (winter)
- Clothing
- Controls menstrual period (giant panda skin)
- Coverings
- Decoration
- Dog traces and harness reins
- Doors (house)
- Fragments (polish sled runners)
- Ground mat
- Hats (drum major and other type of headware)
- Hunting blinds
- Linings for expensive sleeping bags
- Louse mops
- Mantles (clothing)
- Muffs
- Overcoats
- Pants (waterproof)
- Parlor rugs
- Pay taxes (giant panda; ancient China)
- Robes (clothing; carriage and sleigh)
- Sled (rolled and frozen)
- Sled covers
- Sleeping mats
- Sleeping robes
- Status symbols
- Souvenirs for visitors
- Trophies
- Wall hangings

Gall Bladders   aphrodisiac and medicine

Head   food (a delicacy)

Intestines   thongs (cords); window "glazing" (stretched over window; translucent covering)

Meat   Dog food and people food

Paws

- Boots (included some of leg skin)
- Ceremonial; part of a necklace
- Food (delicacy)
- Gloves (shaman)
- Medicine bag (shaman)
- Religious gloves
- Souvenirs for visitors

Sinews   sewing "thread"

Skulls   ceremonial; trophies; ritual magic

Teeth   amulets, jewelry, necklaces, ornaments

Bear Meat

▲ Described as coarse pork

▲ Greasy

▲ Polar bear cub meat similar to veal

▲ Seldom eaten by Indians

▲ High level of *Trichinella* worm (trichinosis)

▲ Polar bear liver has high levels of Vitamin A

In *The History of Four-footed Beasts* (1607), Edward Topsell describes several uses of bear parts. Mythical or factual, these were applications of physical or psychological medicine.

Blood   "If the blood or grease of a Bear be set under a bed, it will draw unto it all the fleas, and so kill them by cleaving thereunto."

Eyes   "The right eye of a Bear dryed to powder, and hung about childrens necks in a little bag, driveth away the terror of dreams, and both the eyes whole, bound to a mans left arm, easeth a quartain Ague."

Fat   "They are exceedingly full of fat or large-grease, which some use superstitiously beaten with Oyl, wherewith they anoynt their Grape-sickles when they go to vintage, perswading themselves that if no body thereof, their tender Vine-branches shall never be consumed by Caterpillers."

Fur

Though present-day North American bear hides have little commercial value as "fur" and are most used as "bear rugs" and wall hangings (trophies), early Native Americans possessed different opinions and values. "The only Bears of this country, are the small black Bear, with a chance Yellow Bear," Bessie Haynes and Edgar Haynes, in *The Grizzly Bear*, quote the "Old Indians" as saying. "This latter has a fine furr and trades for three beavers in barter, when full grown."

"These robes [bear] wear much longer than those of the Buffalo, being in texture much stronger, and more impervious to rain," Cardoza quotes Emmons, "and, besides, they are considered much handsomer and richer in appearance."

"Nanook's fur also might be tied on the end of a long caribou bone to make a kumak-sheun, a louse mop," writes Charles Feazel in *White Bear*, referring to a use by the Eskimos. "When drawn through the hair of the family . . . the fur would attract the little pests. . . ."

Thousands of bear furs have been shipped from North America since the 1700s. In 1702, bear skins were of equal value to beaver pelts. 16,512 furs arrived in the French port of Rochelle in 1743, and in 1763, 8,340, were exported from the East Coast of the United States. However, the majority of pelts stayed in the United States.

During the 1860s, bear hides sold in the general range of two dollars to $20 each. In 1992, American black bear hides (fleshed and salted, not tanned) have been sold in the range of $55 to $340, with an average of $165.

Asian Uses Today

The early subsistence use of bears has evolved and now the taking, trading, and use of bear parts is an important international business in many countries, with major economic benefits for all involved. Unfortunately, bear populations have rapidly declined due to this trade, as thousands of bears are killed annually. The trade is primarily Asian, and most bears and bear parts originate in Malaysia and Thailand, however, the United States and Canada are significant sources. All eight species of bears are employed, with parts used for clothing, decoration, food, and medicine.

"Chinese medicine" is practiced by more than three billion people in the Orient, with over a billion Chinese consumers alone. There are millions of other users in non-Orient countries.

A FEW USES OF PARTS IN THE 17TH CENTURY

". . . cure confulsed and distracted parts, spots, and tumors in the body."

". . . helpeth pain in the loyns, if the sick part be anoynted. . ."

Cures ". . . all Ulcers of the legs or shins . . . feet . . ."

". . . it is soveraign against the falling of the hair . . ."

Liver ("gall") The liver is ". . . trod to powder under ones shooes easeth and defendeth Cripples from inflamation . . ."

A remedy when ". . . bitten by a mad dog . . ."

". . . against the Palsie, the Kings Evill, the Falling-sickness, and Old Cough, the Inflamation of the Eyes, the running of the Ears, the difficulty of Urine, and delivery in Childebirth, the Hemorrhoides, the weakness of the Back."

"The stones in a Perfume are good against the Falling evill, and the Palsie . . ."

A Siamese prescription in the nineteenth century for "morbific fever" was an exotic cocktail, according to Jeffrey McNeely and Paul Wachtel in *Soul Of The Tiger*. "One portion of rhinoceros horn, one of elephants's tusk, one of tiger's, and the same of crocodiles's teeth; one of bear's tooth; one portion composed of three parts bones of vulture, raven, and goose; one portion of bison and another of stag's horn, one portion of sandalwood. These ingredients to be mixed together on a stone with pure water; one half of the mixture to be swallowed, the rest to be rubbed into the body; after which the morbific fever will depart."

Parts and Specific Uses in Asia Today

"Use of bears and bear parts in folk medicine is common with the fat being used for bone bruises, and claws and baculi used for strength and fertility [also as an aphrodisiac]," notes Chris Servheen in *The Status and Conservation of the Bears of the World*. "The use and the association of the bear with machismo. . . ."

Fat   Bear fat is used for other maladies, including rheumatism, and may be found bottled in liquid form. Records of bear fat as a medicine in China date back as early as 3494 BC.

Blood and Bones   Strength is enhanced by the consumption of bear blood, while bone products are purchased as souvenirs in the tourist trade and used as food supplements—including a pulverized form that is added to baby formula in the belief that the child will grow up strong like a bear. Tools are made from bones, for example, scythes for cutting grass made from shoulder bones (sharp blades).

Claws   Bear claws bring good health, including strength and fertility. They are worn in Sri Lanka as protection from evil; in other countries they are often sewn on infant backpacks for good luck. Pendants and souvenirs are made of claws, popular with tourists.

Gall bladders   Bear gall bladders are the most dominant and prized bear part—the mainstay—in the parts trade. A gall bladder is the size of an average human thumb, and, according to Judy Mills and Christopher Servheen in *The Asian Trade in Bears and Bear Parts*, "Fresh gallbladder looks like a balloon filled with water. Once dried, it more closely resembles a fig. . . ." The dried bile of the bladder, the gall, is most often found on the market in a crystalline form ranging in color from golden brown to near black. Golden gall is

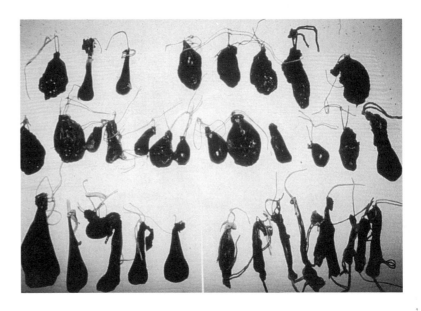

Gall bladders taken from American black bears illegally killed in southeastern United States
Courtesy William Cook, National Park Service

considered superior to dark colored. Dried gall bladders weigh between 50 (1.76) and 150 grams (5.29 ounces).

According to Mills and Servheen, "Bear gallbladder may have entered the Chinese pharmacopoeia as many as 3,000 years ago." Gall is considered a cure for most anything and is even a registered medicine in Japan, where forty-two pharmaceutical companies sell some form of gall. It is an ingredient of ninety-five heart medicines, sixteen stomach medicines, a digestive aid, and several children's medicines. Gall is also used in Japan as a poison. Koreans are the most avid users, where it is available at thousands of clinics.

Gall is derived from bears worldwide, and bear farms raise and maintain bears to "milk" gall. Seven factories in China alone produce fifty-six different medicines containing gall.

"Bile salts are taken in chunks melted on the tongue or downed with water, dissolved in liquor, mixed with other traditional ingredients such as musk and pearl, stuffed in capsules, molded into manufactured tablets, and blended into ointments and creams," write Mills and Servheen. Gall is also found as a powder and in suppositories, oil compounds, tinctures, and wine mixtures.

Bear gall bladder, in its many forms, is a treatment for a vast number of ailments, including conditions of the blood, liver, heart, lungs, spleen, skin, throat, intestines, and bladder. It is a remedy for fatigue, colic, cancer, diabetes, internal parasites, poor appetite, infection, fever, fractures, hemorrhoids, and excessive drinking (alcohol) and smoking.

The price of gall from street sources ranges considerably among different countries and within each country, depending on the specific source and circumstances.* In China gall averages $3,500 per whole gall bladder (up from $200 in 1972) and may sell at $9 per gram, or for $26 to $1,000 per gram from a park. ". . . the standard price for farmed bear gall was $2,000 per kilo—one-sixth the price of galls from wild bears offered to us earlier on the black market," noted Mills and Servheen.

South Korean gall prices range from $1 to $210 per gram, though it is doubtful that gall sold at the lower prices is from bears. Most gall sells between $42 to $139 per gram. One gall bladder was auctioned for $64,000.

Gall in Taiwan sells for between $8 and $30 per gram, with the average-sized gall bladder selling in the range of $800 to $3,000. Prices for gall are approximately $3 per gram in Nepal, $1 to $14 per gram in Malaysia, and $4 to $10 per gram in Thailand. Whole gall bladders sell at approximately $450 in Singapore, with a gram at $1 to $33; a gram sells for about the same in Hong Kong. Again, the low end of that range may mean the gall is from a pig or some other animal. The average price of gall in Macau is $21 per gram. In Laos a small amount costs $20 to $40, and in Japan, gall bladders sell at $1,500 to $4,000 each.

"I believe in the curative powers of bear products," explained zoologist Wu Jia-yan, a professor at Shaanzi Institute of Zoology (China), to Judy Mills and Christopher Servheen (*The Asian Trade In Bears and Bear Parts*) during their investigation and survey of the Asian parts trade.

Meat Bear meat is considered medicinal—a tonic food. It strengthens the body, fights weakness, enhances health and vigor, and provides energy for a person's general mental and physical well being. "For the 1988 Olympics . . . thirty Thai bears were illegally shipped to South Korea to fortify Korean athletes with their meat and galls," according to Mills and Servheen.

There are hundreds of bear meat recipes including spare ribs, steaks, stews, and preparation by grilling. Bear liver is eaten raw with spices. Bear meat is a novelty dish in many restaurants in Japan, and a bearsteak dinner costs around $15. The meat of a whole bear may sell for $3,000 in Japan. In South Korea fifty-one kilos (112 pounds) costs more than $2,000 or $17.86 per pound. Prices in much of Southeast Asia commonly range from $64 to $139 per pound.

Canned bear meat (105 grams) is sold in souvenir shops in Japan for $14, which includes a matching can of deer. Bear meat is also used as a dog food.

*United States dollars at 1991 exchange rates. Prices indicate a range of price quotes and sales; a kilo equals 2.2 pounds; a gram equals .0353 ounce)

Paws Paws, like the meat of a bear, are also considered medicinal tonic food to prevent various ailments, such as the common cold, and to provide strength. However, they are mostly prized as a delicacy, a restaurant cuisine, a banquet food.

In Bangkok, Thailand during the late 1980s, notes Servheen, "... restaurants procure bears for ... meals using the paws and meat and sometimes reportedly killing the bear in front of the guests to assure them the meal is authentic and fresh."

The primary source of market paws are Asiatic black bears. The paws are used in soup, stew, or braised and served with vegetables, and soft-fried as in a restaurant in the Beijing, China zoo.

"... Korean tourists come in groups to Thailand to eat bear paw soup and meat," according to Servheen. "A single serving of bear paw soup sells for several hundred U.S. dollars." A bear paw dinner in Thailand is $400.

In South Korea braised paws are $700 per dish. In Hong Kong it costs $380 for a restaurant entree. Restaurants in Japan have bear paws at $416 to $833 per serving, and in Singapore $170 for a one-paw dish.

On the market in China, paws (1-1/2 to 2 kilos each and raw) sell for $10 to $80 each and in Hong Kong at $146 to $162 per kilo.

Hides Bear hides (furs) have several uses including coverings and decorations for floors, wall hangings, and furniture. They are worn in traditional dances, and pieces of hide are ground-up and placed in pouches that are worn around

Paws and claws removed from American black bears illegally killed in southeastern United States
Courtesy William Cook, National Park Service

the neck as black magic to ensure good health. Hides sell at $400 to $2,500 ($3,000 as a rug with head and paws attached) each in Japan. One million dollars was offered for a single hide in South Korea (the owner retained the hide and had it mounted), and $10,000 was paid for a giant panda hide in Southeast Asia.

Teeth   Bear teeth are sold to tourists as souvenirs, and sewn on infant backpacks in the same manner as bear claws, for good luck.

Bears   Whole bears, normally Asiatic black bears, dead or alive, are sought for various purposes. They are used for their parts—including the meat—as pets, in zoos and circuses, as performers, in bear farms, and to attract customers to businesses.

In China, adult bears sell for $41 per kilo with some sales ranging from $1,400 to $2,700 per bear (dead or alive). An Asiatic black bear in Thailand brings in $2,000 to $4,000, approximately $7,100 in South Korea. Recently in Asia, one was auctioned for $9,722.

Cubs sell for $400 (sun bear) in Thailand, $100 to $180 in Laos, $1,800 to $2,600 in Taiwan, and $31 each as pets in Sumatra.

A high markup exists in the bear parts trade as a retailer will pay the hunter $2,000 for an adult Asiatic black bear and in turn sell it (total parts) for $6,000 to $10,000.

"Some Bangkok [Thailand] animal dealers and restaurants charge between $600 and $1,000 for a live bear," write McNeely and Wachtel, "which is sometimes tied to a post outside the shop for inspection by customers and then . . . beaten to death when purchased."

Pets and Performers

Sun bears and Asiatic black bears are the species typically used where live bears are performers, pets, or otherwise live in a domestic situation. Some are street performers, and several performing bear troupes exist and appear in circuses around the world. "Captive bears are taught to wrestle and dance for groups of 'gypsies' who earn their sole living from the bears," notes Servheen. "Pet keeping also affects bears by creating a market for live bears, especially cubs, that are sold in local markets."

Bears are used in a promotional capacity, attracting customers to gasoline stations, restaurants, brothels, and stores. As pets, bears are sometimes taught to assist with household chores and serve as watch "dogs." The British military in Malaysia has used bears as mascots. Thai Bud-

---

MAJOR BEAR AND PARTS TRADE COUNTRIES

Bangladesh	*supplier*
Bhutan	*supplier*
Burma (Myanmar)	*supplier*
Cambodia	*supplier*
China	*major consumer/ supplier*
Hong Kong	*major consumer*
India	*supplier*
Indonesia	*supplier*
Japan	*major consumer/ supplier**
Laos	*supplier*
Macau	*supplier*
Malaysia	*supplier*
Nepal	*supplier*
North Korea	*supplier*
Singapore	*major consumer*
South Korea	*major consumer*
Sri Lanka	*supplier*
Taiwan	*major consumer*
Thailand	*supplier*
Vietnam	*supplier*

*Trade not restricted or regulated; all other countries involved in major trade regardless of restrictions and regulations.

dhists harbor and care for bears as a "good deed" that will provide them credit after death.

And, when performance and pet bears become too old and difficult to manage, they are sold to restaurants and other businesses for medicine and food.

A broad range of fluctuating prices normally exists for these bears, and during the late 1980s an Asiatic black bear cub sold for $180, a sun bear cub $100, an adult sun bear $2,000 and an adult Asiatic black bear $5,500.

Eating Bear Meat

Bear meat has been used as food since humans and bears shared common areas. The North American settlers often sought bears as a desirable and reliable source of meat.

When their crops failed in 1772, the California colonists at the missions established by Gaspar de Portola slaughtered their cattle. When supply galleons did not arrive, a hunting party spent three months hunting grizzly bears, jerking the meat and providing over nine thousand pounds to northern settlements. A story in an 1855 edition of *Harper's New Monthly* Magazine describes bear meat: "Bar meat is best . . . in the fall. Cotch a bar, then when he has had a cornfield to hide in, and his spar ribs taste like rostin' ears."

"A steak cut from the haunch of the grisly bear, and roasted on a stick by a camp fire, is by no means despicable fare . . . ," relates T.J. Farnham in *Life, Adventures and Travels in California* (1849).

"Roast grizzly and bear steaks were always prominent features of the bills-of-fare in mining camp restaurants [California goldrush period]," commented B.F. Herrick in *Grade-school Grizzly*, "selling at a dollar a share, payable in gold dust."

". . . Our Camp Keeper had prepared an elegant supper of Grizzly Bear meat . . . ," noted mountain man Osborne Russell, in *Journal of a Trapper*, on August 10, 1837 while camped along the Stinking River in present day Wyoming. John Muir also enjoyed grizzly bear, commenting that it was the "best meat in the mountains."

Bear meat is not now the popular meal nor the necessity it was then, though it is consumed by many hunters and their families. The flavor is considered to be somewhere between pork and beef, though it varies with the bear's diet, and is tastiest if from two-year-olds that are feeding on berries or roots rather than on fish. The meat is high in fat, therefore pork recipes are good guides for cooking.

8 Bears and People

The interactions between people and bears have long been high-intensity conflicts, and most have included dramatic and varied reactions by the bears. Though the Lewis and Clark expedition believed the grizzly bear would rather attack than avoid humans, most evidence indicates that bears will typically flee at the sound or smell of people. However, to rely on each individual bear to be "typical" would be quite foolish.

Interactions

bear's interactions with people may include:

▲ Approaching for a better view

▲ Avoidance—secretively move away; remain in location allowing people to pass; visibly and/or noisily, rapidly flee

▲ Curiousness—approach or watch from distance

▲ Aggression—bluff charge to closer distance

▲ Attacks—to lessen the threat to cubs, depart without persistence; persist in attack, depart; persist in attack, consume victim

▲ Food conditioning—bears that associate people with food; bears that seek and eat people's food and garbage

▲ Habituation—bears that are accustomed to people and willing to approach

A study of brown bears in Kamchatka, eastern Commonwealth of Independent Nations, analyzed the response of bears to 230 encounters with humans. The results showed that: 70.7% avoided humans; 18.8% identified humans and moved away; 12.1% were indifferent; 2.2% reacted with a threat demonstration; and 1.2% attacked.

Bears' impacts on people may be described in three basic ways. 1) They have direct contact with people, inflicting injury or death. 2) They damage crops and property and kill domestic livestock. 3) They are nuisances; habituated and conditioned to human foods, they approach people and are unafraid, but they are not tame.

"Foolhardy settlers, contemptuous of the bear's abilities or puffed up with self-righteous bravado," writes James Cardoza in *The Black Bear in Massachusetts*, "attempted to overcome bears with such varied instruments as jack-knives, axes, oxgoads, pitchforks, and hoes."

Sources and Causes of Conflicts

Agriculture Bears seek crops such as carrots, corn, strawberries, raspberries, cranberries, and grains (oats), and they trample crops. Orchards are damaged as bears eat apples, pears, and plums, often inflicting more serious damage by tearing limbs from the trees. Bee hives are a common attraction to bears and serious economic losses are annually sustained.

Begging People feed bears, conditioning them to human foods and developing beggars. Injuries occur when a bear becomes persistent while in close contact with people, or when the person stops feeding them. Begging has long existed in parks and near developments.

"When pressed to find food in the summer," writes Koch, "polar bears have been known to swim to the sides of ships and beg for scraps of blubber."

Camping Campers in the front- or backcountry may be confronted with bears due to unsecured food and garbage, or because previous campers provided bears with food rewards and the bear is habituated and food-conditioned.

Dogs Dogs, hunting or pets, conflict with bears by chasing or barking, drawing a reaction from the bear. The dog normally retreats to its master, bringing along his newfound "friend." Dog food is an attractant when outside at a residence or cabin, and sometimes when inside.

A grizzly bear in Denali National Park rapidly walks toward park visitors who have approached too closely (note the blond fur typical of a "Toklat")
© Gary Brown

A garbage dump grizzly bear in Yellowstone National Park during the 1960s
Courtesy Yellowstone National Park

Bears that approach people are habituated, possibly food-conditioned, and definitely dangerous.

In a remote area of Alaska, a bear broke into a storage shed where 450 pounds of dog food were stored for sled dogs. The entire supply was consumed, according to park ranger Bruce Wadlington, with "slightly less than that many pounds" deposited only a few feet away on the porch in the form of feces.

Dumps   Commercial or household garbage is a major attractant, and when in the quantities found in dumps, will provide bears with a long-term source of unnatural foods. Livestock carcasses in dumps or ranch "carcass pits" provide an additional attractant.

Forest Industry   Bears damage and kill trees by biting, stripping the bark, and eating the sapwood. Such damage may result in major economic impacts on the timber industry. Frank Dufresne, in *No Room for Bears*, relates a comment by bear hunter "Bear" Bill Hulet, in Washington State. "I've knowed a single b'ar to wreck five hundred firs [Douglas] in a season."

Fishing   Bears challenge fishermen for their catch and compete with commercial fishermen at their nets, also sometimes damaging the nets.

Hiking   Hiking in bear country provides the potential of surprising and/or threatening a bear, with subsequent attack by the bear. The perceived threat may be to cubs or a food source.

Trunk of a tree stripped of bark by a bear
Courtesy Yellowstone National Park

Human Foods   Human foods at residences, camps, lodges, hotels, ranches, or villages may provide an attractant for bears if not properly stored. Such foods are normally high in protein, and bears become conditioned to them, seeking comparable foods from similar sources.

Hunting   Though hunting is an accepted and valuable bear-management tool, the activity often leads to conflicts. Hunters are often not as careful in bear country because they have protection—their gun. Hunting dogs attract unwanted bears. And wounded bears can be a major problem.

Livestock   "Although comparatively few bears become stock killers . . . the habit apparently persists in those individuals acquiring it," notes Cardoza. "Claimed losses, however may greatly exceed the actual damage caused by bears . . . discrepancies . . . arise from the bear's habit of feeding on carrion."

Parks   National parks in the United States and Canada have long been sources of human/bear conflicts, as bears have been fed in feeding grounds and at roadsides, and have raided unsecured human food and garbage.

Photography   Photographers attempting to attain the perfect close-up often find themselves invading a bear's "space" and are attacked, mauled, and killed.

Actions of Bears

AMERICAN BLACK BEARS
- Break into buildings seeking food
- Damage bee hives and honey production
- Damage gardens
- Kill domestic livestock
- Seek human food and garbage
- Strip bark from trees
- Suspicious of any intruder

"They are diabolically clever at gaining entry to locked buildings," notes Roger Caras in *North American Mammals*, describing the American black bear.

BROWN BEARS
- Challenge fishermen for their catch
- Damage bee hives and honey production
- Damage commercial fishing nets and catches
- Kill domestic livestock
- Seek game harvests of hunters
- Seek human food and garbage
- Live in peaceful coexistence with people and their animals in the Caucus and Carpathian Mountains (Romania)
- Powerful; break into buildings, through windows or tear out walls

POLAR BEARS
- Less afraid of people than other bears
- Seek garbage

ASIATIC BLACK BEARS
- Seek garbage
- Kill livestock

GIANT PANDAS
- Known to enter camps

SLOTH BEARS
- Viciously attack when startled

SUN BEARS
- Damage coconut plantations

SPECTACLED BEARS
- Damage young palm trees; eat new leaves
- Kill young llamas
- Kill cattle and other domestic animals

Human Injuries and Fatalities

When a confrontation with a bear results in human injuries and deaths, the occasion regularly attracts extraordinary headlines that take bears to task as serial killers. In reality, vehicle accidents, many diseases, falls, homicides, and numerous other incidents each injure and kill thousands more individuals every year than do bears. We seem to be more aware and concerned about being attacked by a wild animal than about a vehicle that runs us down with a "wild animal" at the wheel.

"In Ontario, in November 1929," Cardoza quotes Ernest Thompson Seton, "a trapper was killed by a 'monstrous' black bear whose face and neck were laced with festering porcupine quills."

In Yellowstone National Park, during 1967, a "bear-feeding" visitor lost two fingers when a black bear failed to distinguish where the victim's food ended and the fingers began.

In Glacier National Park, a photographer pursued and approached a grizzly bear sow with cubs. The sow, perceiving a threat to her cubs—and possibly herself—attacked and killed the individual. He had attempted to climb a tree, but the quickness and speed of the bear were too great.

INJURIES AND DEATHS IN NORTH AMERICA

Some North American states and provinces maintain records of bear-caused injuries and fatalities. (Average per year; 1981–1990)

	Injuries	Fatalities		Injuries	Fatalities		Injuries	Fatalities
American black bears								
Alabama	0.0	0.0	Montana	*	*	Utah	0.5	0.0
Alaska	0.7	0.0	Nevada	1.0	0.0	Vermont	0.0	0.0
Arizona	*	0.0	New Hampshire	0.0	0.0	Virginia	0.1	0.0
Arkansas	0.0	0.0				Washington	*	*
California	2.5	0.0	New Jersey	0.0	0.0	West Virginia	0.1	0.0
Colorado	0.1	0.1	New Mexico	0.5	0.0	Wisconsin	1.5	Fewer than 1.0
Connecticut	0.0	0.0	New York	Fewer than 1.0	0.0			
Florida	0.05	0.0				Wyoming	0.0	0.0
Georgia	0.0	0.0	North Carolina	0.0	0.0	Alberta	0.75	0.3
Idaho	Fewer than 1.0	0.0	North Dakota	0.0	0.0	British Columbia	Fewer than 1.0	Fewer than 1.0
			Oklahoma	0.0	0.0			
Kentucky	0.0	0.0	Oregon	Fewer than 1.0	0.0	Manitoba	Fewer than 1.0	Fewer than 0.1
Louisiana	0.0	0.0						
Maine	1.5	0.0	Pennsylvania	Fewer than 1.0	0.0	New Brunswick	0.0	0.0
Maryland	0.0	0.0				Newfoundland	0.0	0.0
Massachusetts	0.0	0.0	Rhode Island	*	0.0	Northwest Territories	0.0	0.0
Michigan	Fewer than 1.0	0.0	South Carolina	0.0	0.0	Nova Scotia	0.0	0.0
Minnesota	1.0	0.0	South Dakota	0.0	0.0	Saskatchewan	0.1	0.1
Mississippi	0.0	0.0	Tennessee	*	0.0	Yukon	Fewer than 1.0	0.0
Missouri	*	0.0	Texas	0.0	0.0			
Grizzly bears**								
Alaska	0.5	0.0	Alberta	0.5	.25	Yukon Territory	Fewer than 1.0	0.0
Idaho	*	0.0	British Columbia	Fewer than 1.0	0.0			
Montana**								
Washington	0.0	0.0	Northwest Territories	1.0	Fewer than 0.1			
Wyoming	0.26	0.0						
Polar bears								
Alaska	Fewer than 1.0	Fewer than 1.0	Newfoundland	0.0	0.0	Yukon	Fewer than 1.0	*
Manitoba	Fewer than 1.0	0.1	Northwest Territories	Fewer than 1.0	Fewer than 0.1			

*Information unavailable
**Alaskan brown bear 0.75 injuries, 0.25 fatalities

Treatment of Wounds
Inflicted by Bears

In California, during 1828, wounds were first washed, then dressed with plasters of soap and sugar.

Today, wounds are carefully irrigated and flushed, and if necessary, sutured. The victim is placed on antibiotics, and rabies treatment is a consideration.

Property Damage

"In New Hampshire, about 1955," according to Cardoza, "a single 208.8-kilogram (450-pound) male [American black bear] killed at least 27 cows over a two-year period."

In Yellowstone National Park, a grizzly bear tore off a wall of a wooden building where garbage from a hotel kitchen was stored.

Damage to crops, and personal and public property is quite substantial. Often, identification of the responsible species is not possible. Many states and provinces do not maintain property damage records, and brown bear and polar bear information is scarce.

During the period of 1981 to 1991, recorded annual property damage by American black bears ranged from $300,000 in Oregon (primarily forest damage), to no losses in other states.

National Park Service sign often used to warn hikers of bear activity in a specific area
Courtesy Yellowstone National Park

Traveling, Camping and Living in Bear Country

The key to successfully sharing bear country with those who were there first—the bears—is *Prevention*, which actually is preparation. "Your best weapon to minimize the risk of a bear attack is your brain," explains Stephen Herrero in *Bear Attacks*. "Use it as soon as you contemplate a trip to bear country, and continue to use it throughout your stay."

First mentally prepare yourself—there is a risk when you are in bear country. However, you probably took a greater risk traveling the world's highways getting to bear country.

Obtain a copy of Herrero's *Bear Attacks: Their Causes and Avoidance*. It is considered by many bear authorities as the most important "bear management document" written in the last twenty years. Not only will it provide a perspective to being in bear country, but it is an excellent How-to and How-not-to publication.

National Park Service sign used to provide information for backcountry hikers and campers in bear country
Courtesy National Park Service

Hiking—Overnight or Day Trips

Be prepared physically and mentally so you are alert and aware, and able to use good judgement to make sound decisions. To begin with, discuss your itinerary with someone who knows about the country and its bears, and obtain all bear information and warnings for the particular area you are entering. It is advisable to travel with a group as they are less apt to have encounters with bears. A single person hiking sustains 57% of all injuries; parties of two sustain 29%. Also, do not hike with pets.

Travel during the day; bears use human trails at night. Do not surprise a bear; talk, sing, or make other noises as you travel to alert bears of your presence. Travel in the open if possible. Remember: bears normally avoid humans if forewarned.

If you observe a bear, avoid it and detour well around it. Keep in mind that the bear may be moving in a direction that intersects your detour route. If in doubt, turn around and hike another day.

Backcountry Camping

Use the hiking measures above since backcountry hiking and camping are closely related. Obtain the necessary camping permit. Carry non-odorous foods that are well packaged and freeze dried. Do not camp where there is sign of bear or in a messy camp. Camp away from trails if possible and cook and store your foods at least 100 yards from where you sleep. Hang your food (human, pet, and horse) and garbage out of reach of bears and keep a clean camp.

Cook on stoves, not open fires, and never in your tent. Do not sleep in the same clothes you wore while cooking. Do not place food, cosmetics, deodorants, or any other odorous items in your tent. Use the pack-in and pack-out method of handling garbage and never bury it. If you must burn it, do so totally in a fire pit until there are no remnant food odors. Remember, a bear is able to smell considerably better than you are. In hunting camp, hang game meat out of reach of bears.

Do not surprise a bear; use a flashlight if moving about in the dark.

Vehicle Camping

Be prepared mentally so you are alert and aware, and able to use good judgement to make sound decisions. Obtain the necessary camping permit and all bear information and warnings for the campground and particular area you are visiting. Do not camp where there is sign of bear, or in a messy camp. Keep your camp site clean.

Do not cook in your tent and do not sleep in the same clothes you wore while cooking. Secure your food in your vehicle or in a storage locker provided in the campground, or hang it out of reach of bears. Dispose of your garbage promptly and in bearproof receptacles provided by the campground; if these are not available, hang your garbage out of reach of bears. Do not place food, cosmetics, deodorants, or any other odorous items in your tent.

Do not surprise a bear; use a flashlight if moving about in the dark.

Living in Bear Country

Recognize that you live in "bear country," and that your existence must be compatible with the existence of bears. Appreciate and enjoy the fact that you live in a unique place, and respect the bears as other residents. Store all human, pet, and livestock foods away from bears, and properly store and dispose of garbage so it is not an attractant. Specifically, ranches must properly dispose of livestock carcasses. Fence all gardens and bee hives to keep out bears.

Viewing and Photographing Bears

These are serious activities as you are intentionally seeking and possibly approaching bears. Obtain local and agency information regarding the locations of bears and how to best view and photograph them.

Viewing bears can be very exciting and rewarding, but you must accept the fact that it may be at a long distance. *Do not approach bears*. Use binoculars or a spotting scope and remain near your vehicle or in it if a bear is within one hundred yards.

Photographers should use long lenses; if you do not have this equipment, enjoy and be proud of your "bear in the distance" photograph, or, if necessary, purchase a photograph or painting!

The Encounter

Again, **Prevention!** Detect the bear from a long distance or allow it to detect and identify you from a long distance. Avoid the bear—do not approach. If the bear is approaching, you may want to climb a tree, which under hurried conditions is difficult at best, and should be attempted while you have adequate time.

Bearproof garbage cans prevent bears from obtaining this common unnatural food
© *Gary Brown*

However, if you find yourself in a close encounter, do not run. (Running seems to incite bears.) Talk softly to the bear, letting it know you are a human and not a threat. Slowly back away and keep going. If the bear follows you or bluff-charges, throw down a glove, hat, or some other item to distract it and continue backing away. *Do not throw food.*

If the bear continues its charge and attacks, play dead by lying on your stomach and interlocking your fingers at the back of your neck. Keep your pack on—it provides protection for your back. Remain absolutely silent and still. (At least try!) The bear is trying to lessen your threat, and your movements and/or sounds may cause the bear to persist in its attack. Remain silent and still until you are sure the bear is gone. Be careful because it may be a short distance away, watching. Be patient, listen, and be certain!

Remember, these are not the only precautionary measures necessary if you're in bear country. Read as much as possible on the subject and check with local authorities and residents to learn all you can about bears and the country where you will be traveling, camping, or living. Be smart and enjoy the fact that you are sharing an area with bears.

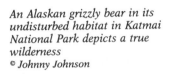

An Alaskan grizzly bear in its undisturbed habitat in Katmai National Park depicts a true wilderness
© *Johnny Johnson*

9 Today's Bears

The Status of Bears

Bears are in a time of rapid change, and are disappearing from today's world. Interacting with humans, and already eliminated from fifty percent to seventy-five percent of their historic range, their future in many countries is uncertain; some populations are assured of disappearing. Many populations remain only in reserves and parks, where their status is localized. Six of the world's eight species of bears are in worse condition than they were in the early 1970s.

"Man and bears are direct competitors for space and resources worldwide," explains Christopher Servheen in *The Status and Conservation of the Bears of the World*. "This competition is mediated by resource availability and the adaptability of both species. Man is certainly more adaptable and effective at resource exploitation when in competition with bears. Man continues to develop new and effective mechanized resource use strategies while bears continue to attempt to use resources in 'natural' ways. Under such a system of interaction, the efficient adaptable species will eventually eliminate the competitor."

By the year 2025, the world's human population will be double what it is now, primarily in Southeast Asia. All species of bears will be highly impacted, but three species may vanish.

The importance people have placed upon bears has not always been beneficial for the animals. Today, as well as in the past, bears are viewed in a broad range, from elements of wilderness to tangible benefits in the form of subsistence and of commercial value. There are nontangible benefits as well, as they provide enjoyment and excitement, and serve as religious symbols.

". . . the sequoia of the animals. . . ."

NATURALIST JOHN MUIR, 1901

The 1889 Annual Report of Yellowstone National Park Superintendent Captain F. A. Boutelle recommended control of predators because they were plentiful like the other animals. "I am more than ever convinced that the bear and puma do a great deal of mischief and ought to be reduced in numbers. While they may be something of a curiosity to visitors to the park, I hardly think them an agreeable surprise. Very few who come here 'have lost any bear'."

Nearly all countries where bears live have at some time placed bounties on them. "As long as bears and men have shared the earth," wrote George Laycock in *The Wild Bears*, "there has existed between them a special adversary condition. Although we sometimes ignore the small wild animals around us and let them go their way, the bear is a special case. Until recent years we have, almost universally, looked upon these animals as if they somehow threaten our territorial dominance." Some people continue to view bears in this light. As human development and activities spread, the large carnivores are the first to die due to loss of habitat and direct killing.

Major Concerns	American Black	Brown	Polar	Asiatic Black	Giant Panda	Sloth	Sun	Spectacled
				SPECIES				
Human Population		C		C	C		C	
Agriculture activities				C				
Competition with Other Species	C	C		U		U	U	U
High Mortality		C		U		C	C	C
Insufficient Research								
Isolated Populations	C **b**	C		U			U	
Oil & Gas Development	C		C					
Livestock Depredation	C							C
Low Numbers		C **c**		U	C	U	U	U
Parts Sales	C			C		C	C	
Poaching				C		C	C	
Poisoning	C							
Sports/Subsistence Hunting	C		C			C		
Timber Harvest	C			C		C	C	C **d**
Use as Food	C	C **a**		C		U	C	
Use as Medicine	C			C		C	C	
Use as Pets						C	C	

Patricia Brown

■ Concern
● Unknown

a—Primarily paws
b—Few populations
c—European brown bears

d—Also defoliation; government action against drug cartels hidden in forests

Present Condition of the Bear Species

AMERICAN BLACK BEAR

Survival assured. They are flexible to human pressures; most populations relatively secure although some individual populations endangered by isolation, lack of food, and overall habitat loss; populations stable (or increasing) in many places, except in southeastern United States—e.g. Louisiana black bear listed as threatened in Louisiana, Mississippi, and Texas under Endangered Species Act; also listed under CITES (Convention on International Trade in Endangered Species of Wild Fauna and Flora, 1973; see Appendix B)

Mexico: Population impacted by logging practices; shot by ranchers, loggers, miners, and sportsmen

Alaska and Yukon: Glacier bear (isolated subspecies/different color phase) listed in IUCN (International Union For Conservation Of Nature and Natural Resources; see Appendix B) Red Book

BROWN BEAR

Survival assured. Some subspecies and individual populations extinct and others threatened with extinction; low numbers in Europe

Canada: Presently secure in remaining areas that have minimal access to humans

China: Protected as a conserved animal under the Wildlife Protection Law of the People's Republic of China; listed under CITES

Czechoslovakia: Population increasing

Finland: Some populations in the country protected; overall increasing

France: Small perilous, but protected population in Pyrenees Mountains

India: Protected under Wildlife Protection Act of 1972; listed under CITES

Japan: Considered pests; listed under CITES

Mexico: Probably extinct

Nepal: Protected under the National Parks and Wildlife Conservation Act; listed under CITES

Norway: Protected in areas where the only permitted activity is bear research; 11% of the country is proposed for preserves

Poland: Some individual populations protected

Spain: Protected

United States: Protected (listed as threatened under the Endangered Species Act of 1973) in the contiguous 48 states where it has been eliminated from over 99% of its original range

POLAR BEAR

Occupies most of original habitat (more than any other world bear species); protected under 1973 (affirmed 1978, reaffirmed 1981) International Agreement on the Conservation of Polar Bears and Their Habitat—Canada, Denmark (Greenland), Norway, former Soviet

Union, United States; major international management cooperation exists through the Polar Bear Specialist Group (under auspices of the IUCN in 1965; consists of biologists from polar bear countries specializing in research and management); listed in IUCN Red Book; international trade regulated under CITES

Canada: Protected; hunting limited to Eskimos and other Native Americans for subsistence and sale of skins; harvests regulated by quota

Commonwealth of Independent Nations: completely protected in Russian arctic; hunting prohibited

Greenland: Protected; hunting limited to Eskimos and other long-time residents for subsistence and sale of skins

North America: Hunting controlled; protected under US Endangered Species Act and US Marine Mammals Protection Act, 1972

Scandinavia: Hunting controlled

ASIATIC BLACK BEAR

Endangered and generally declining; uncertain future in most of range

Bangladesh: Protected under Bangladesh Wild Life Preservation Act, 1974, but fast perishing; listed under CITES

Bhutan: Hunting banned

Burma: Protected under Burma Wild Life Protection Act, 1936

China: Protected as a conserved animal under Wildlife Protection Law of the People's Republic of China; listed under CITES; decreasing

Commonwealth of Independent Nations: Protected

India: Regulated as special game; listed under CITES

Japan: Population considered safe (highly questionable); no protection; unlimited hunting harvest; considered pests; listed under CITES

Laos: Protected under Decree of the Council of Ministers, in Relation to the Prohibition of Wildlife Trade

Pakistan: Baluchistan subspecies listed in IUCN Red Book

South Korea: Protected by Authority of the Wildlife Protection and Hunting Law; near extinction

Taiwan: Protected under Wildlife Conservation Law

Thailand: Protected under Wild Animals Reservation and Protection Act; listed under CITES

Vietnam: No protection or management

GIANT PANDA

Rare (probably always has been); endangered with fragmented population; survival outside parks doubtful due to Chinese population expansion—100 million people nearby; "completely protected," but with few protective measures; listed under CITES and in IUCN Red Book; protected as a second class conserved animal under the Wildlife Protection Law of the People's Republic of China; some sanctuaries established.

Bears of North America
Status and Trend

	AMERICAN BLACK		GRIZZLY*		POLAR	
	Status	Trend	Status	Trend	Status	Trend
UNITED STATES						
Alabama	Threat	Stable				
Alaska	Game	Stable	Game	Stable	Protected	Stable
Arizona	Game	Stable	Extinct			
Arkansas	Game	Increase				
California	Game	Increase	Extinct			
Colorado	Game	Increase	Extinct			
Connecticut	Threat	Increase				
Delaware	Extinct					
Florida	Game/Threat	Stable				
Georgia	Game	Increase				
Hawaii**						
Idaho	Game	Stable	Threat	Decrease		
Illinois	Extinct					
Indiana	Extinct					
Iowa	Extinct					
Kansas	Extinct		Extinct			
Kentucky	Threat	Increase				
Louisiana	Threat	Rare				
Maine	Game	Stable				
Maryland	Game	Increase				
Massachusets	Game	Stable				
Michigan	Game	Stable				
Minnesota	Game	Increase				
Mississippi	Endangered	Increase				
Missouri	Game	Increase				
Montana	Game	Stable	Threat	Increase		
Nebraska	Extinct		Extinct			
Nevada	Game	Increase	Extinct			
New Hampshire	Game	Increase				
New Jersey	Game/Threat	Increase				
New Mexico	Game	Stable	Extinct			
New York	Game	Increase				
North Carolina	Game	Stable				
North Dakota	Endangered	Rare	Extinct			
Ohio	Extinct					
Oklahoma	Game	Increase	Extinct			
Oregon	Game	Increase	Extinct			
Pennsylvania	Game	Stable				

Bears of North America
Status and Trend

	AMERICAN BLACK		GRIZZLY*		POLAR	
	Status	Trend	Status	Trend	Status	Trend
Rhode Island	Endangered	Rare				
South Carolina	Game	Increase				
South Dakota	Endangered	Rare	Extinct			
Tennessee	Game	Increase				
Texas	Endangered	Increase	Extinct			
Utah	Game	Increase	Extinct			
Vermont	Game	Increase				
Virginia	Game	Stable				
Washington	Game	Increase	Threat	Unknown		
West Virginia	Game	Increase				
Wisconsin	Game	Stable				
Wyoming	Game	Stable	Threat	Increase		
CANADA						
Alberta	Game	Stable	Game	Increasing		
British Columbia	Game	Increasing	Game	Stable		
Manitoba	Game	Stable	Extinct		Protected	Stable
New Brunswick	Game	Stable				
Newfoundland	Game	Stable			Game	Stable
Northwest Territories	Game	Stable	Game	Stable	Endangered	Stable
Nova Scotia	Game	Increasing				
Ontario	Game	Stable			***Vulnerable	Stable
Quebec	Game	Stable			***Vulnerable	Stable
Saskatchewan	Game	Stable	Extinct			
Yukon	Game	Stable	Game	Stable	Game	Stable
MEXICO						
Baja Calif Norte			Extinct			
Chihuahua	Endangered	Decrease	Extinct?			
Coahuila	Endangered	Decrease	Extinct			
Durango	Endangered	Decrease	Extinct			
Nuevo Leon	Endangered	Decrease				
San Luis Potosi	Endangered	Decrease				
Sinaloa	Endangered	Decrease				
Sonora	Endangered	Decrease	Extinct			
Tamaulipas	Endangered	Decrease				
Zacatecas	Endangered	Decrease				

*Alaskan and Kodiak Brown Bears are listed as "game" and with general stable populations.
**Bears have never existed
***Growing awareness of the polar bear's requirements.
Information source: State and Provincial wildlife management agencies.
Compilation: Patricia Brown

SLOTH BEARS	Faced with expanding human population; habitat diminishing rapidly due to human encroachment.
	Bangladesh: Protected under Bangladesh Wild Life Preservation Act, 1974; listed under CITES
	Bhutan: Hunting banned
	India: Regulated as special game; listed under CITES
	Sri Lanka: Listed under CITES; some protection provided under the Fauna And Flora Protection Ordinance of Sri Lanka
SUN BEAR	Endangered; one of the rarest tropical forest animals (probably always has been); faced with 5th largest, and expanding human population; minimal government management or research; protection primarily in nature reserves; listed in the IUCN Red Book; future bleak
	Bangladesh: Protected under Bangladesh Wild Life Preservation Act, 1974; listed under CITES
	Burma: Protected under Burma Wild Life Protection Act, 1936
	China: Survival in doubt; protected under Wildlife Protection Law of the People's Republic of China; listed under CITES
	India: Totally protected under Wildlife Protection Act of 1972; listed under CITES
	Indonesia: Completely protected under Wildlife Protection Ordinance of 1931; faces 180 million people; listed under CITES
	Laos: Considered protected under Decree of the Council Of Ministers in Relation to the Prohibition of Wildlife Trade, however receives virtually no protection
	Malaysia: Listed as a game animal; listed under CITES
	Thailand: Protected under Wild Animals Reservation and Protection Act; listed under CITES
SPECTACLED BEAR	Overall population endangered; listed as endangered in northern Bolivia, Colombia, Venezuela; rare in Venezuela; undisturbed environment in eastern Ecuador and Peru, and northern Bolivia; possibly small population in northern Argentina
	Peru: Hunted extensively; two thirds of habitat lost in last 30 years (1,000 feet of lower elevation every 3 years due to elimination of food sources)

Status and Trend of Bears in Mexico

Very little is known and understood of the population distribution and status of the American black bear in Mexico. A few bears may exist farther south and in states additional to those listed.

Extinction of the grizzly bear (brown bear) in Mexico is highly probable. Recent investigation to determine the bear's status has been minimal. Any continued existence of grizzly bears would most likely be in the Sierra del Nido, State of Chihuahua.

The Last Bears—Extinction

T he last" is difficult to assess. The final black or grizzly bear of a population may have been an unreported or undocumented kill, or may have died naturally without human awareness, and "rumors" always seemed to follow the last documentation. Some bear populations were eliminated, but a transient straggler from elsewhere may have passed through the subject area. Grizzly bears were, and remain, in conflict with the activities of humans and were considered pests, threats, and vermin. The black bear populations of the East were the first to go. Then the grizzly bears of the Plains vanished as the herds of bison, an important food source, were eliminated.

The American black bear is presently in all of the United States and Canadian provinces, except as noted in the sidebar and in Hawaii, where it has never existed. It may have at one time been gone from some of the New England states, but has since reestablished itself. In Mexico, it may have previously existed in other states beyond those in which it is currently found.

Grizzly bears originally existed in seventeen states of the United States, five Mexican states, and six Canadian provinces and territories. According to David Brown and John Murray in *The Last Grizzly*, the time frame of the grizzly bear's demise was, "from the arrival of Anglo-Americans in the 1820s to the present, thus spanning the period from 'Westering Man's' initial encounters with the Great Bear to his eventual and absolute victory—a feat that, once attained, was never celebrated; only the conflict would be cherished.

"And so the future of the grizzly in the Southwest hangs on the belief—one might say faith—that a few of the great beasts are holed up in some remote part of Mexico," notes Brown, "or that a couple of individuals still hang on in Colorado's San Juan Mountains."

LAST OBSERVED OR RECORDED

American Black Bear

Delaware 1700s	*Kansas* 1880s (2 transients observed 1965)
Illinois Information unavailable	*Nebraska* 1908
Indiana 1888	*Ohio* Late 1800s (occasional transient observed)
Iowa Approximately 1880	

American Black Bear

Rhode Island   1880

Prince Edward Island   Shot by George (Geordie) and Bernard Leslie in 1927 with 12-gauge shotguns; killing shell had a 3/4-inch ball bearing

Mexico   May have existed in states besides those presently with bears

Grizzly Bear

Arizona   Shot by Richard R. Miller (cowboy/hunter) September 13, 1935; two-year-old, 200 pounds; Greenlee County (evidence of two other bears found at the site, but they were never seen)

California   Shot by Jesse B. Agnew (rancher) August, 1922, in Horse Corral Meadow, Tulare County; evidence exists of "possible" observations in Sequoia National Park area until 1924

Colorado   Killed by Ed Wiseman (outfitter/hunting guide) September 23, 1979, with arrow in hand, while being mauled; San Juan Mountains

Kansas   Previously existed but minimal documentation; gone well before 1890

Nebraska   Previously existed but no documentation; gone well before 1890

Nevada   No official record of previous existence—strange since large populations existed in surrounding states and some suitable habitat existed; one source describes grizzly bear killed in 1907 near Silver Creek by Charles Foley

New Mexico   Shot by Tom Campbell, 1933, in the Jemez Mountains

North Dakota   Shot by Dave Warren, fall 1897, near Oakdale, eastern edge of Killdeer Mountains

Oklahoma   Previously existed but no documentation; gone well before 1890

Oregon   Killed by Evan Stoneman (government trapper) September 14, 1931, in Wallowa County, northeastern part of state; unconfirmed report recorded in 1933

South Dakota   Pre-1900; no official record

Texas   Shot by C.O. Finley, John Z. Means in October 1890. A pack of 52 dogs tracked down a 1,100-pound, very old male

Utah   Trapped and shot by Frank Clark (sheepherder) August 22, 1923, in northern Utah— 1,100-pound stock-killer called Ephraim; Old Ephraim's memorial is of natural stone in Logan Canyon, a nine-foot 11-inch, 9000-pound monument with a plaque erected in 1966 by local Boy Scouts, their parents, and other supporters of the Scouting program.

Washington   Considered extinct in 1913; 10–20 animals have now emmigrated from Canada

Canada

Manitoba   Approximately 1825 but minimal documentation

Saskatchewan   Information unavailable

The grave of old Ephraim, the last grizzly bear in Utah. A stone monument has since been erected in the general area to recognize the sadness in the destruction of these magnificent bears
Courtesy The Five Heirs of Newell J. Crookston

Mexico

Baja California Norte   Information unavailable

Chihuahua   Present existence questionable; possibly along Chihuahua/Sonora border.

1928 and 1932: last grizzly bears killed in Colonia Garcia-Colonia Pacheco area

1932: last-known grizzly bear killed in the Sierra Madre, Chihuahua/Durango

1954: grizzly in the Friar Mountains

1957: grizzly bears killed in the Sierra del Nido, Chihuahua, in June, and, on October 4

1957–1961: Starker Leopold investigated Sierra del Nido and estimated a population of thirty

1960: John Nutt and Curtis Prock killed large grizzly bear in Sierra del Nido

1969: last confirmed report of grizzly bear in Sierra del Nido, Chihuahua

1982: David Brown investigated the Sierra del Nido and found no evidence; a foreman of the Rancho El Nido claimed that there had been no grizzly bears in "20 years"

Coahuila   Information unavailable

Durango   Information unavailable

Sonora   1918; apparently in the Sierra de los Ajos

Brown Bears

Atlas Mountains, Africa   1891; another unverified report of bear observation in the 1920s

England   Eleventh century

Great Britain   1,000 years ago

Scotland   Over 900 years ago

Holland   300 years ago

Germany   Nineteenth century

Switzerland   Early twentieth century

Austria   Decreed extermination in 1788

Most of Europe   By 1850

Bavaria   1836

Denmark   3,000 BC (5,000 years ago)

French Alps   1937

Human Impacts on Bears

Conflicts between bears and people have occurred since the two species began sharing the same habitats. The bears held their own, to a small degree, until technology provided the repeating firearm. Early mortality was by direct killing, while in recent times the impacts are, in some areas, due more to the loss and degradation of bear habitat.

Early settlers in North America began eradicating bears as they cut forests and intensely hunted the American black bear for subsistence, and as a pest. Grizzly bears were killed out of fear and for sport.

Whalers provided the first major human impact on polar bears when they shot and trapped the bears for the hide trade. They also provided the Eskimos with rifles, which improved the hunting ability of these arctic residents. "It was in the seventeenth century, when whalers first penetrated the Norwegian and Russian sectors of the Arctic, that their [polar bear] survival as a species began to be threatened."

Present Worldwide Impacts on Bears

We are a "resource intense society," and our world population is rapidly increasing. The impacts and pressures affecting all bear species are varied but severe:

▲ Expansion of human population

▲ Hunter and trapper conflicts with bears

▲ Bears forced into isolated and fragmented pockets, which is a precursor to extinction

▲ Forestry practices

▲ Habitat exploitation and destruction; habitat shrinking

▲ Lack of adequate preserves

▲ Lack of cooperation; agencies unwilling to compromise their jurisdictions

▲ Lack of human value for bears

▲ Lack of knowledge

▲ Lack of research funding and resource planning programs, especially in South America and Eurasia

▲ Lack of support for conservation

- ▲ Mineral exploration and extraction practices

- ▲ Poaching

- ▲ Pets and products trade

- ▲ Poison dispersed for other animals

- ▲ Poorly managed hunting programs

- ▲ Poorly enforced laws, minimal fines, and light jail sentences

- ▲ Recreation activities

- ▲ War

"In a country with one billion people the demand for agricultural land, timber, and other resources is so great that the panda's wilderness home continues to shrink," notes George Schaller *et al.* in *The Giant Pandas of Wolong*.

"The most potential contributing factor in the destruction of the grizzly in the United States," writes Harold Mc-Cracken in *The Beast that Walks Like Man*, "was the introduction of domestic cattle and farm stock into the grassy mountain valleys and more open ranges west of the Great Plains." The Indians originally called the great central valley of California, "the home of the bear."

Bear Mortality

Bears die from a variety of natural and human-related causes.

Causes

Asphyxiation Bears have been found dead (suffocated) in hot spring areas (Yellowstone National Park) where they entered a draw or other depression in which carbon dioxide had displaced the oxygen.

Electrocution Bears have occasionally been electrocuted by coming into contact with fallen power lines or exploring high-power junction boxes that have been left open.

Enemies Deaths occur due to other animals capable of inflicting mortal wounds.

Falls In Italy, a biologist witnessed a brown bear stumble and fall over a 1,000-foot cliff.

A grizzly bear intentionally killed in Yellowstone National Park because it had become a nuisance—the fault of park visitors providing it food
Courtesy National Park Service

A small American black bear fell to its death while scrambling on the ledges next to Yellowstone Falls. Paul Schullery, in *Yellowstone Bear Tales*, relates park ranger F.T. Johnston's description: "... climb up to a point even with the top of the Falls. Here he slipped when a rock came loose, and slid and fell back into the canyon, and then down into the river under the falls."

James Jonkel, in *Animal Accidents and Deaths*, notes, "... an adult polar bear dead in the Northwest Territories that had broken its back while sliding down a snowfield."

Internal Hemorrhage A grizzly bear died while digging for prey under a rock and was found, with its head in a pool of blood, by author A. Russell, *Grizzly Country*.

Management Bears are often destroyed as nuisances, or they die during other management and research actions due to immobilization problems.

Natural Natural deaths are obviously difficult to determine, as humans are normally not witness to the event. Bears are able, however, to remain in balance with natural mortality and their natural enemies, but when humans interfere natural compensation is often inadequate to maintain the population.

Poisoning Bears die from poisons intended for other animals, or from eating carrion of animals killed by poisoning efforts to rid a ranch, farm, or other development of pests and nuisance animals.

Starvation Bears ill-prepared for hibernation may die in their den, or those with teeth problems may be unable to eat enough. When teeth become worn or abscessed, bears are unable to chew the necessary foods, and adequate nutrition is no longer possible. They often just do not emerge from their dens, as they have hibernated without an adequate storage of fat.

Trapping Traps set for other animal species are the second largest cause of giant panda deaths.

Vehicle Accidents Bears crossing roads are occasionally killed by vehicles, and those using railroad right-of-ways are struck by trains. Corn spills from derailed train cars in Montana have attracted bears that were subsequently killed by passing trains, as well as cars and trucks.

War Bears die during international and civil wars.

Wounds Natural wounds from fighting other bears and enemies, or broken tree limbs, may cause death.

Poaching Poaching—the illegal taking of wildlife—is prevalent around the world, and is a significant cause of bear mortality in many countries. Fifty-four giant pandas were poached during the period 1983 to 1987. In Eurasia, as bears are forced into isolated pockets, poachers find these well-defined populations easy shooting.

"We talked with a researcher who witnessed hunters carrying a poached bear back to camp inside Thailand's Khao Yai National Park," relate Judy Mills and Chrisotpher Servheen, "home to nearly 60 poacher camps at the time...."

Some North American state and provincial wildlife management agencies maintain poaching records. Statistics reflect a ten-year average and are based on estimates, known cases, percentages of known cases and undercover law enforcement actions. (See next page.)

Commercial Poaching of Bears

Poaching of bears originally was synonymous with family subsistence, but now is controlled and influenced to a major extent by commercial operations. International bear poaching rings are impacting bear populations in Eurasia and North America. "Wildlife poaching has become so pervasive and difficult to combat that it threatens to ruin animal

ACCIDENTAL AND NUISANCE DEATHS (AVERAGE PER YEAR) OF AMERICAN BLACK BEARS

United States	Accidental	Nuisance
Alabama	2	0
Arizona	10	15
California	100	70
Colorado	*	10
Connecticut	0	0
Maine	20	50
Maryland	2	0
Massachusetts	5	5
Minnesota	100	600
Mississippi	1	0
Missouri	1	1
Nevada	3	2
New Hampshire	15	3
New Jersey	10	0
New York	24	16
North Carolina	95	7
Oklahoma	0	1
Oregon	8	13

BEARS POACHED IN NORTH AMERICA

United States	American Black Bear	Grizzly Bear	Polar Bear
Alabama	1	—	—
Alaska	10	0	0
Arizona	5	—	—
Arkansas	Low	—	—
California	300	—	—
Connecticut	0	—	—
Kentucky	3	—	—
Maine	200	—	—
Maryland	3	—	—
Massachusetts	23	—	—
Missouri	2	—	—
Nevada	1	—	—
New Jersey	15	—	—
New York	12	—	—
North Carolina	18	—	—
Oklahoma	3	—	—
South Carolina	2	—	—
Texas	2	—	—
Utah	4	—	—
Virginia	10	—	—
West Virginia	50	—	—
Wisconsin	30	—	—
Wyoming	2	—	—

Canada

	American Black Bear	Grizzly Bear	Polar Bear
Alberta	*	5	—
British Columbia	*	150	—
Manitoba	100	—	0
New Brunswick	20	—	—
Newfoundland	50	—	2 or 3
Northwest Territories	Low	—	—
Quebec	16	—	*

Mexico

Significant illegal hunting of American black bears occurs in Mexico.

*Information unavailable

populations around the American West and the world, a top wildlife law officer says." (Associated Press, 4/30/92)

- ❖ Traditional poaching by hunters is on the decline
- ❖ Poaching by commercial interests is out of control
- ❖ Poaching is a menace to all bear populations
- ❖ Bears illegally taken for their parts
- ❖ More than 3 billion people in the Orient use bear parts as medicinal remedies
- ❖ Committed by international poaching rings

- ❖ Poaching often in conjunction with drug cartels and bear farms
- ❖ Forty to 60% of the American black bears in the United States are being taken by poaching
- ❖ American black bears are the source of the greatest profits for international poachers
- ❖ Bears from United States and Canada are prized in Asia
- ❖ Bears are taken because they represent cultural and spiritual values

Hunting

Hunting is a major element in bear management, helping to control the size of populations, and problem bears. Some countries continue to allow indiscriminate hunting, a serious cause of mortality that jeopardizes bear populations. Hunting is allowed without the appropriate population and other management data, and many countries prohibit hunting but are unable to control the illegal taking of bears.

ACCIDENTAL AND NUISANCE DEATHS (AVERAGE PER YEAR) OF AMERICAN BLACK BEARS

United States	Accidental	Nuisance
South Carolina	2	2
Utah	2	11
Vermont	6	6
Virginia	27	2
West Virginia	25	15
Wisconsin	13	15
Wyoming	1	3

Canada	Accidental	Nuisance
Alberta	*	258
British Columbia	*	250
Manitoba	*	150
New Brunswick	40	300
Quebec	46	28
Yukon Territory	*	13

*Accidental deaths unknown

COUNTRIES THAT PROHIBIT BEAR HUNTING

Bhutan (special permit for bears damaging crops)

Bulgaria

Burma

Czechoslovakia

China (special permit for bears damaging crops or livestock)

Finland (northern)

India (brown and sun bears may be killed under a

dangerous animal permit, and there is limited hunting of sloth and Asiatic black bears)

Indonesia

Japan (limited restrictions)

Korea, Democratic Peoples Republic of (North)

Laos (subsistence only)

Malaysia (aboriginal subsistence only)

Nepal (defense of life and property only)

Norway

Romania

South Korea

Sri Lanka (special permit only)

Sweden

Taiwan

Thailand (may hunt sloth bears with impunity)

Turkey

Habitat Loss

Habitat loss includes the displacement of bears from their habitat, degradation of habitat quality, and the destruction of the habitat, and is one of the major problems confronting the world's bears. Bears are forced into areas that have inadequate food, small isolated areas, and into conflict with humans. "The historic impacts of man on bears were more related to direct killing," writes Christopher Servheen in *The Status and Conservation of the Bears of the World*, "whereas recent impacts are more related to habitat loss. Man and bears are direct competitors for space and resources worldwide." In Burma alone, notes Servheen, "at least 1.2 million acres of Burma's forests are being felled each year . . . which undoubtedly reduces bear habitat and increases bears' vulnerability to uncontrolled hunting."

Causes of Habitat Loss

▲ Agricultural practices

▲ Forestry activities

▲ Gas and oil exploration and operations

▲ Human development (residential, commercial)

▲ Increasing human populations

▲ Mining activities

▲ Recreation activities

Levels of Habitat Loss

North American state and provincial wildlife management agencies evaluate and describe the level of habitat loss.

American Black Bear—United States

Serious	Not Serious	Serious	Not Serious
Alabama	Alaska	New Mexico	Oregon
Arizona	California	New York	Texas
Arkansas	Connecticut	North Carolina	West Virginia
Colorado	Idaho	Oklahoma	Wisconsin
Florida	Kentucky	Pennsylvania	Wyoming
Georgia	Maine	Rhode Island	
Louisiana	Maryland	South Carolina	
Massachusetts	Michigan	Tennessee	
Mississippi	Minnesota	Utah	
Missouri	Nevada	Vermont	
Montana	New Hampshire	Virginia	
New Jersey	North Dakota	Washington	

American Black Bear—Canada and Mexico   With the exception of British Columbia, habitat loss is *not* at a serious level in Canada's provinces—Alberta, Manitoba, New Brunswick, Newfoundland, the Northwest Territories, Nova Scotia, Ontario, Quebec, Saskatchewan, and the Yukon Territory.

In Mexico, habitat loss *is* at a serious level in all of the states—Chihuahua, Coahuila, Durango, Nuevo Leon, San Luis Potosi, Sinaloa, Sonora, Tamaulipas, and Zacatecas.

Grizzly Bear   In the United States, grizzly bear habitats are diminishing in the states in which the bear lives: Alaska, Idaho, Montana, Washington, and Wyoming.

In Canada, grizzly bear habitat is losing ground in Alberta and British Columbia at a serious rate, but remains stable in the Northwest Territories and the Yukon Territory.

Polar Bears   Habitat loss is serious in the Canadian Northwest Territories but is stable in Manitoba, Newfoundland, Ontario, Quebec, and the Yukon Territory. In Alaska, habitat loss is not considered serious.

Bear Management in North America

The management of bears is actually people management, providing a situation whereby humans and bears can co-exist in the same territory. Management is also directed by cooperation—the mutual and cooperative efforts of the involved agencies, private land owners, and the general public.

THIS AREA IS CLOSED TO ALL HUMAN TRAVEL

This area provides critical habitat for grizzly and black bears emerging from winter hibernation. Bears depend upon this food-rich area in the spring due to the concentration of winter-killed bison and elk, large numbers of bison calves, and the availability of early snow-free vegetation.

Research has shown that the presence of people displaces bears, reducing the bears' ability to use the area. Also, the presence of people may be viewed by the bears as a threat to their food. Therefore, for your safety and that of the bears, this area is closed.

Bear management area sign identifying and explaining an area set aside in Yellowstone National Park for the benefit of grizzly bears
Courtesy Yellowstone National Park

A translocation release of a nuisance grizzly bear, captured in another area, is made with the hopes it will stay out of trouble
© Gary Brown

A "bear management" program has six basic elements:

1. **Awareness**   Every effort is made to educate those who live, travel and visit bear country about how to act when in this realm that is shared with the bear. We must understand bears, appreciate them, and know how to preserve and maintain natural, wild populations. Awareness is accomplished by agencies and others by disseminating information in the form of publications, verbal messages, television, and signs.

2. **Reduction of Unnatural Bear-Human Contacts**   Encounters and conflicts are detrimental to people and bears, and must be minimized, if not eliminated. The sources of conflict have been previously addressed. We prevent bears from obtaining unnatural foods (human, pet, stock, and garbage) by proper storage. Bears should not be fed.

3. **Bear Management Areas**   Bear management areas are identified and established to reduce human–related impact on bears in high-density bear habitat, and to provide for human safety. Human activities are limited or eliminated in these areas; thus bears are provided opportunities to pursue natural behavior patterns and activities (feeding, breeding, resting, and traveling) free from human disturbance.

4. **Control Nuisance Bears**   Bears that become habituated and unafraid of people, conditioned to non-natural foods, and even those that seek natural foods in developed areas are relocated or removed from the population.

5. **Enforcement of Regulations**   Appropriate regulations must be in place to provide "guidance" for people to properly conduct themselves in bear country. These regulations and laws must be enforced, and the courts must address violations with penalties that are strong deterrents.

6. **Research**   Appropriate research—research that addresses management needs—is necessary. Bear management must be based on valid research. However, on occasions certain drastic actions, prior to achieving research results, may be necessary to protect bears.

Bear Research in North America

Bear research may be described as "getting to know bears better," and it is critical to the management of all bears. Credible knowledge of the species provides the necessary direction for managers to balance the requirements of humans and bears. "Research on bears, especially their space and habitat needs," observe Paul Shepard and Barry Sanders in *The Sacred Paw*, "is essential in order to provide for their survival in a world of competing land uses."

Bear research has progressively increased in North America during the past forty years, both to meet management requirements and as more interest has been centered around the plight of bear species.

All species of bears are quite difficult to study in the wild because they are shy, cautious, and in many instances scarce. A myriad of ongoing bear studies includes anatomy, physiology, and behavior, with strong emphasis on repro-

 A radio collar is placed on a grizzly bear for research purposes. Upon the bear's release, its location and movements will be monitored to determine its range, habitat, and activities
© Gary Brown

duction and survivorship, sex and age structure of populations, and bear habitat characterization and utilization (including feeding and nutrition). Population studies include bear distribution, movements, densities, and ranges. Studies address bear/human activities, interactions, and management methods. Bear evolution, hibernation, and genetics receive considerable attention. These studies are only a few of the multitude of bear research projects.

Bear Research Contributions to Wildlife Literature

Period	Years	Total Citations[2]	Number of Papers[1]	Per Year	Percent[3]
1935–51	17	10,000	17	2	0.4
1952–60	9	14,481	85	9	0.6
1961–70	10	24,440	157	16	0.6
1971–80	10	54,802	309	31	0.6
1981–90	10	125,967	905	91	0.7
Totals	56	229,690	1,493	27	0.6

[1]Bears primary subject.
[2]Bears included, but not necessarily primary subject.
[3]Percent of total citations.
Source: Martinka, C.J. Contributions to a Contemporary History of Bears. International Conference on Bear Research and Management. 9: (No date; in press).

Important Contributions to Bear Literature

Scientists and managers with a professional interest in bears listed and ranked published technical documents considered to be outstanding contributions to bear management and research literature during the period 1967 to 1992. Though scientific in their application, most documents provide practical knowledge for the layperson.

1. *Bear Attacks: Their Causes and Avoidance.* Stephen Herrero. New York: Lyons & Burford, Publishers, 1985. (Book)

2. *Population Dynamics of Bears: Implications:* F. N. Bunnell and D. E. N. Tait. New York: John Wiley and Sons, 1981. (Book, chapter)

3. "The Black Bear in the Spruce-Fir Forest." C. J. Jonkel and I. M. Cowan. Wildlife Monograph 2, 1971.

4. "Effects of Food Supply and Kinship on Social Behavior, Movements, and Population Growth of Black Bears in Northeastern Minnesota." L. Rogers. Wildlife Monograph 97, 1987.

5. "Effects of Mast and Berry Crop Failures on Survival, Growth and

Reproductive Success of Black Bears." L. Rogers. Transactions of the North American Wildlife and Natural Resources Conference 41, 1976.

6. "The Northern Interior Grizzly Bear *Ursus Arctos* L." A. M. Pearson. Canadian Wildlife Service Report Series 34, 1975. (Bulletin)

7. "Black and Brown Bear Density Estimates Using Modified Capture-Recapture Techniques in Alaska." S. D. Miller, E. F. Becker, W. D. Ballard. International Conference on Bear Research and Management 7, 1987. (Conference proceedings)

8. "A Population Analysis of the Yellowstone Grizzly Bears." J. J. Craighead, J. R. Varney, F. C. Craighead. Montana Wildlife Cooperative Research Unit Bulletin 40, 1974. (Bulletin)

9. "Factors Affecting the Evolution and Behavioral Ecology of the Modern Bears." I. Stirling, A. E. Derocher. International Conference on Bear Research and Management 8, 1990. (Conference Proceedings)

10. "Bears in Models and Reality—Implications to Management." F. L. Bunnell, D. E. N. Tait. International Conference on Bear Research and Management 4, 1980. (Conference Proceedings)

11. "The Dynamics and Regulation of Black Bear *Ursus Americanus* Populations in Northern Alberta." G. A. Kemp. International Conference on Bear Research and Management 3, 1976. (Conference Proceedings)

The Future of Bears

onservation of bears requires human intervention in the competitive interaction between man and bear to assure resource availability for both species to the exclusion of neither," notes Servheen.

Why shouldn't a person in Thailand whose annual income is $140 (U.S.), kill a bear and sell it for $2000 to prevent his family from going hungry? "Since one bear brings in more than the average Thai earns in a year, Thai poachers are not deterred by the risk of fines if they are caught," write Jeffrey McNeely and Paul Wachtel in *Soul of the Tiger*.

Conservation Measures

Bear managers in all countries need to find a way to balance bear and human needs, addressing biological, economic, and social concerns. They must initiate, continue, or enhance the broad spectrum of management measures that addresses the survival of all species of bears. A strategy must be developed focusing more on social, economic, and cultural issues, whereby people are not hindered nor burdened with hardships due to bear conservation. The keys are education and values, and humans valuing the presence of bears.

Social questions must be addressed—targeting the people who live with bears—providing incentives for them to change and balance the risks of this dual occupancy. The "local" people must support the long-term maintenance of the various species, developing an economic value of bears that is an alternative to killing them, and where the degradation of bear habitat is not necessary for humans to survive. Compensation payments for bear-caused damage are necessary. Social issues must be managed in a manner beneficial to bears as well as people. As stated earlier, bear management is actually the management of people.

We must adjust the present management of people and bear relationships, and utilize experimental management concepts. And we must improve land use planning, including the implementation of proactive planning measures, and the enhancement of cooperative planning and management between governments (counties, states, provinces, cities and countries). The plans must include the general public.

We also must balance the consumptive and non-consumptive uses of land, and move and resettle people (critical in Asia) and control human access into important bear areas. We have to take measures to deter bears from developments, and protect people and property. We will fail if we do not control unnatural bear attractants and assure the proper storage and disposal of food and garbage that can create human/bear conflicts. We should also realign roads and have governments pay for depredation losses.

Finally, we have to enable research that addresses proper compatibility of people and bears; initiate, enhance, and refocus such research, directing it to management problems, especially social and economic concerns; and carefully evaluate the impact of the research process on bears, and develop programs that have minimal or no negative influence.

Education is critical in helping people develop an understanding of bears and their positive value and importance in the world as wild animals. However, the social, cultural, and economic concerns of people must also be addressed.

Bear habitat can and must be improved. Human activities in critical habitat should be reduced, and in some situations eliminated, with habitat quality optimized and degraded areas restored. The number of reserves for bears should be increased, and existing areas enlarged. Lands for bears must be contiguous, with continuity between populations. Buffer areas around reserves are critical. There should be strategies developed to protect bears on private lands.

Bear-hunting programs must be compatible with bear populations and habitat. Hunters' knowledge and understanding of bears must be improved, especially concerning identification of species. Baiting should be eliminated, spring hunting closely managed, and the use of hunting dogs regulated in brown bear habitat. The use of sport hunting for selective removal of nuisance bears should be carefully managed.

Regulations and laws that provide protection for bears and their habitat must be enhanced and strictly enforced. Courts and judges must apply appropriate fines and jail terms, considering not only punitive measures, but the value of preventing other detrimental impacts on bears.

The human population is the primary culprit impacting bears around the world. Control it!

Future of the Species

AMERICAN BLACK BEAR	Populations relatively secure; species survival assured.
BROWN BEAR	"The future of the species [brown bear] worldwide can only be assured in the northeastern and northwestern Soviet Union, Alaska, and Canada," according to Servheen. And Duncan Gilchrist, in *All About Bears*, notes, "Human attitudes and management policies towards the grizzly are generally the most positive that they have ever been."
POLAR BEAR	Species survival is probably assured, although sport hunting and oil spills are serious threats to populations.
ASIATIC BLACK BEAR	By the year 2025, the world's human population will have doubled, with most of the growth in Southeast Asia. "Without controls on trade and the initiation of management on the harvest," writes Servheen, "it appears that species could become extinct throughout most of its range in the very near future."
GIANT PANDA	"The panda provides a living blueprint for extinction," writes Schaller et al. "We face now the scientific and moral challenge of producing a blueprint for its survival."
SLOTH BEAR	Survival outside parks doubtful.
SUN BEAR	The combination of increasing habitat destruction and direct killing and capture with minimal knowledge and the lack of management interest," comments Servheen, "makes the sun bear's future bleak and uncertain."
SPECTACLED BEAR	Inaccessibility of remaining spectacled bear habitat may protect them for many years, but population fragmentation may have already doomed the species.

"There seems to be a tacit assumption that if grizzlies survive in Canada and Alaska, that is good enough. It is not good enough for me," wrote Aldo Leopold in *A Sand County Almanac*. "Regulating grizzlies to Alaska is about like regulating happiness to heaven; one may never get there."

Epilogue

Bears were on the earth before us but today cling to shrinking habitats around the world as human technology and certain philosophies challenge their ability to survive. We could someday be without bears, except in zoos and other captive situations, as is already the situation with many other animal species of the world. The grizzly bear is gone from most of its original North American habitat, the giant panda is soon to be extinct in the wild, and the sun bear is no better assured of survival.

Marvelous creatures, bears have long been extremely important components in our lives—mythical, religious, exciting and humanlike. They have provided subsistence, sport, excitement, death, comfort, and values. They are an integral aspect of our cultural world and unquestionably in nature and wilderness—they belong.

"Wilderness is the raw material out of which man has hammered the artifact called civilization," notes Aldo Leopold in *A Sand County Almanac*. He described wilderness as the theater of evolution, and the grizzly bear as its outstanding achievement. Early cultures, and maybe no single one as much as the Native Americans, have considered the bear a symbol of nature.

Bears evolved in wilderness—a natural, expansive, diverse, and precarious region, unsettled and in an untamed state. "They [bears] represent a natural world without controls, the dangerous side of nature," writes David Rockwell in *Giving Voice to Bear*.

"Nature has few creations like the great bear to enforce respect for the order she has wrought," explains Douglas Chadwick in *A Beast the Color of Winter*. "Few remaining works whose very spoor, once seen, can make the mountains suddenly higher, the valleys wider, the wind louder as it bends around a rise."

> *"It would be fitting, I think, if among the last man-made tracks on earth could be found the huge footprints of the great brown bear."*

E.J. FLEMING, 1958
(As quoted in The Grizzlies of Mount McKinley, by Adolph Murie)

© *Johnny Johnson*

Bears require undisturbed expanses for survival, and humans, whether we know it or not, also need wilderness. "Knowing that we are in the presence of bears adds spice to the outdoor adventure," notes George Laycock in *The Wild Bears*. "Whenever we go where the wild bear lives, we feel a keen sharpening of the senses, an unforgettable level of alertness."

Bears *are* wilderness—the element that must be there in order to have a complete natural scheme. It would not be wild without them. But, during the last few hundred years, bears have been reduced in numbers, slowly at first, but now more drastically, as species are eliminated from areas and threatened with extinction, primarily due to the rapid reduction of isolated and wild areas.

We should be able to coexist with and enjoy bears, but we happen to have the technology to be the dominant species. We do not have to like the bears, but should respect them for what they are. View and experience this long-time symbol of our culture, and enjoy them as wild animals, an important ingredient of our lives and our world. Humans are challenged to be creative, and address the worldwide social situations that are necessary to assist and support the bears.

American black bears and the brown bears of the world will survive if people improve their understanding and appreciation for bears. The polar bear will be here in the future, because of the inability of the human population to reach, develop, and exist in their habitat. Most bears, and very likely some species, in Eurasia will be gone unless preservation measures are soon enacted.

This "bear almanac" is not all-inclusive, and hopefully the cast of characters and facts have intrigued the reader—perhaps enticed you to investigate, to have a bearlike curiosity, and learn more about these remarkable animals. If you gain but a single thing from this book, it should be an understanding and appreciation for the bears in this world—a world big enough for bears and people.

Appendix A

ERA	PERIOD/EPOCH	DURATION
MEZOZOIC ERA 230,000,000 to 63,000,000 years ago	**Triassic Period** **Jurassic Period** **Cretaceous Period**	230,000,000 to 180,000,000 180,000,000 to 130,000,000 130,000,000 to 63,000,000
CENOZOIC ERA 63,000,000 years ago to present	**Tertiary Period** **—Oligocene epoch** **—Miocene epoch** **—Pliocene epoch**	63,000,000 to 2,000,000 to 500,000 years ago* 63,000,000 to 25,000,000 years ago 25,000,000 to 13,000,000 years ago 13,000,000 to 2,000,000 to 500,000 years ago
	Quaternary Period **—Pleistocene epoch** **—Holocene epoch**	2,000,000 to 500,000 years ago to present* 2,000,000 to 500,000 to 11,000 years ago 11,000 years ago to present

*There are no definitive beginnings or endings for some periods or epochs due to the enormous amount of time considered, as well as different dating methods utilized around the world.

Appendix B

Convention on International Trade in Endangered Species of Wild Fauna and Flora (CITES)

The Convention on International Trade in Endangered Species of Wild Fauna and Flora (1973) serves as an oversight body, and regulates, to some degree, the international trade in most bear species (although individual countries must be "parties" to CITES). All bears are listed under CITES except the American black bear (listed in Louisiana only), and the brown bear in the Commonwealth of Independent Nations.

Appendix I

". . . all species threatened with extinction which are or may be affected by trade. Trade in specimens of these species must be subject to particularly strict regulation in order not to endanger further their survival and must only be authorized in exceptional circumstances . . ."

Appendix II

". . . all species which although not necessarily now threatened with extinction may become so unless trade in specimens of such species is subject to strict regulation in order to avoid utilization if compatible with their survival . . ."

"... other species which must be subject to regulations in order that trade in specimens of certain species referred to ... above ... may be brought under effective control ..."

Appendix III (1991)
"... all species which any party identifies as being subject to regulation within its jurisdiction for the purpose of preventing or restricting exploitation, and as needing the cooperation of other parties in the control of trade ..."

Several bear trade countries are not parties to CITES, and among those that are, many do not have laws to enforce trade restrictions. Where laws do exist, enforcement is often negligible.

International Union for Conservation of Nature and Natural Resources (IUCN)

The world's largest conservation organization, IUCN maintains a Red Book (a worldwide listing of species of concern). The organization does not have enforcement powers, but identifies, lobbies and promotes protection and conservation of all threatened species of plants and animals.

Appendix C

Organizations Involved in the Preservation, Research, and Management of Bears

ALLIANCE FOR THE WILD ROCKIES
   Box 8731, Missoula, MT 59807
   Grizzly bear
AMERICAN ASSOCIATION OF ZOOLOGICAL PARKS AND AQUARIUMS
   Oglebay Park, Wheeling, WV 26003
   All bear species
AMERICAN COMMITTEE FOR INTERNATIONAL CONSERVATION, INC
   Room 500, 1725 De Sales Street, NW, Washington, DC 20036
   All bear species
ANIMAL PROTECTION INSTITUTE OF AMERICA
   P.O. Box 22505, 6130 Freeport Boulevard, Sacramento, CA 95822
   American black bear, brown bear, polar bear
BLACK BEAR CONSERVATION COMMITTEE
   P.O. Box 52477, Shreveport, LA 71135
   American black bear
BROWN BEAR RESOURCES, INC
   315 South 4th East, Missoula, MT 59801
   Grizzly bear
CANADIAN WILDLIFE FEDERATION
   2740 Queensview Drive, Ottawa, Ontario, Canada K2B 1A2
   American black bear, brown bear, polar bear
COMMISSION ON NATIONAL PARKS AND PROTECTED AREAS
   (suborganization of IUCN)
   IUCN Headquarters, CH1196 Gland, Switzerland
   All bear species
CONSERVATION INTERNATIONAL
   1015 18th Street, NW, Suite 1000, Washington, DC 20036
   Spectacled bear, sun bear

(continued)

COSEWIC (The Committee on the Status of Endangered Wildlife in Canada); a Federal/Provincial committee that study, report on and assign a status to various species in Canada
Ottawa, Ontario, Canada K1A OH3

DEFENDERS OF WILDLIFE
1244 19th Street, NW, Washington, DC 20036
American black bear, brown bear, polar bear

FUDENA (*Fundacion para la defensa de la naturaleza*)
Apartado 70376, Caracas 1071-A, Venezuela
Spectacled bear

THE FUND FOR ANIMALS, INC.
200 West 57th Street, New York, NY 10019
American black bear, brown bear, polar bear

GREAT BEAR FOUNDATION
P.O. Box 2699, Missoula, MT 59806
All bear species

GREATER YELLOWSTONE COALITION
P.O. Box 1874, 13 South Willson, Bozeman, MT 59771
Grizzly bear

THE HUMANE SOCIETY OF THE UNITED STATES
2100 L Street, NW, Washington, DC 20037
American black bear, brown bear, polar bear

INTERNATIONAL ASSOCIATION FOR BEAR RESEARCH AND MANAGEMENT
c/o Michael Pelton, Department of Forestry, Wildlife and Fisheries, University of Tennessee, Knoxville, TN 37901
All bear species

IUCN (International Union for the Conservation of Nature and Natural Resources), World Conservation Union, Avenue du Mont-Blanc, CH-1196 Gland, Switzerland
All bear species; maintains a Red Book list of endangered animals

MARINE MAMMAL COMMISSION
1825 Connecticut Avenue, NW, Suite 512, Washington, DC 20009
Polar bear; established under the Marine Mammals Protection Act

NATIONAL AUDUBON SOCIETY
950 Third Avenue, New York, NY 10022
American black bear, brown bear, polar bear

NATIONAL FISH AND WILDLIFE FOUNDATION
Main Interior Building, 18th and C Streets, NW, Washington, DC 20240
American black bear, brown bear, polar bear

NATIONAL WILDLIFE FEDERATION
1400-Sixteenth Street, NW, Washington, DC 20036-2236
American black bear, brown bear, polar bear

THE NATURE CONSERVANCY
1815 North Lynn Street, Arlington, VA 22209
American black bear, brown bear; purchases and preserves bear habitat

NORTH AMERICAN BEAR SOCIETY
P.O. Box 9281, Scottsdale, AZ 85252
American black bear, brown bear, polar bear

SIERRA CLUB
730 Polk Street, San Francisco, CA 94109
American black bear, brown bear, polar bear

THE SOCIETY FOR MARINE MAMMOLOGY
c/o British Antarctic Survey, High Cross, Cambridge CB3 0ET, United Kingdom
Polar Bear

VALHALLA SOCIETY
    Box 224, New Denver, BC, Canada V0G 1S0
    American black bear (including Kermode black bear), grizzly bear
VITAL GROUND FOUNDATION
    P.O. Box 447, 558 Little Sweden Road, Heber Valley, UT 84032-0447
    American black bear, grizzly bear
THE WILDERNESS SOCIETY
    900 17th Street, NW, Washington, DC 20006-2596
    American black bear, brown bear, polar bear
WILDLIFE CONSERVATION INTERNATIONAL
    (Conservation program of the New York Zoological Society)
    New York Zoological Society, 185th Street and South Boulevard,
    Building A, Bronx, NY 10460
    All bear species
WORLD SOCIETY FOR THE PROTECTION OF ANIMALS
    29 Perkins Street, P.O. Box 190, Boston, MA 02130
    All bear species
WORLD WILDLIFE FUND
    1250 24th Street, NW, Washington, DC 20037
    All bear species
YELLOWSTONE GRIZZLY FOUNDATION
    581 Expedition Drive, Evanston, WY 82930
    Grizzly bear

This list represents those organizations that devote considerable effort to the conservation of the various species of bears around the world. Some have no other purpose. Many other groups, though not listed, are involved with bear preservation on a collateral basis if not totally.

Glossary

alimentary canal: the mucous-membrane-lined tube of the digestive system.

anthropomorphism: **1** the attribution of human feelings to nonhuman beings. **2** A being or object having or suggesting human traits.

aphrodisiac: a substance that stimulates or intensifies sexual desire.

arboreal: **1** living in trees. **2** An animal that spends the majority of its time in trees.

bile: bitter, alkaline secretion of the liver, stored in the gall bladder; aids digestion.

binocular vision: both eyes are used at the same time and have the same movement and direction.

bipedal: walking on two feet as opposed to four (quadpedal).

BP: Before Present

Bromeliade: a plant, such as an orchid or fern, that grows on other plants for mechanical support rather than nutrition.

Bunodont: refers to the molar teeth of bears; flat cusps, broad and grinding type of teeth.

carnivore: animals that are predominantly flesh eaters; belong to the classification order Carnivora.

carrion: dead and decaying flesh; refers to dead animals available as food.

crepuscular: active at twilight or before sunrise.

dressed: a dead animal that is gutted and cleaned; intestines removed; hunting term.

embryogenesis: growth and development of an embryo.

estrus: period of ovulation and sexual activity in female mammals; in "heat."

game animal: an animal managed by fish and game departments for the purpose of hunting harvest.

habitat: the area or environment in which a bear or other animal normally lives or exists.

herbivore: animal that eats mostly vegetation.

invertebrate: an animal without a backbone or spinal column.

New World: the western hemisphere; North and South America and adjacent islands.

Old World: the eastern hemisphere; Eurasia, Africa; commonly refers to Europe.

olfactory: contributing to, or of, the sense of smell.

omnivore: animal whose diet consists of a balance between flesh and vegetation.

plantigrade: to walk with the entire sole surface of the paw on the ground.

pseudobulbs: **1** false bulbs; bulbs similar to true bulbs. **2** A bear food.

temperate: zones of moderate climate; the two middle latitude zones of the earth.

translocation: bear management term; to capture a bear in one area and release it at another location.

vertebrate: an animal with a backbone or spinal column.

vestigial tooth: a degenerate, nonfunctioning, and unnecessary tooth.

Bibliography

Books

Adams, Ramon F. *Western Words*. Norman, Oklahoma: University of Oklahoma Press, 1968.

Armstrong, Richard B., and Mary Willems Armstrong. *The Movie List Book*. Jefferson, North Carolina: McFarland & Company, Inc., Publishers, 1990.

Auel, Jean M. *The Clan of the Cave Bear*. New York: Bantam Books, 1980.

Bakeless, John. *Lewis and Clark: Partners in Discovery*. New York: William Morrow & Co., 1947.

Banfield, A.W.F. *The Mammals of Canada*. Toronto: University of Toronto Press, 1974.

Bassett, W. *History of the Town of Richmond, Cheshire County, New Hampshire*. Boston: C.W. Calkins Company, 1884.

Bauer, Erwin. *Bear in their World*. New York: Outdoor Life Books, 1985.

Boone and Crockett Club. *Records of North American Big Game*, 9th ed. Dumfries, Virginia: Boone and Crockett Club, 1988.

Brown, David E. *The Grizzly of the Southwest*. Norman: University of Oklahoma Press, 1985.

Brown, David E., and John Murray. *The Last Grizzly*. Tucson: The University of Arizona Press, 1988.

Bull, Peter. *The Teddy Bear Book*. New York: Random House, 1970.

Burnaby, A. *Travels Through the Middle Settlements in North America in the Years 1759 and 1760*. Ithaca: Cornell University Press, 1968.

Cahalane, Victor H. *Mammals of North America*. New York: The Macmillan Company, 1947.

Caras, Roger A. *North American Mammals*. New York: Galahad Books, 1967.

Cardoza, James E. *The Black Bear in Massachusetts*. Westborough: Massachusetts Division of Fisheries & Wildlife, 1976.

Chadwick, Douglas H. *A Beast the Color of Winter*. San Francisco: Sierra Club Books, 1983.

Chartrand, Mark R., and Helmut K. Wimmer. *Skyguide, A Field Guide to the Heavens*. Racine, Wisconsin: Western Publishing Company, 1982.

Cherr, Pat. *The Bear in Fact and Fiction*. New York: Harlin Quest, Inc., 1967.

Clarkson, Peter, and Linda Sutterlin. *Bear Essentials*. Missoula: School of Forestry, University of Montana, 1984.

Clutton, Cecil, Paul Bird, and Anthony Harding. *The Vintage Car Guide*. New York: Doubleday & Co., 1976.

Coffin, Tristram Potter, and Henning Cohen. *The Parade of Heros*. Garden City, New York: Anchor Press/Doubleday, 1978.

Craighead, Frank C., Jr. *Track of the Grizzly*. San Francisco: Sierra Club Books, 1979.

Craighead, Karen. *Large Mammals of Yellowstone and Grand Teton National Parks*. Karen Craighead, 1978.

Craighead-George, Jean. *Beasty Inventions*. New York: David McKay Company, Inc., 1970.

Cramond, Mike. *Killer Bears*. New York: Charles Scribner's Sons, 1981.

————. *Of Bears and Man*. Norman: University of Oklahoma Press, 1986.

Crampton, William. *Flags of the United States*. New York: W. H. Smith Publishers, Inc., (198-?).

————. *Flags of the World*. New York: Dorset Press, 1990.

Crookston, Newell J. *The Story of Old Ephraim*. North Logan, Utah: Newell J. Crookston, 1959.

Cummins, John. *The Hound and the Hawk*. New York: St. Martin's Press, 1988.

Cushing, Frank Hamilton. *Zuni Fetishes*. Las Vegas: KC Publications, 1990.

Dary, David A. *The Buffalo Book*. New York: Avon Books, 1974.

DeHart, Don. *All About Bears*. Boulder, CO: Johnson Publishing Co., 1971.

Dellenbaugh, Frederick S. A *Canyon Voyage, The Narrative of the Second Powell Expedition*. Tucson: University of Arizona Press, 1988.

Dewey, Donald. *Bears*. New York: Michael Friedman Publishing Group, Inc., 1991.

Domico, Terry, and Mark Newman. *Bears of the World*. New York: Facts on File, 1988.

Drimmer, Frederick. *The Animal Kingdom*, Vol. 1. New York: Greystone Press, 1954.

Dufresne, Frank. *No Room for Bears*. New York: Holt, Rinehart and Winston, Inc., 1965.

East, Ben. *Bears*. New York: Outdoor Life Books, 1977.

————. *The Ben East Hunting Book*. New York: Harper & Row, 1974.

Evans, Ivor H., ed. *Brewer's Dictionary of Phrase and Fable*. New York: Harper & Row, 1959.

Farnham, T. J. *Life, Adventures and Travels in California*. New York: Nafis and Cornish, 1849.

Feazel, Charles T. *White Bear*. New York: Henry Holt Company, 1990.

Finnerty, Edward W. *Trappers, Traps, and Trapping*. New York: A. S. Barnes and Company, 1976.

Flint, Richard Foster. *Glacial and Quaternary Geology*. New York: John Wiley & Sons, Inc., 1971.

Funk, Charles Earle. *Thereby Hangs a Tale*. New York: Harper & Row, 1950.

————. *Horsefeathers*. New York: Harper & Row, 1958.

————. *A Hog on Ice*. New York: Harper & Row, 1948.

Gard, Wayne. *The Great Buffalo Hunt*. Lincoln: University of Nebraska Press, 1959.

Gilchrist, Duncan. *All About Bears*. Hamilton, Montana: Outdoor Expeditions and Books, 1989.

Gowans, Fred R. *Mountain Man & Grizzly*. Orem, Utah: Mountain Grizzly Publications, 1986.

Greener, W. W. *The Gun and its Development*. Secaucus, New Jersey: Chartwell Books Inc., 1988.

Griggs, Robert F. *The Valley of Ten Thousand Smokes*. Washington, D.C.: The National Geographic Society, 1922.

Grosswirth, Marvin. *The Heraldry Book*. Garden City, New York: Doubleday & Co., 1981.

Grzimek, H.C. Bernard, ed. and contributor. *Grzimek's Encyclopedia of Mammals*, Vol. 3. New York: McGraw-Hill Publishing Company, 1990.

Halfpenny, James. *A Field Guide to Mammal Tracking in Western America*. Boulder: Johnson Publishing Company, 1986.

Hanna, Warren L. *The Grizzlies of Glacier*. Missoula: Mountain Press Publishing Co., 1978.

Haynes, Bessie D., and Edgar Haynes. *The Grizzly Bear*. Norman: University of Oklahoma Press, 1966.

Herrero, Stephen. *Bear Attacks*. New York: Lyons & Burford, Publishers, 1985.

Hill, W. W. *An Ethnography of Santa Clara Pueblo New Mexico*. Albuquerque: University of New Mexico Press, 1982.

Hoh, LaVahn G., and William H. Rough. *Step Right Up!: The Adventures of Circus in America*. Crozet, Virginia: Betterway Publications, Inc., 1990.

Hornaday, William T. *Camp-Fires in the Canadian Rockies*. New York: Charles Scribner's Sons, 1907.

————. *The American Natural History*. New York: Charles Scribner's Sons, 1904.

Hoyt, Olga. *Witches*. New York: Abelard-Schuman Ltd., 1969.

Hubbard, W.P., and Seale Harris. *Notorious Grizzly Bears*. Chicago: The Swallow Press Inc., 1960.

Ingles, Lloyd Glenn. *Mammals of California*. Stanford: Stanford University Press, 1947.

Jamieson, David, and Sandy Davidson. *The Colorful World of the Circus*. London: Octopus Books Limited, 1980.

Kane, Joseph Nathan. *Famous First Facts*. New York: The H. W. Wilson Company, 1950.

Kaniut, Larry. *More Alaska Bear Tales*. Anchorage: Alaska Northwest Books, 1989.

Koch, Thomas J. *The Year of the Polar Bear*. New York: The Bobbs-Merrill Company, Inc., 1975.

Kurten Bjorn. *Pleistocene Mammals of Europe*. Chicago: Aldine Publishing Company, 1968.

Kurten, Bjorn, and Elaine Anderson. *Pleistocene Mammals of North America*. New York: Columbia University Press, 1980.

Laycock, George. *The Wild Bears*. New York: Outdoor Life Books, 1986.

Lehner, Ernst. *Symbols, Signs & Signet*. New York: Dover Publications, Inc., 1950.

Lekagul, Boonsong, and Jeffrey A. McNeely. *Mammals of Thailand*. Bangkok: Sahakarnbhat Company, 1977.

Leonard, Rhoda. *Arctos the Grizzly*. Sacramento: California State Department of Education, 1969.

Leopold, Aldo. *A Sand County Almanac*. New York: Oxford University Press, 1949.

Lopez, Barry. *Arctic Dreams*. New York: Charles Scribner' Sons, 1986.

MacDonald, Margaret Read. *The Folklore of the World Holidays*. Detroit: Gale Research, Inc., 1992.

Marty, Sid. *Men for the Mountains*. New York: Vanguard Press, Inc., 1979.

Matteucci, Marco. *History of the Motor Car*. New York: Crown Publishers, 1970.

Matthiessen, Peter. *The Snow Leopard*. New York: The Viking Press, 1978.

McCoy, J.J. *Wild Enemies*. New York: Hawthorn Books, Inc., 1974.

McCracken, Harold. *The Beast that Walks Like Man*. Garden City, New York: The Garden City Press, 1955.

McGuire, Bob. *Black Bears*. Blountville, Tennessee: Bowhunting Productions, 1983.

McIntyre, Rick. *Grizzly Cub*. Anchorage: Alaska Northwest Books, 1990.

McNamee, Thomas. *The Grizzly Bear*. New York: Alfred A. Knopf, 1984.

McNeely, Jeffrey, and Paul S. Wachtel. *Soul of the Tiger*. New York: Doubleday, 1988.

Medawar, P.B, Medawar, J.S. *Aristotle to Zoos*. Cambridge: Harvard University Press, 1983.

Menzel, Donald H. *A Field Guide to the Stars and Planets*. Boston: Houghton Mifflin, 1964.

Miles, Alfred H. *The Universial Natural History*. New York: Dodd, Mead & Co., 1895.

Mills, Enos A. *The Spell of the Rockies*. Lincoln: University of Nebraska Press, 1989 (Originally Houghton Mifflin, 1911).

————. *Wild Life on the Rockies*. Lincoln: University of Nebraska Press, 1988 (Originally Houghton Mifflin, 1909).

————. *The Grizzly—Our Greatest Wild Animal*. Boston: Houghton Mifflin, 1919.

Morris, Desmond, and Ramona Morris. *Men and Pandas*. New York: McGraw-Hill Book Company, 1966.

————. *The Mammals*. New York: Harper & Row, 1965.

Muir, John. *The Mountains of California*. New York: Dorsett Press, 1988.

————. *Our National Parks*. New York: Houghton Mifflin, 1901.

————. *Wilderness Essays*. Salt Lake City: Peregrine Smith, Inc., 1980.

Murie, Adolph. A *Naturalist in Alaska*. New York: The Devin-Adair Company, 1961.

————. *Ecology of the Coyote in Yellowstone*. Fauna Series No. 4. Washington, D.C.: United States Government Printing Office, 1940.

————. *The Grizzlies of Mount McKinley*. Washington, D.C.: United States Department of the Interior, 1981.

Murie, Olaus J. *A Field Guide to Animal Tracks*. Boston: Houghton Mifflin, 1954.

Napier, John. *Bigfoot*. New York: E. P. Dutton & Company, Inc., 1972.

Nielsen, Leon, and Robert D. Brown (editors). *The Translocation of Wild Animals*. Milwaukee: Wisconsin Humane Society, Inc., 1988.

Ormond, Clyde. *Bear*. Harrisburg, Pennsylvania: The Stackpole Company, 1961.

————. *Complete Book of Hunting*. New York: Outdoor Life Books, 1962.

Osteen, Phyllis. *Bears Around the World*. New York: Coward-McCann, 1966.

Paradiso, John L. *Mammals of the World*. Baltimore: John Hopkins University Press, 1975.

Partridge, Eric. *A Dictionary of Slang & Unconventional English:* New York: Macmillan Publishing Co., Inc., 1976.

Peacock, Doug. *Grizzly Years*. New York: Henry Holt & Company, 1990.

Perry, Richard. *The World of the Giant Panda*. New York: Bantam Books, Inc., 1969.

————. *Bears*. New York: Arco Publishing Company, Inc., 1970.

Peterson, Thomas Carl. *Heaven and Earth*. New York: Prentice Hall Press, Inc., 1986.

Prodgers, Jeanette. *The Only Good Bear is a Dead Bear*. Helena, Montana: Falcon Press Publishing Company, 1986.

Riley, William, and Laura Riley. *Guide to the National Wildlife Refuges*. Garden City, New York: Anchor Press/Doubleday, 1979.

Robinson, Sandra Chisholm. *The Everywhere Bear*. Niwot, Colorado: Roberts Rinehart, Inc., 1992.

————. *The Last Bit-Bear, a Fable*. Niwot: Roberts Rinehart Inc., 1984.

Rockwell, David. *Giving Voice to Bear*. Niwot: Roberts Rinehart, Inc., 1991.

Roosevelt, Theodore. *The Works of Theodore Roosevelt* (Elkhorn Edition). New York: G.P. Putman's Sons, 1893.

Russell, Andy. *Grizzly Country*. New York: Lyons and Burford, Publishers, 1984.

Russell, Osborne. *Journal of a Trapper*. Lincoln: University of Nebraska Press, 1955.

Samson, Jack. *The Bear Book*. Clinton, New Jersey: The Amwell Press, 1979.

————. *The Grizzly Book*. Clinton: The Amwell Press, 1982.

Savage, Candace. *Grizzly Bears*. San Francisco: Sierra Club Books, 1990.

Schaller, George B., Hu Jinchu, Pan Wenshi, and Zhu Jing. *The Giant Pandas of Wolong*. Chicago: The University of Chicago Press, 1985.

Schneider, Bill. *Where the Grizzly Walks*. Missoula: Mountain Press Publishing Company, 1977.

Schullery, Paul. *American Bears*, Selections from the Writings of Theodore Roosevelt. Boulder: Colorado Associated University Press, 1983.

———. *The Bear Hunter's Century*. New York: Dodd, Mead & Co., 1988.

———. *Mountain Time*. New York: Lyons & Burford, Publishers, 1984.

———. *The Bears of Yellowstone*. Niwot: Roberts Rinehart, Inc., 1986.

———. *Yellowstone Bear Tales*. Niwot: Roberts Rinehart, Inc., 1991.

———. *Pregnant Bears and Crawdad Eyes*. Seattle: The Mountaineers, 1991.

Scott, M. Douglas, and Suvi A. Scott. *Heritage from the Wild*. Bozeman: Northwest Panorama Publishing, Inc., 1985.

Service, Robert W. *Ballads of a Bohemian*. New York: Barse & Hopkins, 1921.

Seton, Ernest Thompson. *The Biography of a Grizzly*. New York: Grosset & Dunlap, 1919.

Sheldon, Charles. *The Wilderness of Denali*. New York: Charles Scribner's Sons, 1930.

Shepard, Paul, and Barry Sanders. *The Sacred Paw*. New York: Viking Penguin Inc., 1985.

Silverstone, Paul. *U.S. Warships of World War I*. Garden City, New York: Doubleday, 1970.

Skinner, M. P. *Bears in the Yellowstone*. Chicago: A. C. McClurg & Company, 1932.

Speaight, George. *A History of the Circus*. San Diego, California: A. S. Barnes & Co., 1980.

Stefansson, Vilhjalmur. *Arctic Manual*. New York: The Macmillan Company, 1944.

———. *Hunters of the Great North*. New York: Harcourt, Brace & Co., 1922.

Stein, Ralph. *The World of the Automobile*. New York: Random House, 1973.

Stevens, Montague. *Meet Mr. Grizzly*. San Lorenzo, New Mexico: High-Lonesome Books, 1987.

Stewart, George R. *Ordeal by Hunger*. New York: Pocket Books, Simon & Schuster, 1974.

Stimpson, George. *A Book About a Thousand Things*. New York: Harper & Brothers, 1946.

Stirling, Ian. *Polar Bears*. Ann Arbor: University of Michigan Press, 1988.

Stone, Irving. *Men to Match My Mountains*. Garden City, New York: Doubleday & Co., 1956.

Storer, Tracy I., and Lloyd P. Tevis, Jr. *California Grizzly*. Berkeley: University of California Press, 1955.

Talocci, Mauro. *Guide to the Flags of the World*. New York: William Morrow & Co., 1982.

Tomkins, William. *Universal Indian Sign Language*. San Diego: William Tomkins, 1926.

Tracy, Jack. *Scherlockiana, the Encyclopedia*. New York: Avenel Books, 1977.

Van Wormer, Joe. *The World of the Black Bear*. New York: J. B. Lippincott Company, 1966.

Walker, Ernest P. *Mammals of the World*. Volume II. Baltimore: The John Hopkins Press, 1968.

Wasserman, Paul, and Edmond L. Applebaum. *Festivals Sourcebook*. Detroit: Gale Research Company, 1984.

Wilson, Herbert Earl. *The Lore and the Lure of Yosemite*. San Francisco: Sunset Press, 1923.

Woodcock, Thomas, and John Martin Robinson. *The Oxford Guide to Heraldry*. Oxford: Oxford University Press, 1988.

Wright, Banton. *Kachinas, A Hopi Artist's Documentary*. Flagstaff, Arizona: Northland Press, 1973.

Wright, William H. *The Black Bear*. New York: Charles Scribner's Sons, 1910.

———. *The Grizzly Bear*. Lincoln: University of Nebraska Press, 1977.

Young, Robert. *Analytical Concordance to the Bible*. Grand Rapids, Michigan: Wm. B. Erdmans Publishing Company, 1972.

Yukon Wildlife Branch. *The Bear Facts*. The Government of the Yukon Territory.

Zappler, Lisbeth. *Nature's Oddballs*. New York: Doubleday & Co., 1978.

Articles, Bulletins, Papers, Reports

Banci, Vivian, 1991. "The Status of the Grizzly Bear in Canada in 1990." A COSEWIC Status Report. Governments of Alberta, British Columbia, and Yukon.

Barnes, Victor G. and Olin E. Bray. 1967. "Population Characteristics and Activities of Black Bears in Yellowstone National Park." A Final Report. Fort Collins: Colorado Cooperative Wildlife Research Unit.

"Bears and Bear-Hunting." *Harper's New Monthly Magazine*, Vol. XI, No. IXV, October 1855.

Bell, W.B. "Hunting Down Stock-Killers." Yearbook of Agriculture for 1920, Washington, D.C.: U.S. Government Printing Office, 1921.

Blanchard, Bonnie M. and Richard R. Knight. "Reactions of Yellowstone Grizzly Bears, *Ursus arctos horribilus*, to Wildfire in Yellowstone National Park." *The Canadian Field-Naturalist*, Vol. 104, 1990.

Bolgiano, Chris. "Do Appalachia's Bears Have a Future?" *Defenders of Wildlife*, November/December 1987.

California (state of) 1987. "A Plan for Black Bear in California." Sacramento: Department of Fish and Game.

———, 1991. "Final Environmental Document, Bear Hunting." Sacramento; Department of Fish and Game.

Ceballos-G., Gerardo. "The Importance of Riparian Habitats for Conservation of Endangered Mammals in Mexico." Paper read at First North American Riparian Conference, 1985, at University of Arizona.

Craighead, J.J., and F.C. Craighead, Jr, 1972. "Grizzly Bear-Man Relationships in Yellowstone National Park." A report in Bears—Their Biology and Management, IUCN.

Dalquest, Walter W., and O. Mooser. "Arctodus Pristinus Leidy in the Pleistocene of Aguascalientes, Mexico," 1980. *Journal of Mammalogy*, Vol. 61, No. 4, Nov. 1980.

Demaster, Douglas P., and Ian Stirling. "*Ursus Maritimus*." *Mammalian Species*, No. 145. The American Society of Mammalogists, The Johns Hopkins University Press, 1981.

Erdbrink, D.P. "A Review of Fossil and Recent Bears of the Old World." Paper. Deventer, Netherlands, 1953.

Hall, E. Raymond. 1984. "Geographic Variation Among Brown and Grizzly Bears in North America." Lawrence: University of Kansas Museum of Natural History.

Harlow, Richard F. 1961. "Characteristics and Status of Florida Black Bear." From proceedings at 26th North American Wildlife and Natural Resources Conference, 1961. Washington, D.C.: Wildlife Management Institute.

Herrick, B. F. 1946. "Grade-School Grizzly." *California Historical Society Quarterly*.

Home, W. S. 1977. "Color Change in a Growing Black Bear." *The Murrelet*, Winter 1977.

Jonkel, C., and I. McTaggert Cowan. "The Black Bear in the Spruce-fir Forest." *Wildlife Monograph* No. 27, 1971.

Jonkel, James J. "Animal Accidents and Deaths." *Outdoor Life Magazine*, January 1987.

Kiliaan, H.P.L., and Ian Stirling. "Observations on Overwintering Walruses in the Canadian High Arctic." *Journal Of Mammalogy*, Vol. 59, No. 1, 1978.

Knight, Richard R., Bonnie M. Blanchard, David J. Mattson, 1992. "Yellowstone Grizzly Bear Investigations," Annual Report of the Interagency Grizzly Bear Study Team, 1991, Bozeman, Montana.

Kurten, Bjorn. "The Evolution of the Polar Bear, Ursus Maritimus Phipps." Acta Zoologica Fennica 108. Helsinki, Finland: Institute of Zoology and Institute of Geology and Paleontology of the University, Helsingfors, 1964.

Kurten, Bjorn, and Elaine Anderson. "Association of Ursus Arctos and Arctodus Simus in the Late Pleistocene of Wyoming." Abstract in the periodical, *Breviora*, No. 426. Cambridge, Massachusetts: Museum of Comparative Zoology, 1974.

Laurie, Andrew, and John Seidensticker, 1977. "Behavioural Ecology of the Sloth Bear." *Journal of Zoology*.

LeCount, Albert, 1986. "Causes of Black Bear Mortality." Arizona Game and Fish Department.

Lentfer, Jack W. "Polar Bear." Article in *Wild Mammals Of North America*, Eds. Chapman, Joseph A. and George A. Feldhamer. Johns Hopkins University Press, 1982.

Lindzey, Frederick G., and E. Charles Meslow. "Winter Dormancy in Black Bears in Southwestern Washington." *Journal of Wildlife Management* 41 (3), 1976.

———1977. "Population Characteristics on an Island in Washington." *Journal of Wildlife Management*.

Martinka, C. J., 1992. "Contributions to a Contemporary History of Bears." Paper presented at 9th International Conference on Bear Research and Management, Missoula, Montana.

Mattson, David J. 1991. "An Evolutionary and Ecological Interpretation of the Life Histories and Distributions of Northern Bears." Unpublished paper for Interagency Grizzly Bear Study Team, Bozeman, Montana.

———. 1988. "Human Impacts on Bear Habitat Use." Paper presented at the 8th International Conference on Bear Research and Management. Victoria, British Columbia.

McIntyre, Thomas. "American History—Grizzly." *Sports Afield*, Sept. 1983.

Meagher, Mary, and Sandi Fowler, 1987. "The Consequences of Protecting Problem Grizzly Bears." Paper presented at Yellowknife, Northwest Territories. Bear-People Conflicts Symposium.

Merriam, C. H. 1918. "Review of the Grizzly and Big Brown Bears of North America." *North America Fauna* 41. United States Department of Agriculture, Biological Survey, Washington, D.C.

Mills, Judy A., and Christopher Servheen, 1991. "The Asian Trade in Bears and Bear Parts." A project report. World Wildlife Fund, Inc., Washington, D.C.

Pelton, Michael R. 1987. "The Black Bear in the Southern Appalachian Mountains: An Overview." Exerpts from a paper presented at conference, Is There A future for the Southern Appalachian Black Bear? Asheville, North Carolina.

Poelker, Richard J., and Harry D. Hartwell, 1973. "Black Bear of Washington." Biological Bulletin No. 14. Washington State Game Department.

Proceedings of the 9th Working Meeting of the IUCN/SSC Polar Bear Specialist Group, Edmonton, Alberta, 1985. International Union for Conservation of Nature and Natural Resources, 1986.

Revenko, Igor A, 1992. "Brown Bear Reaction on Man on Kamchatka." Paper presented at Missoula, Montana. Ninth International Bear Conference on Bear Research and Management.

Rogers, Lynn. "Shedding of Footpads by Black Bears During Denning." *Journal of Mammology*, Vol. 55, No. 3, 1974.

———. 1976. "Effects of Mast and Berry Crop Failures on Survival, Growth, and Reproductive Success of Black Bears." Paper read at 41st North American Wildlife and Natural Resources Conference. Wildlife Management Institute, Washington, D.C.

Schullery, Paul. "Bear Myths." *Field and Stream*, December 1984.

Servheen, Christopher, 1989. "The State and Conservation of Bears of the World." Paper read at 8th International Conference on Bear Research and Management, Victoria, British Columbia.

Stirling, Ian. "Sleeping Giants." *Natural History*, January 1989.

Topsell, Edward. "The History of Four-Footed Beasts." 1607

Urquhart, D.R., and R.E. Schweinsburg, 1984. "Polar Bear, Life History and Known Distribution of Polar Bear in the Northwest Territories up to 1981." Yellowknife, Northwest Territories: Department of Renewable Resources, Northwest Territories.

Voorhies, M. R., and R. George Corner. "Ice Age Superpredators." Museum notes, University of Nebraska State Museum, 1982.

Vyse, E. R., 1989. A report on the "Feasibility of 'DNA Fingerprinting' Grizzly Bears." Montana State University.

Other References

American Heritage Dictionary of the English Language, The. New York: American Heritage Publishing Co., Inc., 1975.

Book of Mormon, The. The Church of Jesus Christ of Latter-day Saints. Salt Lake City, 1981.

Holy Bible, The. King James Version. New York: Thomas Nelson & Sons.

Webster's New Collegiate Dictionary. Springfield, Massachusetts, G. & C. Merriam Co., 1953.

World Book Encyclopedia, The. Chicago: Field Enterprise Educational Corporation, 1969.

Index

Note: Page numbers in *italic* refer to illustrations

I'm so excited to learn about the Outer Banks, thought Denali as she jumped eagerly into the backseat of the car.

After a long car ride, Denali started to see signs for the ocean. She practically flew out of the car when they finally arrived at the beach.

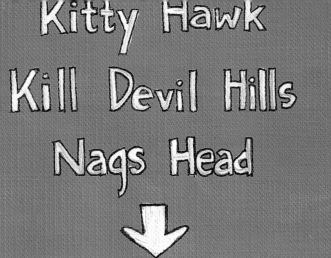

Denali ran so fast she didn't notice that she was sinking into the ground.

"Help!" cried Denali. "I'm sinking!"

Suddenly, Denali saw a shadow pass over her and she looked up into the sky. There, flying above her, was a white bird with long legs and webbed feet. He giggled and said, "You silly kitty, you're not sinking. You are stepping on sand. The beach is made up of sand that comes from the ocean. The sand is made of ground rocks, minerals, and seashells."

"Wow, I have never seen anything like this! It feels so strange between my paws," said Denali.

"My name is Sam, Sam the Seagull. I know everything about this beach. I fly above the ocean and shoreline looking for food and learning new things. Did you know there is a beach that has horses on it not far from here?"

"What? Horses? You must be joking!" said Denali.

"No, I'm not joking. But I need to meet my friends farther down the beach so enjoy the rest of your vacation and be careful of Clawde the Crab," called Sam as he flew off over the ocean.

Clawde the crab? Who's that? thought Denali.

Before she could take a step she heard, "WHO GOES THERE?"

Denali jumped and turned to see a creature with a large claw and eyes on top of his head.

"You are trespassing on my beach!" cried Clawde the Crab.

"This is my first time here. I didn't know I was trespassing," said Denali.

"No one comes here without asking permission. I'm Clawde and I say who comes and goes on this beach."

"Excuse me, but you're a strange-looking creature. What are you?" asked Denali.

"You don't know what I am? I'm a crab. I live in the ocean and on land. I use this big claw, called a pincher, to defend myself against large creatures, like you, who try to bother me."

Denali laughed. "Mr. Clawde, what is that large statue over there?"

"Well that, my friend, is the Wright Brothers Memorial. Back in the early 1900s, two brothers named Wilbur and Orville dreamed of flying. They worked and worked, and after several years, they were the first to take flight. Right here, on my beach!"

"Wow, that's amazing!" said Denali. Denali needed to move on so she thanked Clawde and continued her adventure. Suddenly, she saw something moving slowly up the beach.

It looked like a green rock with four flat legs that slowly moved through the sand. A little head popped out of the top and said very slowly, "Heeellooo theeere. I'm Tiiim the Greeen Seeaa Tuuurtle."

"Hi, Tim. I'm Denali. I'm visiting the beach with my family."

"Weeelcooome. My voice is waaarming up. Can I help you with anything?" asked Tim.

"Actually yes. What is a sea turtle exactly?" said Denali.

"A sea turtle is a creature that lives in the ocean. We can swim underwater and hold our breath for up to five hours at a time. We float along the ocean currents and eat things like crabs, jellyfish, and sea grass," said Tim.

"Every year, each female turtle lays about 100 eggs on the beach. When the eggs hatch, the baby turtles run to the ocean," said Tim the Turtle.

"Wow, 100 eggs? That is a lot!" Denali yelled.

"It sure is," Tim the Turtle said. "Oh my, look at the time, it's getting late and it takes me a long time to get to where I need to go. Enjoy the rest of your vacation!"

As Denali watched her new friend make his way down the beach, she saw something in the ocean trying to get her attention. It had a long skinny nose, made loud noises, and jumped in and out of the water.

"Hello there. I'm Delores the Dolphin."

"Hello, Delores. I'm Denali. Are you a fish?"

"No," said Delores. "I am a mammal just like you. I live in the ocean and eat fish and squid. I breathe air through a hole on the top of my body. Some people say I am the smartest animal in the ocean."

"Wow, you live in the ocean all the time?" asked Denali.

"I sure do, and I love to play and swim up and down the beach. I use that lighthouse way over there as my guide."

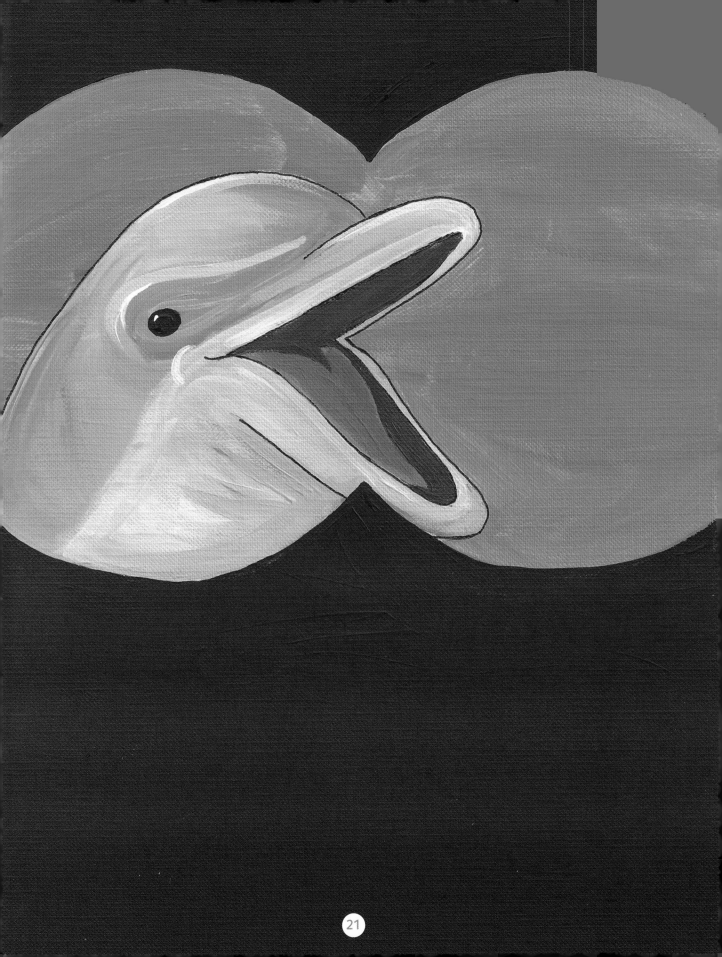

Denali looked down the beach and saw a tall, black and white building with a light on top.

"A lighthouse? That doesn't look like a house," Denali said.

"It's not actually a house. It's called a lighthouse because it has a huge light on top that helps ships navigate when it is too dark to see where they're going," said Delores.

"There are five lighthouses in the Outer Banks, each one with its own unique design and pattern. That way, boaters and dolphins like me know where they are just by looking at each lighthouse. One of the most famous lighthouses in North America is located right here in the Outer Banks and it's called Cape Hatteras," said Delores.

"That is amazing!" cried Denali as she stared out at the ocean.

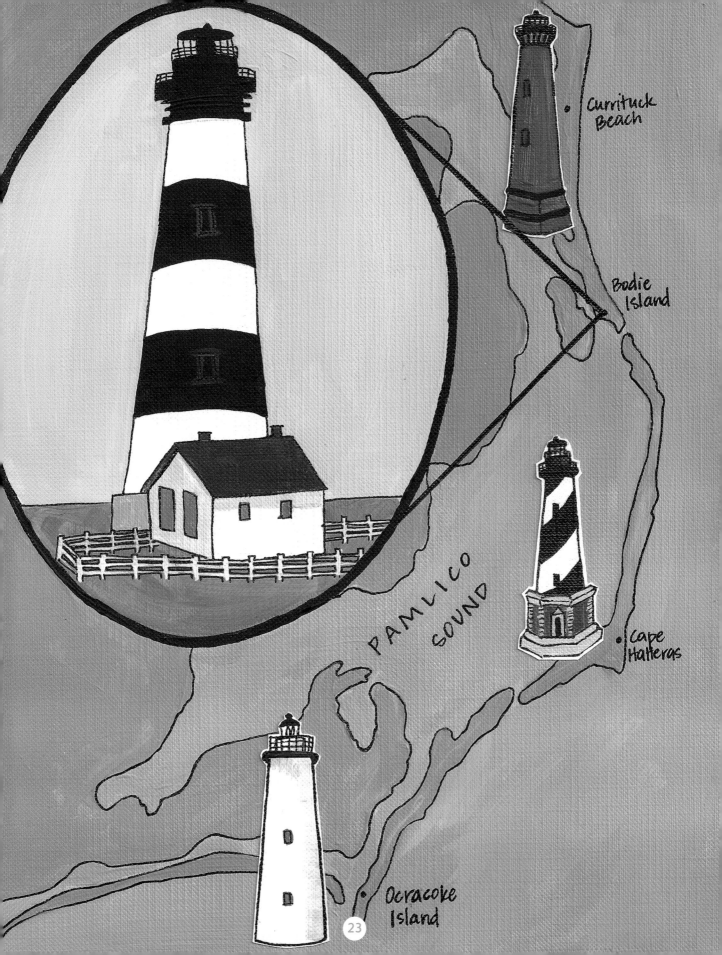

Currituck
Beach

Bodie
Island

PAMLICO SOUND

Cape
Hatteras

Ocracoke
Island

Just then, Denali noticed the sun was starting to set. She had spent so much time walking around the beach, learning about the Outer Banks, and meeting new friends that she didn't realize how late it had gotten.

"Sorry, Delores, but I have to go and meet my family," said Denali.

"No problem. Take care, Denali," said Delores as she swam away.

Denali ran as fast as she could past Jockey's Ridge State Park, the largest sand dune on the East Coast, and the beach cottages that lined both sides of the road.

Denali ran to the spot where her family had parked, but their car was gone. "Oh no, where did they go?" cried Denali. Denali was on her adventure and didn't realize how late it had gotten and now her family was looking for her. *Oh where did they go?* thought Denali. She looked down the beach and down the road but she didn't see them. "Well, I guess I will go look for them," said Denali, and off she went down the road.

Denali's family is looking for her and she is looking for her family.

Find out where Denali's goes next!

Where do you think Denali will go?

Questions

What is sand made of?

What are the names of the Wright brothers?

How many eggs does a sea turtle lay?

What is the name of the most famous lighthouse in North America?

What state is the Outer Banks located in?

About the Author

Gretchen Schuyler Brenckle is an elementary school counselor in Virginia. The inspiration for her books came from the students at her school who needed a fun way to learn more about geography. Gretchen lives in Virginia with her family and two cats, Denali and Kenai.